ABOUT THE AUTHOR

John Wesley Thompson Faulkner III (1901-1963) was a life-time resident of Mississippi, and grew up in Oxford with his three brothers, William, Murry, and Dean. John was a widely-published author, civil engineer, self-taught painter, and an aviator intensely interested in the South and loyal to a literary family steeped in tradition. He is best known for *Dollar Cotton* and several other novels, as well as his memoir, *My Brother Bill*.

ALSO BY JOHN FAULKNER

Men Working
Dollar Cotton
Chooky
Cabin Road

My Brother Bill

My Brother

Bill

John Faulkner

Foreword by Jimmy Faulkner

d

HILL STREET CLASSICS   HILL STREET PRESS   ATHENS, GEORGIA

HILL STREET CLASSICS
Published by Hill Street Press, LLC
191 East Broad Street
Suite 209
Athens, Georgia 30601-2848

First printing

1 3 5 7 9 10 8 6 4 2

ISBN 1-892514-00-1
LC# 98-73550

Printed in the United States of America by R. R. Donnelley & Sons Company
Set in 10/12 Sabon
The paper in this book contains a significant amount of post-consumer
recycled fiber.

Text and cover design by Anne Richmond Boston

First published by Trident Press (New York) 1963

Cover photographs of William Faulkner courtesy of J. M. Faulkner

Foreword

WILLIAM, JACK, JOHN, AND DEAN WERE THE FOUR
Falkner boys in that order of age. My Uncle William (Brother
Will, as I always called him) and my father John were more
alike than the other two. Brother Will had brown eyes and
parted his hair on the left. John had blue eyes and parted his
hair on the right. Brother Will was a realist while John was an
optimist. That was about the only difference. Many people
couldn't tell them apart and confused one for the other. When
John and Dolly married they bought a sewing machine on time
and sometimes would miss payments. The sewing machine
salesman kept dogging Brother Will for money, thinking he was
John, until Brother Will finally paid him off.

I grew up listening to John and Brother Will telling stories
about the Old Colonel, their great-grandfather, who owned a
railroad and was shot and killed in Ripley, Mississippi. I knew
these stories would lead to tales about the Young Colonel, Big
Dad, Aunt Bama, Nanie, and other family members.

As I listened, I learned who my people were, where they
had come from, what had shaped them; the roots of their
talent, strong will, and dignity. These stories had been handed
down to them, and they passed them on down to us.

Some of these stories were about their early years. When
the Falkner boys were growing up, Brother Will was the leader
and would make up games for them to play, such as baseball on
pony-back, wet corn cob fighting, and shinny (that's like
hockey-using sticks and a tin can for a puck). He also got the
others to help him build an airplane out of Nanie's bean poles,
tomato stakes, and newspapers. That airplane did not make it
through its first flight. When they threw it off a hill with
Brother Will in it, the plane crashed in a sand gully.

In the 1930's John and Brother Will got the real flying bug, and Brother Will bought an airplane. Dean was killed in it on November 10, 1935, but that didn't stop make either of them stop.

During the Depression, it was hard to make a living flying, so Brother Will bought a farm and John moved there to manage it for him. That is where John started writing. He would write stories on rainy days, so he could read them to Chooky, my younger brother, when he came home from school.

The farm was in the country, so in the ninth grade, I went to live with Brother Will at Rowan Oak, so I could go to school in town.

Later on, there were times when Brother Will and I wanted to get up before daylight to go hunting, so I would stay with him to save time getting in the woods or on the river to hunt ducks. What I learned from Brother Will while growing up was to be a good sportsman, to know and respect nature, and to stand on my own two feet.

He gave me my first cowboy chaps, hat, and pistol, my first airplane flight (he was the pilot), and my first gin and tonic.

When I was on the West Coast during World War II, getting ready to go to the Pacific as a Marine fighter pilot, Brother Will wrote these words of advice to me on the back of a blank check: "Listen to the old heads [pilots], keep the revs up. Good luck and good hunting. I love you, boy."

John was a man of many talents—a civil engineer, a writer, a pilot, and a painter. Everybody liked John, and he liked them. He was a friend, buddy, and teacher to Chooky and me. He was the best daddy two boys ever had. I knew him well. I loved him. He was my father.

John and Brother Will were both very compassionate men, especially towards children, young people, and animals. They always had time to talk to and listen to children. When we were growing up, they would get involved with what we were doing. They wouldn't say no to us, but were around to help if we got into trouble.

Sometimes they would start the trouble. Around 1950 Oxford was dry, not even beer was allowed within the city limits, and a beer election was coming up. Brother Will believed that we should at least have beer here, so he got on the "wet side." He had 5,000 flyers printed up in opposition to a flyer signed by three Oxford ministers who opposed the legalization of beer. John got interested in getting beer voted in, too, so he and Brother Will recruited me and some younger members of the family to go around town handing out these flyers. We all worked for it, but we still lost the election. You still can't buy cold beer in stores in Oxford.

One of the last times we (Brother Will, Jack, John, Chooky, and me) were all together was when my grandmother Nanie, was in a coma for about a week in October 1960. I flew down to Mobile to bring Jack back to Oxford. That week we spent most of the time sitting outside on the hospital steps, waiting.

The talk turned to death. Brother Will said to his brothers, "One of us will bury the other two." He was the first one to go.

Jack asked Bill,"How do you think you are going to recognize Dad when you go? You are older now than he was when he died."

Brother Will said, "I don't know. I think our souls will be like little radio waves."

I took Brother Will on that last trip to the hospital in Byhalia on July 5th the night before he died. On July 4th, he asked to go to Byhalia. That was the first time he had ever done that. We decided to wait until the next day, maybe it would be cooler then. The next morning I went down to see how he made it through the night. He still wanted to go, so I laid him down on the back seat of the car with a pillow under his head. We left late that afternoon and got to Byhalia just before dusk. We had driven through a rainstorm that cooled things down a little.

I checked him in, and stayed with him until about 10 o'clock that night.

When I was ready to leave, I went to his bedside, and reached down and took his hand. I told him, "Brother Will, when you're ready to come home, let me know and I'll come get you."

He said, "Yes, Jim, I will."

He never got home alive. He died around 2 o'clock in the morning on July 6th.

Between Brother Will's death in July 1962 and his own death in March 1963, John wrote this book, *My Brother Bill*. He had just made revisions on the galleys and sent them back to the publisher in New York, when he went into the hospital and died. The book, which John called an affectionate reminiscence of Brother Will, was released about two months later. He never saw it in print.

John said: "I have never known anyone who identified himself with his writings more than Bill did. He seemed to be as much a part of the stories he was telling as were the characters in it. When we would see Bill, we would see him surrounded by his stories." In the pages of this book are the sources of those stories.

Jimmy Faulkner
Oxford, Mississippi
June, 1998

If there be grief, let it be the rain
And this but silver grief, for grieving's sake,
And these green woods be dreaming here to
    wake
Within my heart, If I should rouse again.
But I shall sleep, for where is any death
While in these blue hills slumbrous overhead
I'm rooted like a tree? Though I be dead
This soil that holds me fast will find me
    breath.

From "A Green Bough"
by William Faulkner

Chapter 1

BILL'S DEATH OCCURRED ON A SUMMER NIGHT that could have been taken straight from the pages of his *Light in August*, except that it was July, in the early part of the month. It was soon after midnight in the beginning hours of July 6th.

He had been in the hospital for several days. Earlier he had had a bad fall from a horse and he was in there for a general checkup as was usual, periodically, the last few years of his life. He had been given his final tests, they had found nothing radically wrong and he was ready to come home. Then death struck.

It was unexpected, the kind of thrombosis that is undetectable until it strikes. If the first attack is light enough, the victim survives and treatment can be instituted that will correct the condition in the future. In such cases the patient can look forward to a future of almost normal years. About half the time in such attacks the patient does survive. In the other half he dies. Such was Bill's case. He died that morning in spite of all the doctors could do.

As the doctors explained it to us, a thrombosis is a stoppage of the veins. Fat has formed on the inner walls of them and in time pieces of it flake off. If the piece is small enough the heart can pump it on through the blood stream. There is a light heart attack, the first warning of the fat condition in the veins, yet the heart is able to maintain its function. Medical treatment is then begun that melts the fat still adhering to the veins' inner walls, and the victim lives. But if that first flaked-off piece is large enough completely to stop up the vein, the heart action can produce no blood flow through it. Without blood the well goes dry, the pump stops. So it happened to Bill. They worked over him for forty-five minutes but it was to no avail. The block could not be budged, and Bill was gone.

My phone rang that soft July night. It is in the room next to where we sleep. It waked us both, my wife and me. She went to the phone and I sat up on the edge of the bed and lit a cigarette. I heard her answer the phone, and then silence as she listened. Finally I heard her say, "I don't know how I can tell him."

Some of us have premonitions at such times. I did not. I knew Bill was in the hospital but I knew, too, that he was about ready to come home. I did not think of him at all. Actually I did not know at the moment what time it was. We get calls at odd times. I did not think one way or the other about this call even after I heard her say she did not know how she could tell him. I did not even know she was referring to me. Then, after replacing the receiver, she came to stand beside the bed.

That was Jimmy. Bill just died."

We had not put on a light. In the familiarity of our bedroom we did not need it. Now I rose from the bedside, flicked on the wall switch and began pulling on my clothes.

"Do you want me to fix you some coffee while you dress?" she asked, still standing beside the bed.

"No," I said. "I'll go on down there now."

I went over to Bill's house. It was about two-thirty. Jimmy, my oldest son, was already there. He met me at the door. Estelle, Bill's wife, had called him as soon as the hospital had called her. They had not had time to summon her to the hospital. They were all too busy working with Bill. Jimmy, as soon as she called, had called me and Chooky, my younger son, and my other brother, Jack, in Mobile. Chooky was not there yet. Jimmy had called me first and he had not quite had time to arrive.

"Where is he?" I asked Jimmy.

"They're bringing him to the funeral home from the hospital," he said.

"I'll go up and speak to Estelle."

"Chester is up there with her," Jimmy said. "I called him as soon as Aunt Estelle called me."

Chester was Dr. Chester McLarty, our family doctor.

I went upstairs to Estelle's room. Chester was there with her, watching her. He had given her a sedative but, as yet, it had

had no effect. She was walking the floor, her hands clenched. She came toward where I was as soon as I entered the room. I put my arms around her, held her a moment. There was nothing I could say. I could only give her the sympathy of my arms.

"I can't believe it," she said. "I can't believe it. He's not gone. He's not gone."

I looked over her shoulder at Chester. He was standing to one side, his whole attention fixed on her. Abruptly she pushed away from me and began walking the floor again. Leaving her with Chester, I went back downstairs to where Jimmy, whom we called Bub, was. I knew Estelle would want him to stay there to take charge for her in all the endless details that accompany death. In her overwhelming grief and shock she would be unable to. Bub was the logical one until Jill, Bill's daughter, could arrive from Virginia, for through the last few years Bill and Bub had been awfully close and during that time I expect he knew more about Bill and his affairs than any man.

We stood a moment without any words. Bub was waiting for me to speak. After several seconds, standing there in Bill's home, knowing he was gone, or at least trying to know it, I said, "I'll go to the funeral home to be there when they bring him in."

Bub nodded.

I left then, driving out Bill's cedar-lined driveway past the entrance post with the PRIVATE-KEEP OUT sign he had painted himself and put up there, and on to town.

They had not yet brought Bill in when I arrived. After going inside and finding this out, I returned to the front and sat on the steps.

The funeral home is just off the edge of the Square. Almost the whole Square can he seen from the steps. I sat there and smoked and thought of Bill. Every spot on the Square I could see contained a memory of him. The area just ahead of me was where the balloonist used to make his ascension at our county fair. I could see the exact spot where Bill and Jack and I used to stand to watch him. Beyond was the section of the Square, unpaved then, that we used to cut across on our way back and forth to school. A concrete watering trough was there then, for the convenience of the farmers, in which to water their mules when they came to town to trade. We used to pass it several times a day.

It was said of us then: "Don't fool with those Falkner boys. If you get one of them down you will have the rest of them coming at you from every corner of the Square."

To my left was the post office. On the steps there I had met Bill many a time as we were entering or leaving after securing our mail. We always stopped and passed the time of day. At all the other places I could see, the same thing had happened. We had come across each other and stopped and talked awhile.

I realized suddenly that I was living, for the moment, in memories. I realized too that that was where Bill would be from now on. And my memories were bringing in my other two brothers: Dean, who was killed in an airplane crash in 1935, and Jack, my remaining brother, who lived now in Mobile. I think it was then, as I sat there in the soft summer night, that I first accepted the fact that Bill was gone.

They brought Bill in. I heard the ambulance as it moved up to the back door down the long hallway from where I sat. I went inside and watched them place Bill's stretcher on a dolly and roll it into the embalming room. They closed the door behind them, of course, and I went back to the front steps.

I remained there with him until they were ready to take him home. One time I left, for a few minutes, to call Phil Stone, Bill's oldest and closest friend. I wanted him to hear of Bill's death from one of us and not from some outside source. It was about six when I called. Phil was not awake. His wife answered the phone and I told her who I was and asked to speak to Phil. When I told him Bill was dead he said, "What!" It was as incredible to him as it had been to me.

He asked where Bill was and I told him, saying that I would stay there with him till they were ready to take him home. Phil said he would come down to Bill's home. I went back to the funeral home then and about eight they said they were ready. I went ahead of them. Bub and Chooky were there and I told them I had brought Bill home.

Mother, who died about two years before Bill, had been very explicit about her funeral. She had told each of us how she wanted it: her family only, no flowers, as simple a funeral as possible and the least expensive. She said the quickest and the cheapest. Bill had asked for the same thing. As he expressed it:

"Just like Mother's." He had told all this to Estelle and Bub. Estelle, in the state of shock she was in, left it up to Bub until Jill could get there from Virginia. She got into Oxford with her husband, Paul, that morning and Paul stood beside Bub in everything. Cho-Cho, Estelle's daughter by her first marriage, and her husband, Bill Fielding, flew in from Caracas and arrived that day. Malcolm, Bill's stepson, also came, from Charleston, South Carolina.

Our mayor, who is also owner of the funeral home, came to the home early that morning while they were still fixing Bill up and I was there on the steps. I asked that a guard be placed at Bill's gate. He asked for how long and I told him as long as Bill lay in his own home. He agreed to send a policeman and he was there on duty soon after we brought Bill from the funeral home.

A great many people tried to get in, but according to Bill's wishes only his family was admitted, though this included his closest friends.

When he had been brought home in a casket like Mother's, it was placed on a wheeled funeral bier and rolled into his parlor and placed across his hearth. It was the same spot in which Mammy, who had raised us, had lain and in the same room where Bill had read her funeral service. He had requested that his coffin not be opened after he was placed in it and only one exception was made. Some of his black friends, dressed in their Sunday best, came to the kitchen and asked permission for one last look at him. Bub went to Estelle and she said, "Yes, of course." They were led in through the dining room and the funeral director opened the casket for them. They looked at him in silence, a few lips moved without sound, and a few dusky tears fell. Then the coffin was closed, not to be opened again.

Wires and cables came from all over the United States and the world. A message from the President arrived, cables from foreign governments and from native and foreign literary societies and other cultural groups. Bennett Cerf, representing Bill's publisher, Random House, arrived from New York. Shelby Foote came down from Memphis to pay his last respects. The University of Virginia sent a representative and a message from its president. He said that since Bill had been a part of its faculty in a lecture course he held there each spring, he would forever be a part of that institution.

My brother Jack got in from Mobile and among the two of us and my two sons, we set up a watch over Bill that lasted as long as he lay before his own hearth. Taking time about, we were his death watch, his closest remaining male relatives, his blood kin.

Reporters and photographers from all the news services had come to town but according to Bill's wishes they were restrained at his gate and not allowed in the house. They, of course, wanted entree but Bill had said no. They appointed Paul Flowers of the Memphis *Commercial Appeal*, a friend of Bub's, as spokesman and he called Bub to meet with them and try to work out some arrangement whereby they could photograph Bill in his coffin and Estelle in her grief. They said that was what they had been sent there for. Bub and Jack met with them and explained that they were simply carrying out Bill's wishes, that according to those wishes he belonged to his family until the hearse passed out his gate on its way to the cemetery. After that moment he belonged to the public, the world.

Bill had not belonged to any church. None of us has ever been a regular churchgoer, with the exception of my wife, my two sons and Jill. They are Episcopalians. Whatever churchly services we have found the need for, we have gone to their church. So the Episcopal rector was asked to read the service over Bill.

The family stood in the parlor beside Bill, his friends stood in the dining room adjoining. The simple service was read and Jack and Bub and Chooky and I moved Bill's casket away from his hearth and out to the waiting hearse. We placed our brother inside, the doors were closed for the final ride to the cemetery. As we passed out Bill's gate, photographers began snapping pictures. Some of them were from the news services, many were those who had come simply to get a shot of Bill's last ride.

All along the way to the Square people with cameras lined the walks. On the Square the flag had been lowered to half mast and the stores were all closed in Bill's memory. Photographers were in all vantage points about the Square. Some, on the ground, ran along beside the hearse; others were on upstairs balconies and the tops of buildings.

Grandfather had bought a cemetery lot for us sixty or seventy years ago. He deemed it large enough at that time but there were too many of us; we had lived here and died here too long. He and Granny were there, Mother and Dad, Dean, my youngest brother, Uncle John's children, who had died soon after birth, and Bill and Estelle's first-born, a girl named Alabama. She had lived only five days. So our cemetery lot had been filled and now there was need for more room.

Uncle John and Aunt Sue had bought a lot of their own for themselves and their son, John, Jr., who died only a few years ago. Now space had to be found for Bill.

Oxford has outgrown its burial space several times. Just recently a new area was opened up. It is raw now. Only a few people have been buried in it so far. It was the only space available, so Bub and Paul went there and selected a plot. It is on the lower slope of a bank that slants down between the old cemetery and the new. A huge old tree is there. They chose this spot for Bill.

The appointed pallbearers were there when we drove up, Phil Stone and Mack Reed, of course, and some of our kinsmen by marriage. They carried Bill to the open grave, where a tent had been pitched and chairs beside it for his family. A place had been set aside for the newsmen. There were almost more of them than there were of us. The rest of the Episcopal service was read. It did not take long. The coffin was lowered. Bill was committed to his native hills and we filed quietly away.

In the quietness of my own home memories began flooding in of Bill and our boyhood. One memory brought to life another till my life was filled anew with forgotten scenes from my years, in all sixty-one of which Bill has played his part. It was then I decided it was time for me to write about my brother Bill.

Chapter 2

THE FIRST MEMORY I HAVE ABOUT MY BROTHER
Bill is what Mother told me about his colic. For his first year he
had it almost every night. We lived at the time in New Albany,
a town about thirty miles northeast of Oxford. At least Mother
and Dad and Bill lived there. Jack and I and Dean hadn't come
along yet. We were born later in Ripley and in Oxford.

Dad was working for the railroad then. He was general
passenger agent at New Albany. It was Grandfather's road. The
Old Colonel, my great-grandfather, the first W. C. Falkner, had
built it and Grandfather and his half sisters had inherited it
when my great-grandfather died. After that Grandfather
became president and managed it until 1902, when he sold it
because he did not have the time to attend to it. It was called the
Gulf and Chicago then; the Gulf, Mobile and Northern now.

Grandfather had not wanted the railroad to begin with. He
had an extensive criminal practice at the law that left him no
spare time to manage anything else, let alone a railroad. Dad was
the only one who wanted it and except for a misunderstanding
would have bought it when Grandfather sold it in 1902.

The only things Dad ever loved were that railroad and horses
and dogs and the Ole Miss football and baseball teams when he
was secretary of the University in the 1920's. But the railroad was
his first and lasting love. He never got over being deprived of it in
1902 and they couldn't keep him in school on account of it in the
early 1890's. They would send him to Ole Miss and the next thing
they would know he would be back on the railroad. After two
years of trying to keep him in classes they gave up. He was
fireman, then engineer, then conductor, then station-master at
New Albany. Bill was born there, in 1897, on the 25th of
September, and had the colic every night for about a year.

Mother said the only way she could ease him enough to stop his crying was to rock him in a straight chair, the kind you have in the kitchen. The neighbors said the Falkners were the queerest people they ever knew; they spent all night in the kitchen chopping kindling on the floor. That's the first thing I remember about Bill.

Dad was appointed auditor and treasurer for the entire road in November of '98 and moved the family back to Ripley where we came from. Jack was born the following June and I came along in September of 1901. My birthday was the 24th, one day ahead of Bill's. It took me a long time to understand how he could be the older when my birthday came before his did. He helped me to not understand it till Mother finally explained it to me one day and after that Bill left me alone about it.

The Old Colonel was killed by a man named Thurmond. Their differences had extended back over the years. They had grown more bitter with time. The final edge was reached when the Old Colonel defeated Thurmond for a seat in the state legislature in 1892. When the Old Colonel came back from Jackson, Thurmond shot him down on the street when he walked up to the Square from the depot. He died three days later.

The town of Ripley, the county of Tippah, took sides in that quarrel. The people were split about half and half. The trial was bitter. The jury had been rigged. Thurmond was freed and the audience was held in the courtroom while he could be got out through the judge's chambers. He left town and did not come back but Granny was afraid of the bitterness that had been generated so she moved us away from Ripley.

Then Grandfather closed his office in Ripley and he and Granny came to Oxford, where he went in practice with Judge Howrey, who was later on the federal bench in Washington. The rest of us stayed on in Ripley until 1902, when Grandfather sold the railroad, and then Dad moved us here too. That was on the 24th of September, 1902, my first birthday.

Mother had been an Oxford girl. Dad had met her after Granny moved Grandfather here from Ripley. He married her in '96 and took her to New Albany, where Bill was born. So when we came here from Ripley in 1902, Mother simply came home again. Mother's home place is north of Oxford, looking back toward the town. Dad never worked for a railroad after that, but I can always remember how he used to listen when a train would pass and when it would blow its whistle.

Bill was one day short of five on the day we moved away from Ripley. He could talk by then, of course. Mother told me about one day we all ate dinner at Pa Murry's. That was Granny's father. Bill insisted on saying the blessing. They let him. He said:

"*Now I lay me down to sleep;*
I pray the Lord my soul to keep.
If I should die before I wake
I pray the Lord my soul to take.
W. C. Falkner."

Granny said he sent his petition up signed.

Granny moved Grandfather from Ripley as soon as she could after old man Thurmond's trial. She wanted no more of bloodshed nor the chance of it. Auntie and Uncle John, of course, came with them. Auntie was as yet unmarried and Uncle John was in his teens. They were Dad's brother and sister. Dad came too and that was when he met Mother.

Grandfather rented a house on North Street across a wood lot from L. Q. C. Lamar's. Mother had moved into town by then. She lived on the same street as the Lamars but nearer town. It was one street over from Grandfather's. The three houses formed sort of a triangle with Grandfather's at the apex. There was nothing but wood lots in between. Mother and Auntie and one of the Lamar girls used to stand on their porches and make arrangements to meet each other uptown at the drugstores, where no doubt they lay in wait for Dad and Uncle Jim and whomever the Lamar girl had her eye on at the time.

Later on Grandfather bought a place on Second South Street, on the opposite side of town; later still he built Granny a house on South Street about two blocks from the Square. It was when he finished this house that the rest of us moved to Oxford, to the new house on Second South.

This new house was three stories high, a landmark that could be seen from miles outside town. It became the center of our lives for as long as Grandfather lived. Years ago it was turned sideways and moved to what was Granny's flower garden and cut up into apartments. We still call it Grandfather's house, crowded in though it is among thirteen other houses and a filling station that occupy what was once his lot.

With Grandfather in Oxford, his duties to the railroad became more irksome than ever. Its headquarters was in Ripley, sixty miles away. The trips back and forth took too much time from his legal practice. He worried with it until '98 and that's when he made Dad auditor and treasurer and moved him to Ripley from New Albany. And that's when Granny put the pressure on to sell the railroad and get Dad away from Ripley, where there still were Thurmond partisans.

When Grandfather told Dad he was going to sell the railroad, Dad went to a banker in Corinth and tried to borrow the money to buy it. The banker laughed at him. He thought Dad was joking. No one who owned a railroad at the turn of the century would be foolish enough to want to sell it. Railroads had just put river traffic out of business and their profits were growing by leaps and bounds. Dad thought the man was laughing at him for his presumption in wanting to borrow so much money. He stalked out of the bank offended.

After the road was sold Dad was in that bank one day and the banker called him aside. He asked him why in the world he didn't tell him he was serious that day he asked to borrow the money; the bank would have been glad to let him have it.

Dad brought his horses with him when we came from Ripley. In fact we drove through the country. The sixty miles of road was easier than the roundabout way you had to come by train, with changes and layovers and such.

Our new home had a big pasture for the stock. Our lot was four hundred feet wide and a thousand deep. It was divided down the middle and one half was pasture and barn lot and the house was on the other half, about five hundred feet back from the street. The whole was enclosed with a crisscross panel fence and a like one divided pasture from front yard. I can remember Dad, arms crossed on the top rail, looking at his horses on the other side, and Bill and Jack and me, climbed up beside him, watching the horses too.

From just behind our lot a woods stretched a half mile to the railroad that linked Oxford and the University. On a spur track from the main line was a cottonseed-oil mill and ice plant and that's the business Dad went into soon after we arrived. A bridle path went through the woods from near where we lived to the oil mill and Dad used to ride back and forth to work and let us ride with him. Bill and Jack had their own ponies, Shetlands, but I was too young to have one of my own. Dad picked one of his horses for me and a black boy, Durwur, rode it and held me on the saddle in front of him.

I remember the hungry smell from the oil mill where they pressed the oil from the cotton seed. It smelled good enough to eat and some of the blacks who worked there did eat it, sopping it on bread like molasses. I remember, too, how Leslie Oliver, who worked at the ice plant, used to take one of the covers from the tank where they froze ice in three-hundred-pound blocks and let us stick our hands down in the water and feel how cold it was. It was the overflow from the ice plant that we dammed in after years to make our swimming hole in Bailey's Woods.

We began our love for horses at that time and our love for the woods too. It was those woods and that swimming hole that Bill used in *Soldier's Pay*, his first published novel. We spent a great part of our early lives in those woods and woods like them around Oxford and came to know them and outdoor life well. It showed up later in Bill's writings in almost microscopic detail.

Dad had dogs too. In Ripley he had foxhounds but by the time we came to Oxford foxes had about been hunted out. I remember his telling us about a fox hunt in Ripley. The dogs ran out of hearing and he and the others waited, but the dogs did not come in. It was late that night when they finally gave up and went home. Then early the next morning Dad rode back to where they had lost the hounds and blew his horn and listened. It was well after daylight when a red fox crossed the road not far from where he was standing. A rail fence stood beside the road. Dad watched the fox, almost too tired to move, laboriously crawl over the fence and, after looking back over its shoulder at him and then at the field behind it, trot, with tongue hanging out, across another field and into a hedgerow. Pretty soon his lead dog came along, tireder than the fox. It couldn't climb the fence and Dad said he helped it over and watched it, still on the fox's trail. He went on back to town then, to work. Late that night the dog came in and he got up and fed it and bedded it down and watched it drop off to sleep.

It was one of the many hunting stories he told us. We stood leaning against his chair and knees and listened and Bill remembered them better than Jack or me.

Dad didn't have hounds now. He had bird dogs. One, old Dick, a black-and-white setter, used to follow him through the woods to the oil mill. I can remember him trotting along beside us as we followed Dad through the woods.

I was about three, I guess, when Bill learned about baseball one day and came home and taught Jack and me how to play. He wasn't in school yet. None of us started until we were eight. And I can remember the game when he taught us, so I must have been about three.

Bill had been up to spend the day with Sallie Murry, our first cousin. She was Auntie's daughter. We pronounced it *Auntee*. They lived with Grandfather. Auntie had married Uncle Jim (he was a doctor), and he died about a year later, leaving her with child. Grandfather brought her to his house after Uncle Jim died and Sallie Murry was born there. Granny died not many years later and Auntie took over the housekeeping duties and kept house for Grandfather for as long as he lived.

Grandfather had a big front yard, as did everybody then. Most of them were full of children. Every neighborhood had enough boys and girls for baseball teams and football teams and any other games it took two sides to play.

With three of us, Bill and Jack and me, we had enough to play the game the way Bill taught us. The only trouble was I was too small to count as a full man. Durwur was there, though, to take my place in a pinch: to pitch for me when I was pitcher, to catch for me when I was catcher and to take my third strike when I was the hitter. If Mary, his mother, our cook, needed him to bring her an armload of stovewood or to run some other errand, we simply sat and waited until he got back and then resumed the game.

The way we played, if the hitter hit the ball he had to run the bases—which were oak trees about twenty feet apart—and get home before the pitcher could chase the ball down and beat him to the plate. A caught flyball was out, of course, but we seldom hit one in the air or caught it if we did. The main thing was to beat the runner to the plate. When the hitter was out, he took the pitcher's place, the pitcher moved to catcher, and it was the catcher's turn to bat.

Bill also told us you could throw a man out at home. If the pitcher could retrieve the ball and throw it to the catcher and he could catch it with one foot on the bag before the runner could get there, the runner was out. That's where Durwur came in handy. I hadn't yet learned to catch a ball so he caught them in my name. Otherwise Bill or Jack never could have got each other out.

Our front yard was full of big old oak trees and the ground was covered with acorns. This latter fact saved our baseball game one day and changed the way we played it.

We had been playing one morning when Mary had called Durwur. We sat down to wait till he got back. He returned and told us Mary had given him some task that would take him till dinnertime to finish. That meant twelve o'clock. That's when we ate dinner. So we were left stranded. We did try to play without Durwur to sub for me but it was no use. I simply could not catch a man out at the plate. Whoever was batting, Bill or Jack, just kept on and on and on while I missed ball after ball after ball.

Then Bill thought up a new way to play so we would not have to give up our game. This new way was: You no longer tried to throw a man out at the plate, you simply hit him with an acorn as he ran the bases. As long as you missed he could keep on running. If you hit him, he was out and it was the next man's time to bat. You were not supposed to throw at his head or face. If you hit him there it was an accident. We ran with our arms folded over our heads and our faces ducked but Bill made one more rule: If and when I got hit I was not to cry. If I did it would bring Mother and she would put a stop to our game.

I'm sure I did get hit with the acorns but, I suppose, not too hard for I never remember breaking up a game. I cried, I'm sure, for I was quite a crybaby in those days, but I always remembered Bill's injunction and never did it loud enough to bring Mother.

From acorn baseball we progressed to horse baseball. Bill usually got these things up for he was oldest. He and Jack worked out the details and I simply followed along.

Bill and Jack's ponies were in the yard that morning. The other horses were over in the pasture. We had been fooling with the little Shetlands, riding them, climbing over them. They were gentle as dogs. Durwur was in the back somewhere, doing something for Mary. We had grown tired of what we were doing and decided to play ball. Bill then thought about using the ponies.

Quickly we made up the rules. You batted standing on the ground. Once you hit the ball everything came to a standstill till you scrambled on your pony. That was the signal to go. You dug your heels in the pony's side and headed for first base as the pitcher opened season on you with acorns.

Bill's first shot hit Jack's pony in the flank and he hunched and sprang. The pony passed first base full out with Jack clinging to its mane and Bill and I screeching at the top of our voices. Of course it brought Mother, and Durwur came running around the corner of the house with Mary not far behind him. Damuddy, Mother's mother, who lived with us, came out on the porch. Mother yelled to Durwur and the two of them chased Jack and the pony down our five hundred feet of front lawn and cornered them against the board fence. Durwur caught the pony and Mother lifted Jack down. Bill and I had watched from the baseball field and were still standing there when Mother led Jack back up the yard by the hand. Durwur put Jack's pony in the pasture and caught Bill's and put it in there too.

Mother lined the three of us up and we went through an inquisition. Jack was scared and crying and Bill stood on first one foot and then another, with his hands behind him, trying to get out from under his part in it, but of course I blabbed everything. When court ended this session, horse baseball was outlawed and acorn throwing under any circumstances was taboo; we might knock each other's eyes out.

I don't remember us playing baseball any more until we moved up on South Street several years later. Without the fillips we had added it was too tame. To simply run the bases with someone chasing us with a baseball was fun no more. We needed the added zip of being pelted with acorns and horses running away beneath us. We turned our energies to other pursuits.

Chapter 3

IT WAS ABOUT THIS TIME THAT MOTHER, FOR THE time being, gave up on trying to get us to Sunday school. It was 1904. Bill was seven, Jack five and I three. There was a Children's Day at the church and Damuddy, Mother's mother, talked Mother into making a special effort to get us there. Mother took some persuading but she finally gave in.

We had one of the first bathtubs in Oxford. Grandfather had had it built for Granny when they lived where we did now. It was made by local carpenters. I don't know that they had ready-made bathtubs at that time. Anyhow, the first porcelain-lined cast-iron tub I ever saw was the one we put in after we moved up on South Street.

This bathtub I'm talking about was pieced together of tin. It had a curved wooden rim around the top. The carpenters sawed it out a piece at a time and fitted it and dressed it down. They even curved the edges, rounded them over. The tin was cut piece by piece and fitted and the seams soldered to prevent leakage. It was set in a wooden frame with fitted hoops running underneath to support it.

Only cold water ran in the tub. There was one pipe running in and a drainpipe running out. The drainpipe itself was an innovation. Until then someone carried your dirty water out and flung it over the garden fence to water the vegetables.

Hot-water tanks were known then but most people were afraid of them. They might blow up. It was safer to heat what water you needed in pots and kettles on the kitchen stove and besides, every range had a five-gallon hot-water reservoir built into the end by the firebox. A constant supply of water was kept steaming there and all you had to do was dip out what you needed.

Our bathroom was what had once been a bedroom. It was across a hall from the kitchen and handy to it for toting water. When a bath was necessary you ran cold water in the tin tub and stepped across the hall to the kitchen for what hot water was needed to temper the cold. When a bath was over you pulled the plug and the used water ran through a pipe laid across the back yard to the garden.

On this morning of which I speak Mother bathed and dressed Bill and Jack and me and then went to take her bath. Damuddy had promised she would look after us and see that we kept clean until Mother could get ready to take us to Children's Day. But Jack got hungry while we waited.

Jack was puny when he was little. He simply wouldn't eat. The only things he would stomach were buttered biscuits and sausage and fried eggs. Any time he would eat, feeding him became the first order of business. Damuddy took Jack on as her problem. She called him Little Brother.

Just as we were turned over to Damuddy that morning for Mother to go take her bath, Little Brother got hungry. Damuddy took him to the kitchen at once and began frying him eggs. She left Bill and me in rockers on the front porch to sit there and behave ourselves until she could finish feeding Jack.

While we were sitting there a coach, or hack as we called it, that Dad had sent from the livery stable to take us to church drove up. The driver was a colored man named Jessie Hayes. Bill and I knew him. He was one of our friends since he drove for Dad. Dad was in the livery business now, having sold the oil mill and ice plant.

We knew all of Dad's drivers. They were all our friends. They would put us on the mules' backs when they led them to water after they harnessed, and slow the wagons at the edge of our lot and let us get in and ride when we met them there in the evenings. We were delighted to see Jessie that morning and immediately ran out to the gate as soon as he stopped. We spoke and grinned and he spoke and grinned and helped us climb up on the seat beside him.

The first thing we settled, of course, was turns about driving. The blacks always let us drive when they stopped for us at the edge of the yard in the evenings and now we naturally presumed the same arrangements. Bill came first because he was oldest. Jack would be second, I knew, even though he was not here to make his claim, because he was older than I. I accepted third. Now there was nothing to do but wait for Mother and Jack and Damuddy and we would be ready to go.

In the meantime, Jessie placed the hack at our disposal with a fine manner and Bill and I, taking advantage, began climbing over it and inside it and under it, too I'm sure, from what Mother said we looked like when she came out the door at last, all dressed in white to go to Sunday school, as we had ben earlier when she dressed us.

Hacks were mostly to meet trains and carry drummers to our hotels. Most people had their own surreys and used them. Dad, being in the livery business, found it easier that morning to send a hack for us than to use our own surrey. Surreys were put away in buggy houses and kept clean. Hacks never were. Some times for a funeral they were dusted out, or after a trip in the mud, washed off. But usually livery stables let the rains take care of what dust accumulated from our unpaved streets and washed them only when they got muddy. It was this accumulated dust that Bill and I had climbed about in.

Mother said when she came to the door and saw us she could not tell us from Jessie's children. We were the same light-yellowish color that they were, all over, just like Jessie himself. Mother said she could not believe her own eyes at first. She came down off the porch and walked up closer to the hack. There was no longer any doubt then.

She made us come down off the hack and dismissed Jessie with a wide sweep of her hand. Jessie ducked his head, tipped his cap, said, "Yes, ma'am," to whatever Mother said and drove off.

Mother bathed Bill and me again and threw our white suits in the soiled-clothes hamper. Dressing us in our play clothes, she turned us out in the yard. I don't know what she said to Damuddy. She was still in the kitchen feeding Little Brother but it was not long before she came out the door in her widow's weeds and hurried away to church. Jack came out later in his play clothes so I guess Mother made a clean sweep and threw his white suit in the hamper too.

I don't remember us going to Sunday school after that until we moved up on South Street and were older. I think Mother gave up formal religion right there. We never had white suits again either. We have a picture taken not too long after that. Bill and Jack and I were taken to a "portrait studio" over Leavell's Plain & Fancy Grocery on the Square. We were dressed in black velvet.

It was later this same summer that Jack's goat ate up our genuine Panama hats that Aunt Willie sent us from Havana, and Tommy Yates got snake-bit in Miss Mary Lou Neilson's cow pasture next door and ran over Bill.

Aunt Willie was Grandfather's half sister. He had two other half sisters—Aunt Effie and Aunt Bama, who still lives in Memphis—and a half brother, Henry, who was shot by a friend of the Old Colonel's for fooling with the friend's wife. When my youngest brother, Dean, was born, Grandfather wanted to name him Henry, but Mother said, "Over my dead body." So they christened him Dean for Mother's mother.

Aunt Willie was especially fond of Bill. She would have him visit her and one time in Meridian she pointed out the governor to him. Bill never could explain to Jack and me what a governor looked like. That's one time words failed him. When he got through he made the governor sound just like anyone else.

Whenever Aunt Willie would take a trip, and she traveled a great deal, she would send Bill something from wherever she went. She always remembered Jack and me too. When she went to Havana she sent us the hats.

Dad had bought Jack a billy goat that summer. Mother tried to stop him from doing it but he did it anyhow. He also bought a small-scale model of a regular farm wagon with a spring seat just like a real one. The wagon was painted red and green with red wheels. He bought harness for the goat too, just like regular harness.

It took Dad and all the blacks to get Billy harnessed the first time and two of them to lead Billy about while Jack sat on the spring seat and held the reins. After a while they turned Billy loose but he didn't do anything. He wouldn't even move. He just stood there shaking his whiskers and glaring at everybody that moved.

Jack flicked him with the reins. Billy stood there. Jack tapped him with the switch. Billy stood a moment longer then walked slowly through the yard gate and out onto the plank walk that ran to the corner of our lot, where it joined the walk on the street.

Bill and I were walking along beside Jack telling him to make the goat go faster. The blacks were all hanging over the fence watching. Jack hit Billy again. Billy bleated. Jack whacked him once more and Billy came to a stop. Then Bill told me to get a stick and I got one. We took sides by Billy and with the blacks hollering "Stop it," we both laid on him. Billy took off.

He outran Bill and me almost at once. With the miniature wagon rocketing down the plank walk, Jack grabbed the seat to hold on. Bill and I were yelling, "Give him cord, Jack. Give him cord," like Jack was flying a kite. But Jack had already given him cord. He had flung the reins down when billy started down the walk. Billy hit a post with the wagon and damaged it badly, then tore himself loose and Jack shot out over the dashboard and slid along the plank walk on his stomach.

Jack cried, of course, and Mother and Dad and the blacks came running. Mother picked Jack up and the blacks caught billy with no trouble and slipped what was left of the harness off. With the wagon no longer trailing him, he had come to a stop almost at once and was standing there nibbling splinters off one of the fence boards. He said *baa* when the blacks walked up, and paid them no more attention as they stripped him of the broken pieces of leather. They pulled the wagon back to the house.

Bill and I had come up and were standing there, big-eyed at what had happened, and Dad gave us a good talking to for not having any more sense than to beat billy with the sticks. Mother led Jack, sobbing, back to the house. Damuddy met them at the door and took Little Brother and fed him fried eggs and buttered biscuits to quiet him down.

We never harnessed the billy again. The harness was all torn up and anyhow we no longer had a wagon to hitch him to. We simply gave him the run of the house—the outside part, that is—and he spent most of his time from then on out front where we played. He was on the front porch a lot too, and that's where he ate the hats.

We weren't wearing our hats. We wore caps in the winter to keep our heads warm but in the summer we wore nothing. We really did not need the hats and when they came we opened the packages and tried them on, then set them aside.

It was on a Sunday morning that we tried the hats on. The Sunday paper had come, with the funnies in it, and we were grouped about Dad as he read them to us. Nobody was paying any attention to Billy until Mother came to the door and saw what he was doing. It was too late then. He had already eaten some of each hat. She screamed and Dad dropped the paper and together we all chased Billy off the porch.

While Dad and Mother stood there arguing, Bill and Jack and I chased Billy around the house. He outran us back to the porch and was waiting when we turned the last corner. He was just standing there so we picked up the funnies Dad had dropped and sat down on the steps to await his return. He and Mother had gone on in the house, still arguing.

Mother said he would have to get rid of Billy. Dad said every little boy ought to have a goat. Mother said we had had ours. Dad came back out on the porch. We were sitting there holding the funnies and Billy was eating the rest of the paper.

Dad retrieved what was left of the paper and ran billy off the porch again and told us to keep him off. We followed about after billy, reporting back to Dad. He went to the trash pile and ate the labels off some cans. He ate part of an old magazine that had been thrown away. When we would call these happenings back to Dad he would rustle his paper and grunt. We watched billy the rest of that afternoon and the next day Dad sold him or at least got rid of him. We never saw billy again or owned another goat. As Mother said, we had had our goat.

Oxford was unspoiled by pavement and automobiles in those days. Our streets were good dirt as the Lord had made them, good enough to drive our horses over, and if they got dusty in summer and He neglected to dampen them down with a shower we simply sprinkled them with town water.

Second South, the back street on which we lived, didn't have much traffic of any kind on it. We had an occasional dray or a passing surrey or buggy and Mr. Watt Wardlaw, who lived next to us, used to swirl up dust every evening with the rig he had. But the dust was worth breathing just to see him pass. He had what was known as a "spanking bay," though the horse was a good bit darker than bay. It was almost a brownish black with red fire rippling along it when he touched it with the switch.

His buggy always looked like it was shiny new. He had white harness for his mare and when he came by, dressed up with a handkerchief sticking out of his breast pocket and that horse of his stepping out, it was a sight to see. I can remember Bill and Jack and me hanging over the fence to watch him pass and breathing dust until he was far out of sight. And Damuddy and Mother came out on the porch too to watch Mr. Watt each evening as he passed on his way to give some girl a treat. And it was a treat to sit behind that ripple of fire he had harnessed to that speckless chariot of his, though we never understood why he had to have a girl, of all things, beside him to help him enjoy it.

Besides this infrequent traffic, our back street was used as a cow lane. Some of the people in Oxford did not have room enough at home for a cow pasture. Everyone had cows. Those that did not have pasture room at home had their cows driven to pasture at the edge of town. We came to know some of the boys whose chore this was and later became friends with them. There was Whit Rowland, who later made something of a name for himself in the medical world as a pediatrician, and the Leavell boys, all seventeen of them, who mostly went into the Baptist ministry. We still hear of some of them, and all of them later appear in this story.

Other than this traffic the street was ours. We flew kites from it, and played baseball and shinny and paper-chase up and down it. It was because of our flying kites that Tommy Yates got snake-bit in Miss Mary Lou Neilson's pasture next door to our house.

The Yateses and the Standifers lived about halfway to town from where we did. We got to know Tommy and Shack because they were two of the boys who drove their family cows past our house each day. They were both good kite makers, the best we had till Ed Beanland came along, and one day Tommy promised to make me a kite. I had helped him drive his cow to the pasture and coming back he told me he would make me a kite the next day and bring it to me. And sure enough, he did.

Bill and Jack and I were in the front yard when Tommy and Shack came up with the kite. Tommy was flying it over his shoulder. He didn't have more than ten feet of string out on it, but it was flying as he walked along. It was a tiny thing, about a foot long, and he had covered it with silk. He stood there in the front yard and sort of gave it a flip and it went right on up, in almost no breeze too. As soon as it got above the house he let me have the string and almost at once I got the cord hung in one of our oak trees and the kite fell on top of our house. We couldn't get it. Mother came out and told us to leave it alone and when the blacks came in that night she would have one of them get a ladder and haul the kite down for us. A breeze came up later that day and blew the kite off the roof and because the string was tangled in the tree, beat it to pieces against another branch. Tommy made me another one later on but not out of silk. This one was covered with wrapping paper and full-sized and I flew it in the street with the rest of them.

Chapter 4

BECAUSE WE HADN'T BEEN ABLE TO GET MY kite down that morning Mother let us go with Tommy and Shack into the street where the rest of the boys were flying theirs. They were older than we and usually we had to watch them from our yard, hanging over the fence. This morning, however, she let us go clear out to where they were, almost behind Grandfather's. Ike King was there and Ed Beanland and Whit Rowland and I think one or two of the Leavell boys.

What little wind there was was from the north, so from where they were standing, the kites were about over Miss Mary Lou's pasture. We held Tommy and Shack's kites for them while they walked off string, then let them go when they yelled and began running, and watched the kites waft into the air as the long tails whipped off the ground. As soon as the kites were airborne and above the trees, Tommy and Shack stopped running and fed them string until they sailed aloft with the others already up there.

With so many kites up, Tommy's string soon got tangled with somebody else's and he yelled, "First cut!" before Tommy could. He got out his knife and cut Tommy's string to free his kite and Tommy's began falling. Tommy began running, with Bill and me right behind him. Jack was holding Shack's kite and couldn't leave it, so Shack ran after Tommy too.

We saw the kite drop from sight behind the trees in Miss Mary Lou's front yard and knew it would be in her pasture.

The entrance to Miss Mary Lou's pasture was just off the street and right across the street from the corner of our front yard. The entrance was grown up in a thicket but there was a narrow cow path through it. With Tommy leading, we ran past the corner and turned into the entrance. Tommy ducked through with Shack just behind him and Bill was just bending over to go through too when Tommy stepped on the snake. He jumped in the air and yelled, "Snake! Snake!" and hit the ground whirling back the way he had come. He knocked Shack aside and Bill back through the fence into me and we both fell in the ditch. I remember Tommy stooping to go through the fence but he didn't even break stride. Shack regained his balance and came through right behind him.

Tommy led the procession up the street, still yelling, "Snake!" with Shack trying to catch him and Bill and I trailing. We ran through the others flying kites there in the road and they tied their lines to fence posts as quick as they could and followed us. We ran Tommy clear to his own home, trying to catch him. He beat us there. His mother called the doctor and we soon found that snake bites did not necessarily kill you as we had thought.

After about fifteen minutes Tommy came out on the porch with his ankle bandaged (he had been barefoot; we all went barefoot in the summertime) and stood there finishing a glass of milk Mrs. Yates made him drink. So we all went back to flying kites. Tommy's kite was gone so he just sat on the bank and watched the rest of us.

I don't know why we chased Tommy that day, unless it was to be there to watch him die when he did it. And I don't think that Tommy was too persuaded that a snake bite was not fatal, either, even after the doctor tended to him. I remember how pale he was the rest of the day as he sat on the bank and watched us. As Bill and Jack and I, as long as we lived on Second South Street, sure gave that corner of Miss Mary Lou's pasture a wide berth when we had to pass it.

Years later Miss Mary Lou told Mother it was the finest thing that ever happened for her cow. She said that all summer long every time she looked out her window there would be some little Falkner boys after kites and her cow galloping around her pasture. Mother let it go at that. Miss Mary Lou was a kind old soul and getting along in years so Mother didn't think it worth her to remind her there were other little boys on Second South Street besides hers.

By the time August came around each year we were through flying kites or doing anything else that took us far from our front door. August brought "dog days" and that was mad-dog time. Every year we had our scare. We played close to the front porch and the handy front door with a wary eye on the street for any stray dog that might pass.

Each year we would hear of someone being bitten, or someone's stock being attacked, and then everyone began seeing mad dogs all over town. Our good hunting dogs were locked up at this time and every man kept a pistol handy. We were instructed to play close to the house and run in and slam the door if we sighted a dog of any kind.

Terrible stories would be told of those who had been bitten and always the one about the man who was tied to his bed when he went mad and bit his own tongue off clear to the roots. We went around big-eyed with fear and peered long out the door before we ventured forth. Of course most of these scare stories came from the blacks but Dad's pistol was always kept handy.

The cure for mad-dog bite in those days was almost as amazing as was the step-by-step account of the disease itself. We listened fascinated as the blacks told each other about it. None of them had ever seen it, but each one of them knew someone who knew someone who had. And nearly always the "stone" was now over in Arkansas, but they knew how they could send for it if they needed it.

There were no shots for rabies. We called it hydrophobia. The only cure was the stone. The stone was a growth taken from a deer's stomach under certain conditions. Not just any deer had a stone. You had to have the right kind of deer. The stone was like blotting paper and would suck the poison out of a dog bite. You simply placed the stone against the punctured flesh and it went to work immediately, turning a greenish color as it sucked itself full of the venom. When it was full it would become "pure green" and drop away from the wound to which it had attached itself as long as it was sucking.

Once it fell off it had to be put in a pan of coal oil so the oil would dissolve the poison in the stone. Once free of venom, the stone turned pure white again and could be reattached to the wound for more sucking. The stone could be used repeatedly so long as it was washed clean in coal oil each time. The blacks kept track of the stones and always knew where word could be sent for one in case they got bitten.

Actually the only person or thing I ever knew to be bitten was old Dick, Dad's bird dog. That happened after we moved to South Street across from Grandfather's. It was in August of the first summer we were there.

Dad heard a commotion in the back yard one night and it was Dick, in a fight with an invader, another dog. The intruder was gone by the time Dad got there but Dick came whimpering up to him and Dad could tell he had been in a fight. There was a mad-dog scare in Oxford at the time so of course he could take no chances. He locked Dick up for two weeks and Dick went mad and he had to destroy him.

He made us stay in the house while he did so, and we huddled scared around Mother until it was over and the blacks had taken Dick away. Dad kept the pen locked through the following winter and would let nothing, including us, in it.

It was not hard to make us careful about staying in the house after that. Occasionally we would hear shots as our marshals killed stray dogs. Mother and Dad were nervous too and we felt that. In fact most of my memories of our late-August days of that period are of Bill and Jack and me watching a hot bright outside world with our noses pressed to the dusty screens on our windows and doors.

With the coming of fall our late-summer scares were over. It was schooltime and in the fall of 1905 Bill started school. He was within a few days of becoming eight years old at the time school opened and that was the age, as determined by Mother, for his, and later Jack's and my, formal education to begin.

All through that summer the three of us talked of Bill's entry into school the coming fall. Jack and I asked Mother why, since Bill was going, we were not to be allowed too. She told us we were not old enough yet. We asked her what good it was going to do Memmie (that's what we called Bill then) anyhow. She told us that he would learn to read and write, that's what school was for, to teach you how to read and write.

That writing part made no impression on Jack and me but we went for that reading part. And so we made our preparations.

On the Sunday before Bill's first day at school, Jack and I refused to let Dad read the funny paper to us. We would save it for the next day, after Bill went to school and learned to read.

I think Mother would have corrected this assumption of Jack's and mine but Dad would have none of it. He carefully folded the colored sheet depicting Mutt and Jeff, and the Katzenjammer Kids, and Foxy Grandpa, and Buster Brown and his dog Tige, in their comic capers and put it away for the next day's reading. He wanted to hear Bill too.

I remember how Dad laughed when we handed Bill the funnies and he unfolded them and couldn't read any more than he could before he spent that morning in school. Mother couldn't help but laugh either, but not like Dad did. Bill, of course, was a disappointment to Jack and me. Bill might just as well have stayed home and played with us for all the good his morning in school had done him. When Dad had finished laughing he reached the paper from Bill's hand and gathered us around him to read the funnies as always; the only difference was we got them a day late.

It was after we moved up on Main South Street that Mother discovered that I couldn't make out a picture unless I looked at it upside down. It was because of my position around the funny paper. Bill stood on one side of Dad and Jack on the other; that left me only space at the head of the paper, facing Dad. I had never had occasion to look at a picture from any other position.

Mother was reading me a story one day and I moved around to the top of the book so I could see the picture. She turned sideways so I could see better and I again moved around to the top. She handed me the book and said, "Look at this picture." I turned the book upside down and looked at it. Right there she made a new rule about the funnies.

She always tore the double sheets in two and she read one piece and Dad read the other, so all three of us could have places at the sides. She saw that I looked at pictures in the normal way from then on so I would learn to see them as they ought to be looked at. I remember it took me a good many weeks to get to where I could recognize my funny world turned right side up.

The first grade in our school, the one that failed to teach Bill how to read in one day, was called the chart class or the primer. It held session only for half a day. Miss Annie Chandler taught both it and the first grade.

In chart class we learned our letters, how to count to a hundred, and a few sentences such as "Mama loves Baby" and "Baby loves Mama." Mother had taught us most of this before our eighth birthdays, so all of us skipped the chart class after only a few days. Bill went into the first grade almost at once, even though he couldn't yet read the funny paper.

Miss Laura Eades taught second and third and Bill skipped second too, as did Jack and I in our turn. Bill and I made the honor roll regularly our first years in school. Jack did sometimes. He just never did take to learning after Bill's flat failure after his first day in school. Even Mother's earnest explanation of what an education meant to a man in after life didn't quite fade out his distrust after Bill unfolded the funnies and couldn't read a word of them.

And then our first automobile came through Oxford. From then on Jack was not interested in whether eggs cost a penny apiece or a bit a dozen, or what 9 times 6 or 7 times 8 was, or how much two and a half yards of cloth cost if one yard cost nine and three-quarters cents. His world from then on was filled with pistons and sliding gear transmissions and spark plugs and distributor heads and such. Education such as you got in school was a lost cause as far as he was concerned, or he was so far as it was concerned. Either way, neither of them troubled the other much after that car came through.

It was in 1908 when that first automobile came through Oxford. It was a red Winton Six, a touring car. They didn't make anything but roadsters and touring cars then. They both had collapsible tops, like convertibles, and the roadsters had one seat and the touring cars two. We never heard of a sedan or any closed car until the Teens.

We already knew what an automobile looked like from pictures. Jack had a scrapbook of them he had clipped from the slick magazines. And even though Jack spent his time pouring over his car pictures and reading whatever he could find about engines and such, Bill actually knew the principle that made the engines run, and built a steam engine. It ran too, we think. But it burned our playhouse down one Sunday afternoon, so we never could be sure, but we thought it did.

We heard weeks ahead that the Winton was coming. It belonged downstate and was headed for Memphis and would come through Oxford, right up South Street past where we lived. We began watching the street for it, afraid it might pass while we were in the dining room eating. We spent a great deal of our time hanging over the front-yard fence, looking down the road.

The car finally came through too. We saw it pass and ran along the street behind it in the dust till it was out of sight. It got all the way to Memphis, we heard later, but the man who owned it missed the river bridge and drove it off into the river. He never got it out. We heard he'd been living on peanut butter and crackers to save the money to buy the car and now we heard that he had got a job in Memphis and was living on peanut butter and crackers again to buy him another one.

Seeing that car pass, moving under its own power, set Bill to thinking. Mother saw to it that we had things to read. She selected the right books and magazines that would hold our interest. She trained us all in how and what to read. For Bill she subscribed to the *American Boy*, Jack had *Boy's Life*, and I the *St. Nicholas* magazine.

Bill's *American Boy* had an inventor's section in each issue and one of them had had an article on steam engines. That was how Bill came to build a steam engine.

He built it in the back corner of the hall, with Jack and me helping. He used a baking powder can and one of Mammy's (she was with us by then for Dean had just been born) nickelized snuffboxes. I don't remember where he got the small pieces of tubing he used, but I do remember he ordered a soldering iron with some of the money he always managed to have hoarded away for when he needed it.

As soon as Dad moved us up on Main South Street, across from Grandfather's, the first thing he did was to build a big new barn on our lot for his horses and mules. I suppose Bill found some of the stuff he used in his engine out where they were building the barn. I know we all helped with the barn and knew almost every piece that went into it, and with Jack and me helping, the three of us were apt to be able to find enough pieces to build almost anything.

Anyhow I can remember us hunched about that table in the back corner of the hall helping Bill put together that steam engine. I know some of the time we put in back there we were supposed to be devoted to studying and Mother and Dad came in one night from where they had been visiting over to Grandfather's and caught us at the back table and made us quit fooling with the engine and go back to our books. But we finished the engine anyhow and that's what Bill set the playhouse on fire with.

When Dad first began operating his livery business he built a small one-room office uptown that he used for headquarters. Later he bought a livery stable on Depot Street and moved the old office to our back yard for our playhouse. He had never painted it while he used it for his office but decided that we boys should when he turned it over to us. He brought us a big can of red paint and some brushes and when Mother saw the paint and brushes she said, "No, Buddy. No." But Dad said it was time we learned to protect and take care of what was ours.

Neither Mother nor Dad was there when we started painting, just Bill and Jack and I. The side of the building was about ten feet high so of course we had to have a ladder. We got from the barn one that had been used in building it. It was the right height and Bill, being oldest, climbed to the top with his bucket and brush. Jack came second. He went about halfway up the ladder. I came last, on the bottom rung. The only trouble was, the ladder slanted so far back from the house that when I stood on the bottom rung I couldn't reach the wall. So I stood under the ladder.

Of course our brushes dripped some paint but no more than you would suppose. I got a few splashes from Bill's and Jack's brushes and Jack got an occasional splatter from Bill's. And then one of Mother's white chickens that had the run of the back yard saw a drop of paint fall and thought it was a bug of some kind. It came running up and pecked at the red blob on the ground and other chickens saw and came. Soon all of Mother's flock was there at the foot of the wall pecking at the falling drops. Then we began flicking paint at them. Mother, who had by then come home, came to the back door about this time and when she saw what was going on, began screaming. Mammy came running with Dean in her arms.

Between the two of them they got us down off the ladder and me from under it and the paint and brushes away from us. Mother made us strip our clothes off standing in the yard at the edge of the porch. I was almost solid red, Jack was pretty red, and Bill, who had been at the top of the ladder, was scarcely red at all.

Mammy went in the house and put Dean down and she and Mother got coal oil and scrubbed us the best they could. Bill came pretty clean but finally Mother called Dad to send her oil in five-gallon lots and she had the blacks empty several cans into our tub and she simply put Jack and me in there and bathed us in the stuff. Most of the red came off except in the wrinkles and under our toe and fingernails. She couldn't do much about our hair. She finally cut great gaps out of Jack's and cut all of mine off.

The main thing I remember about that episode was those poor white chickens. We had really soaked them. Their wings were so heavy with paint they couldn't raise them. When the paint dried they couldn't go to roost, They couldn't flap their wings to get up on the roost poles.

I remember, when dark would come, how they would trail their wings across the yard and crowd into a corner of the hen house. They wore their feathers about half off scraping them across our back yard. It made the funniest sort of sound. And I remember how the neighbors used to come over in the evenings to watch them trail across the back yard to go to bed in the corner of our hen house. Dad had the blacks finish painting the playhouse and it was shortly after that we built Bill's steam engine.

Since we were just across the street from Grandfather's now, Dad used to visit over there every few nights after supper. He would take Mother with him and we would be left at home, supposedly to study and get up our homework for the next day.

Jack and I would not have studied with Bill tinkering with something like that anyhow, but as it happened, we couldn't. Bill took the light.

We didn't have electricity then. The University did but Oxford had not as yet put in its plant. We used oil lamps.

Our study table was about the size of a card table, though at that time we had never seen what they call a card table now. It was a stiff-legged, square-topped table like you see now in hallways and against walls in living rooms, for putting flowers on and magazines and such. We sat about it with our books open and tablets before us and a lamp in the center. But Bill took the lamp, as soon as Mother and Dad left for Grandfather's, to the back corner of the hall where he had his workshop and, of course, Jack and I tagged along.

This arrangement worked well for a while but then one night, as I said, Mother and Dad came back from Grandfather's before we noticed how much time had passed and that brought an end to Bill's workshop in the hall. It was moved out to the play-house for the daytime. I don't think Mother went to Grandfather's so often after that, either. She stayed home with us after supper, to be sure we got our homework done.

I remember that it was a Sunday afternoon when we finished the engine. It was soon after dinner. That meant about one-thirty or two o'clock. We had a tin biscuit pan to make a fire in under the boiler (the baking powder can) and we had just started the fire when Dad called us. It was time to go riding. We always went riding Sunday afternoons.

Dad had what was called a trap. It looked like a buggy except the back end of it was high, like a box, instead of just a shallow tray to carry luggage and such in. This boxlike affair opened sideways from the middle and formed two lengthwise seats. Four people could crowd in there, so there was plenty of room for the three boys. We scrambled into the trap with Mother and Dad up front and away we went. However, before Bill left he had heaped coal on the fire in the firebox to hold the heat until we could get back.

We rode into the country several miles, stopping along the way to cut stalks of sorghum that we sucked the juice from, and came back in time to see smoke billowing from every crack in our playhouse. Dad flung the reins to Mother and jumped to the ground yelling for the blacks. They came out of their cabins and began running after Dad and Bill, and Jack and I scrambled out of the trap and followed as fast as we could.

When they got the door of the playhouse open, the floor was burning around the edges of a big hole through which the steam engine had dropped. It was on its side under the floor with steam hissing from it, and some of the coals were still red hot.

They put the fire out and left the door open and opened all the windows to clear the smoke out. We all believed that the engine had actually run and it was the vibrations from it that had tilted it over and knocked coals out of the pan to set the floor on fire. Another reason we believed Bill's engine had ran was that when it finally got cool enough to pick up there was very little water left in the boiler. That fire was bound to have made a whole lot of steam and if it hadn't been used up running the engine it would have blown the whole thing up. But we never did know for sure. Dad set his foot down on our building anything else that took fire to run. But I still to this day believe Bill's steam engine ran.

I remember another thing about the ride that afternoon. Bill picked up a snake. It was a cottonmouth. It scared all of us but Dad nearly had a fit. He simply could not stand snakes of any kind.

All the time we were riding Bill and Jack and I were jumping in and out of the trap, running along beside it, letting it get ahead of us and catching up or running ahead and waiting for it. One of our tricks was to pick up a stick and run along beside a wheel and let the stick rattle against the spokes. We were doing this when Bill's stick broke. He saw another one ahead in the road and ran and picked it up, only it was a snake. When it began to squirm he dropped it and yelled.

Dad cussed and Mother made us all get back in the trap. I could see the muscles in Dad's jaws knotting for the next few miles as he clenched his teeth and I remember Mother saying, "Shhh, Buddy. Shhh. The children can hear you." I guess he was glad to have something to stomp when we got home and found the playhouse floor on fire.

Chapter 5

EVERY HOME BACK THEN WAS ON A LOT LARGE enough to devote space to a vegetable garden, a pasture for a cow and a pen for pigs. Every home was a long way toward being self supporting. Our grocery stores were usually labeled "Plain & Fancy." But most of the stock they carried was plain, such as coffee (in bean form, which we roasted and ground as we needed it) and sugar and salt and flour, which we bought by the barrel. All of us had barrel-stave hammocks in our yards then too.

The fancy stock the stores carried was usually for special occasions like Christmas, when they imported bananas by the bunch, coconuts with their funny monkey faces and crates of oranges. Christmas smelled like oranges, for that was about the only time we had them.

Most of our fruits came from our own orchards. They were planted so as to give us plums and early peaches and summertime pears and late-November apples. We put the apples in scraps of newspaper that we saved, each apple wrapped separately because if one spoiled it would rot all the others it touched. Then we stored them away in empty flour barrels against the coming winter.

Mother was a good gardener and with our dubious help raised fresh vegetables for our table for almost every month in the year. March is about the only month you can't have fresh vegetables down here. I always remember how good that first early mess of English peas tasted.

Of all the vegetables we raised, I remember her best as a wonder with pole beans. Hers flourished. She raised so many one year that she sent Bill and Jack and me out selling them in Negro Hollow.

When pole beans come through the ground you have to stick them. If you don't, they grow so long they mat all over the ground and the beans, once in contact with the earth, rot. Some people use trellises to train the vines on but Mother used sticks. Each vine was stuck separately and she didn't use just ordinary old sticks either. Hers came from the sawmill and were cut one inch square and eight feet long. She saved them from year to year, making us pull them carefully out of the ground when bean season was over and stack them neatly in our old barn.

We started out with two gallon cans full apiece, one in each hand. We knew most of the blacks in the Hollow. A great many of them worked for Dad or cooked for us or did our washing. We had a big pasture across the road from our lot and our cow was put out there every day, and Dad's work stock on Sundays. He had built several cabins for his drivers along the fence line and we stopped at Jessie's house first with the beans.

When we knocked on the door the first one to come out on the porch was Eskimay, Jessie's son. Eskimay was about our age and one of our playmates. He grinned when he saw us and we grinned back. Then his mother came to the door. Her name was Cora, think, and we told her we were selling beans for fifteen cents a gallon. She bought a gallon. Eskimay came along when we went on to the next house. He took one of my buckets and one of Bill's and toted them for us.

By the time we got over in the Hollow proper we had sold another gallon or two and then we came to Nancy's house. Her name was Nancy Snowball and she'd cooked for us at one time. She'd washed for us during one period too. She wore a black straw sailor hat winter and summer. When she would come for our wash she would put the sheet load of clothes on her head and her hat on top of the bundle. We used to follow her home just to watch her crawl through a barbed wire fence with that sheet load on her head and her hat on it and never touch it with her hands. Bill wrote about Nancy Snowball in one of his stories, "That Evening Sun."

Anyhow, when we got to Nancy's she wanted a gallon of our beans. Jack still had a gallon left so he made the sale. He gave Nancy the gallon of beans and she gave him a quarter and he gave her back a dime in change. I raised the roof. Jack was giving her a gallon of our beans and a dime of our money too.

Bill and Eskimay had gone on to the next house and when I began crying Jack called them to come over where we were. Bill and Eskimay came. Jack told them what the trouble was and Bill tried to explain to me about making change. I would have none of it. I had seen Jack give Nancy a bucket of our beans and some of our money too with my own eyes.

Eskimay had dropped aside. He didn't open his mouth in the argument. Nancy was standing there with the bucket of beans in her hand and our dime too. Finally she gave them both back to Jack and he gave her back her quarter and we went home. We didn't try to sell any more beans. I don't remember Mother ever sending us out again.

Dean was with us by this time. He came to us in the summer of 1907. His birth date was two days before Dad's and Dad always called him his birthday present. Damuddy was gone. She had died of stomach cancer.

The only thing they knew to do for cancer in those days was to leave small amounts of morphine for the patient to take when the pain became unbearable. Doctors made up their own prescriptions then, from ranked bottles looped inside their black bags. They mixed stuff on a handy table and measured it off on small squares of paper that they folded into little drumlike pill-boxes and wrote the directions by hand on top.

I remember Damuddy's last days and weeks and months, when she spent more and more time in bed. We used to visit in her room often and I remember how gentle and kind she always was, and how patient with us even amid what I know now to have been almost unbearable pain. She never let us see her take any of the morphine and I seriously doubt if she ever took as much as she should have. She was a devout Baptist and, somehow or other, the taking of dope under any circumstances did not fit in with her religious beliefs. Pain wasted her away and she died before Dean was born.

Dean was born completely bald and with a sort of milk crust Mother found all but impossible to cure. Mammy came to us, almost with Dean. I remember how she and Mother worked over Dean's bald head. They made silk caps for him and kept some sort of grease all over his head about till he could walk. He never did have much hair and was beginning to get bald again when he was killed at twenty-eight.

When Mammy came to us she became a daily part of our lives and except for a few infrequent intervals, remained with us till she died. Bill spoke her burial service. He held it in his parlor and she was buried from there. All of us loved Mammy, our shepherdess, at times an avenging angel. She appears in a great many of Bill's books. She it was who was faithful; she was the one who endured.

From the time Mammy came she spent about as much time with the rest of us as she did with Dean. When he was quiet or asleep and she was not needed with him she would be where we were, watching our doings. I remember her, small and black (she weighed only ninety-eight pounds), standing unobtrusively to the side, always with a head rag and some sort of bonnet on, a snuff stick in her mouth, and always in a fresh-starched dress and apron and soft-toed black shoes. I have no doubt that her black wing saved us many a hurt or that her sharp tongue kept us from many a mischief we had no business thinking of getting into in the first place.

Mother trusted her profoundly and we soon learned to mind one of them the same as we would the other.

Bill had a tombstone put on Mammy's grave. It is inscribed from her "white children." A little of each of us lies buried there in the black section of St. Peter's Cemetery.

Mammy's name was Callie Barr. She had belonged in slavery times to old Colonel Barr, who lived cater-cornered across the street from where I live now. He owned nearly all the land from here to Burgess, about twelve miles to the west.

Nearly all slaves, on being freed, took the surnames of their former owners. That's why Mammy chose Barr. She had a brother who lived over in the Hollow, a good friend of ours-Wes Barr.

Mammy always told us she was sixteen years old when she was freed. That would have made her almost a hundred when she died. She might well have been. I know she was old. She married five times but none of them took. She had been married four times when she came to us. She married once after that and her new husband took her to Arkansas and mistreated her and Dad sent Mr. Bennett over there and brought her back. She never again left Oxford or us.

Mammy used to tell us stories of slavery times. Jack didn't pay too much attention to them but Bill and I did, in particular Bill. I can remember him listening by the hour to her. When Dean was big enough to walk, Mammy used to take us to the woods hunting bird eggs, for we all had bird-egg collections. She called it "bird nesting."

She taught us to take one egg from a nest with a spoon so the mother bird would not desert the rest of the eggs because our hands had touched them. As we would walk along, slowly on Dean's account, she would tell her stories and we would stay close and listen. This twined her whole life with ours.

One story Mammy told us was about making candles when she was a child. That was the children's chore. They made them in cane molds. Each mold had twelve cane joints fixed in a wooden frame. The bottoms of the joints were sealed, the tops, level with the frame, open. Wicks were put in each joint, then melted tallow was poured in.

Mammy said all the children would be seated in a half circle about the kitchen fireplace, each with a mold, and "Ol' Mistus" in the center. She sat there with a long-stemmed pipe, the stem long enough to reach any head in the half circle. At any sign of foolishness she could lean over and rap the mischief-maker over the head with the knob of her pipe. Mammy said the main head thumpings she got were for putting water in the bottoms of her molds, because when the hot tallow was poured in it would shoot clear to the ceiling. And usually it was not the one whose head got thumped who had put the water in. It was his next-door neighbor, while be wasn't looking.

Another story Mammy told us was the classic about the ghost from Shiloh, who appeared all over the South during Reconstruction. When the Yankees had come through Oxford on their way overland to Vicksburg, Colonel Barr had moved all his slaves to Pontotoc, about thirty miles to the east. That's where Mammy was when she was freed. After the War, when the Ku Klux Klan rode, she said they were really scared. All the blacks had heard stories about these silent, white-clad ghosts. Some of them had seen the night riders. Every black got his family in the house before dark and shut and barred the doors and windows.

Mammy said that one night someone knocked on their door. They were scared to open it and scared not to, too. Finally her father called, "Who dat?" A groan. It was repeated. Her father opened the door a crack and there was a man in white on a horse draped in white. The man wore a hood with eye holes in it. The horse's head was also covered. Only its ears stuck out.

On seeing Mammy's father the ghost groaned, "Water. Water. I'm in hell. I'm burning. I was killed at Shiloh and I've been burning in hell since. Water. Water."

Mammy's father told the ghost there was water in a bucket on the bench just outside the door. The ghost said that if it got off its horse it would be too weak to remount. It would have to remain there. So Mammy's father slipped outside and handed the man a dipper of water. The man took it and poured it into a rubber bag hidden in its robe, then asked for more. Mammy's father gave it another dipper, then the ghost asked for the bucket and emptied that into the bag. Mammy said that when the ghost handed the empty bucket back it moved away. They couldn't hear it because the horse's feet were tied in burlap. They only saw it seem to fade away. Mammy's father then dropped the bucket and bolted back inside the house and barred the door again. Mammy said they spent the rest of that night huddled together under quilts and it was not too long after that they moved back to Oxford.

Some of Mammy's great-grandchildren and their children still live around here. It is not too many years ago I saw one of them, Molly, and we talked about Mammy.

Old Wes used to always help with our hog killings. Everyone had hogs then and the first hard frost, about the first week in November, you could hear hogs squealing all over town as they were butchered for winter meat. You could get most any black to take charge of the butchering for the chitterlings. They say chitterlings taste like fried oysters. All blacks and some white people seem to love them. I never tasted one nor did we ever cook them at home. All the blacks in the Hollow had certain white folks they helped with hog killing and for a week or more after that first hard frost you could hardly go through that area on account of the stench of chitterlings cooking in almost every house.

I cannot pass over Mammy too quickly because of the tremendous influence she was on Bill's life and outlook and writings. When she came to us he was ten, Jack eight, and I six. Of course she called us by our first names then, a habit she never relinquished, nor did we notice or take it amiss. Even when we were grown men and had children of our own she still called us Memmie and Jack and Johncy. Memmie was a name Jack got up for Bill, trying to say William. That was as near as he could come, and I very naturally took it up from him. Bill did more for Mammy than Jack or I because chance offered him that privilege. Jack and I were away from Oxford during

Mammy's last years and Bill was here. What he did he did in all our names. We were her "white children."

It was by the yardstick of his memory of Mammy, I think, that Bill measured integration. They say we love the blacks as individuals down here and hate them as a class, while up North they love them as a class and hate them as individuals. I know we loved Mammy, and measured by any yardstick she stood as the equal of any of us. I'm sure that now she looks down on us, her still earthbound "children." I am sure that when our time comes she will demand an explanation even of Him if we are denied admittance Up There, and as sure that her staunch vehemence will bring for each of us at least a resigned, "All right. Let them in."

I expect even He has learned by now not to argue with Mammy.

Chapter 6

SINCE I WAS JUST BEFORE TURNING SIX WHEN
Dean was born, I still had two more years to go at home before
I started school. For those two years Mammy became almost as
much a nurse and playmate for me as she was for Dean. She
and Mother still kept Dean's head greased and his silk cap on
on account of the milk crust, but besides that and his feeding
and tending to, she spent a great deal of her time keeping me
entertained. There were long winter days she spent on her old
black knees in the hall playing marbles with me and letting me
win because I would cry if I didn't. She would see that I was
bundled up if I did go outside and if my feet were dry when I
came back in. I never remember her complaining. I only
remember her there when I needed her.

But then there were good days through the winter and on
Saturdays, of course, Bill and Jack were home from school. We
spent most of those Saturdays in the woods. It was easy to get
up a gang in those days. Nearly every home had children and it
took only two or three to produce a gang. Only our main
streets were settled then and the woods came up to most of our
back doors. All you had to do was yodel a few times (each gang
had its particular call) and half a dozen or more of you were
ready for the woods.

Bill and Jack and I found an old Confederate horse pistol
one Saturday morning when we were playing in the woods. We
were down behind the Chandler house in their pasture and
found the pistol in a sand ditch at the foot of a hill we used to
slide down when it snowed. There's no telling how long the
pistol had been buried in the sand. Only part of it was sticking
out when we found it, like it must have been buried for a long
time and a recent rain had washed enough sand away for about

half the barrel to show. We dug it out, Bill claimed it and we took it home.

The pistol was an old cap-and-ball. There was a long rod under the barrel that worked a plunger to ram the loads home. Each chamber had a tube off the back of it for the cap. It was rusty, of course, and when we got it home and cleaned it up with coal oil we found the butt plates eaten away and the mainspring broken. But we got the cylinder loosened to where it would turn and the hammer to where it could be moved back and forth. It was remarkable what good shape it was in for the time it must have lain there, probably ever since the War Between the States.

During that war there was a great deal of cavalry skirmishing back and forth through Oxford. The Yankees were in force at Holly Springs, thirty miles to the north. They kept patrols across the Tallahatchie at Abbeville, eleven miles away, that ranged through our area. We were at Grenada, fifty miles south. The Yocona River was eight miles north on the Grenada Road and we were afraid to cross it in force and kept our patrols this side of it, also ranging through town. These patrols ranged as high as three hundred men. There were running fights all through this No Man's Land and Oxford was the center of it.

Relics were not too uncommon, bayonets and rifles and sabers and such, but this was the only pistol we ever found, and after Bill fired all six chambers one day, we never saw it again. Mother took it away from us and I don't know what she did with it. She never told us or mentioned it after that day.

This was the next Saturday morning. We had been all week cleaning the pistol up and Bill had whittled handles for it out of a piece of cedar we found. We had managed to clean all the sand out of the barrel and the chambers in the cylinders and Bill figured out how to use a slingshot rubber for a mainspring. He simply doubled it around the frame holding the cylinder and looped it back over the hammer. You held the pistol with both hands and pulled the hammer back against the stretch of the rubber bands with both thumbs, and let go. That slapped the hammer against the back end of the percussion tubes with a more than satisfying click. We were ready to fire it.

There were no percussion caps available to us. Some of the stores uptown still sold them, for there were still muzzle loaders around, but we found no need to go as far as town for our caps. Bill simply went to his hoard, which contained a little of everything he had ever owned, and got some paper caps for cap pistols he had been saving. By crimping them properly they could be made to serve. Bill stuffed one in a *phfut* tube, pulled the hammer back and let it go, and the cap said and made smoke, so we were satisfied there was enough fire there to explode a charge of powder in the cylinder.

We loaded the cylinders, all six of them, with black powder taken from some of Dad's shotgun shells. We cut the shells open to get at the powder. It took several of them but we finally got all the chambers loaded and tamped down with pieces of wet newspaper. We had buckshot that we used to shoot in our slingshots so we put some of these on top of each charge of powder and tamped it down with wads of chewed paper. With all six chambers now fully loaded, Bill crimped paper caps into each of the six tubes, and we were ready to go.

Dad had taught us each to hunt as our turn came. Our turn came when we reached eight. We were given an air rifle then and taught to use it like a real gun. We never pointed a gun at anything unless we aimed to shoot at it, whether the gun was loaded or not. We always fired higher than a man's head so there would be no accidental shooting of someone screened from our sight on the other side of a bush. He taught us never to bring a gun in the house loaded.

At ten we got .22 rifles, and at twelve, shotguns. Bill was past ten and already had his .22 and knew how to handle powder guns. He remembered his powder gun training and fired over Jack's and my head that morning, thank goodness. He brought neighbors running to see what in the world us Falkners had done now.

Mother had a fit. Mammy berated us soundly, and would have done worse had it not taken most of her time trying to calm Mother down. I don't remember which one of them actually took the pistol out of Bill's hand, Mammy or Mother. But one of them did and we never saw it again. I do remember that Mother made us come in the house and sit in separate corners of the front room till Dad got home to dinner and decided what to do to us for firing the gun. He got after us mainly about cutting his shells up and made us stay in our own front yard the rest of that Saturday.

We had been using the steps of the back porch as a bench to work on when we'd loaded the pistol. As soon as we were through, Bill had taken it and got up, on the porch, facing the yard. Jack and I were still in the yard, facing Bill from below. He raised the barrel toward the sky, holding it in both hands, and pulled the hammer back. Jack and I shut our eyes and stuck our fingers in our ears. Bill let go.

When the hammer struck the first tube the cap said *phfut* just like before. But then all the other five caps began exploding. They said *phfutphfutphfutphfutphfut*, then the loads began going off, one right behind the other. There was a terrific roar from all that black powder and our back yard was filled with smoke and flying pieces of smoldering newspaper.

Mother said later that she could just see Bill on the edge of the porch disappearing into the smoke cloud and couldn't see Jack and me, down in the yard, at all. She called to Bill and asked him where we were. He could only look at her for a minute before the smoke enfolded him, and stand there with the pistol in his hand. He wasn't so much scared as surprised. None of us expected all those shots to go off at once, least of all Bill. He had invented the rubber mainspring and tested it out. He knew it would work.

I guess probably it was Mother who got hold of Bill and took the pistol away and Mammy who found Jack and me in the smoke. Anyhow, by the time the yard was cleared enough of smoke for Mammy to see how to get Jack and me up on the porch, the yard was full of neighbors. They had heard the explosion, of course, but what really brought them was all that black smoke. They thought we had set the house on fire at last.

Mother told us to go in the front room and sit there until Daddy came home to dinner and decided what should be done with us as punishment for fooling with the pistol. We went, without a word.

We called Dad "Daddy" in those days. We didn't drop the diminutive or change it to "Dad" until we were almost grown. I don't know why we changed then, but we did. But "Dad" or "Daddy," we knew what Mother meant when she said go in the front room and sit down. It was the way she punished us.

I don't remember her ever whipping us but once, and that was one Saturday morning in the winter. We were out in the woods and I fell in the creek with my clothes on and didn't come home and change. She whipped me for not coming home and Bill and Jack for not making me. She was afraid I would catch cold, but I didn't.

Mother wasn't big as a minute. She was less than five feet tall and weighed about the same as Mammy. She couldn't have hurt us if she had whipped us but this punishment she figured out was far worse, we thought, than a whipping. A whipping is over and you go about your business, but this sitting in chairs in the front room could go on for hours sometimes, depending on what we'd done.

She would make us sit in chairs in opposite corners of the room and we couldn't even speak to each other. We couldn't read books. We couldn't do anything but sit there. And most of the time we could hear the other children playing outdoors, sometimes in our very own yard, and we couldn't even go to the window to wave at them or yell that we couldn't come out. It was the worst punishment I know about. And if we so much as made a sound Mother came and took her seat in the middle of the room and extended our punishment another fifteen minutes.

It was about nine o'clock when we fired the gun. Dad came home at noon. We had been sitting there three hours by then. Of course, all the neighborhood children had come to see what the commotion was in our back yard and had stayed to play. We had been listening to them, with Mother sitting there in her chair in the middle of the room, and Dad decided we had had enough. He merely gave us a good talking to.

I've often wondered what Mother did with that pistol. It would be quite a relic now. But somehow I never could bring myself to ask her. I guess I always figured it was better to let sleeping dogs lie.

We were regular attendants at Sunday school by then. We lived only about half as far from town now as we had on Second South Street and were within easy walking distance. Damuddy was gone now and Mother never was much of a churchgoer. She always claimed she didn't have time. She said she did her part just getting us there every Sunday.

Dad went along with her as far as our going was concerned, though he never went himself either until years later when the Darwin-Bryan "Monkey Trial" in Tennessee scared him into it for a short while, but that spell did not last long.

Dad had a funny idea about God. The One he recognized didn't bother you much during the week and even on Sundays. He didn't pay any attention to anything you did, except on the front porch. Whatever you did in the back yard behind the fence was all right. That's where we played Sunday afternoons, in the back yard.

Dad helped Mother see to our going to Sunday school. It was her job to bathe and dress us but Dad took it on himself to see that our shoes were shined. I can remember Mother, after she had us ready to go, telling us to be sure and go by Dad and let him look at our shoes. If they needed it he would shine them before we left. We were supposed to do it ourselves Saturday night, but we always missed places, especially at the backs where it was hard to reach with the brush. Dad would touch them up and away we would go. I guess that commitment was his sole acknowledgment to formal religion. Except for the time he got scared about evolution, I never saw him make any other gesture toward a church.

Sunday school "took in" at ten and ran for about an hour. A passenger train came through town at eleven. It brought the Sunday paper from Memphis, the one with the funnies in it. Bill and Jack and I, and all the other little boys, would leave the church running as soon as Sunday school was over, to see the train come in and get our Sunday paper. In fact, about half the town would meet that train to see who was coming in or leaving and pick up their papers too.

Our depot had a flagged area around it. It was sort of like a brick porch set six inches above the ground. The edge of the porch away from where the train stopped was "the line" for the hackmen. Each livery stable sent a hack to meet every train. The hacks were backed up against a spur track just beyond the flags and the edge was the advance line for the hackmen. They stood with one foot on it like sprinters, calling, "Colonial Hotel. Oxford House. Knight's Boardinghouse."

They made the rule themselves that none should cross "the line." Each driver must stand behind it to shill. They stood with one hand outstretched, trying to outreach each other for the handbags of the traveling men. All the boys from the Sunday schools used to stand there and watch them shouting the names of hotels, cussing each other out and having tugs of war over bags every now and then. Then we would all run to get our papers before old man Will Browning got away from the depot with them.

I know we almost ran Mr. Browning crazy. He would unload his papers from the baggage car onto a hand truck and open the bundles there and deal them out to his delivery boys, so many to each. About that time fifty or sixty Sunday school boys would rush up before it was too late and begin grabbing papers and calling their names so he could put them down on his list as already delivered. If he failed to get the name then that subscriber got another paper that day and Mr. Browning didn't have enough papers to go around. If he got a name down by mistake, then that subscriber got no paper at all and he raised Cain.

Mr. Browning was a little old squint-eyed, irritable man and I know what we did to him didn't help soften his disposition. Whatever he thought about it though, we were always there the next Sunday to get our papers off the truck and run all the way home with them to read the funnies.

We got another paper on Sundays too, a Sunday school paper they handed us each week just as class was over. It was a weekly newsletter about our diocese and church affairs in general. Ours was called the *Sunday Morning Messenger*, I think. I know it was a folio, on slick paper, and published in Nashville, Tennessee. The sheets were not large and the first page usually had the picture of some new church, and over inside, another of some Sunday school class. In the back there were always a few jokes and advertisements.

Jack and I and most of the other little boys always turned first to the jokes and if there was a funny one immediately turned to whatever little boy was sitting next to us and began reading it aloud to him, hoping he had not already read it first. Bill, however, for some reason, began reading the advertisements. None of the rest of us had ever paid any attention to them.

Most of them were aimed at a group effort on the part of some class, under the supervision of the teacher, for the benefit of the class at large. Under his supervision the entire class was to invade some neighborhood at a predetermined time (Saturday morning, usually) and peddle, house to house, postcards and mottoes and other religious relics for a small commission. The total would be donated to the class itself for some class purpose.

Bill wasn't interested in that. It was another kind of ad that caught his attention. This one was aimed at benefitting the individual and Bill was all for that. In fact he picked out two. He ordered some starched collars for Jack to sell and some bluing, in sheets, for me. He was to supervise and collect and pay Jack and me an even smaller commission than he got. And we fell for it. No wonder he sold stories later on. He sure sold us on that one.

One of Bill's ideas for selecting the collars and bluing, he explained to Jack and me, was that they would work into a repeat business. Once we were established it would be simply a matter of regular visits to our customers, as the products we had sold them would wear out or be used up. We knew more about bluing than we did about starched collars, for the wives of most of Dad's blacks took in washing for white folks and had to have bluing every Monday morning to put in the wash. We had been to Eskimay's or Seemie's house many a Monday when their mothers found they were out of bluing and we went along with Eskimay or Seemie clear to town to get a new supply. We also knew several black preachers who always preached in stiff collars and Bill was sure we could land their business. So he sent away for the bluing and starched collars.

I remember the day the packages came. They both got there the same day, one from Chicago and one from either Cincinnati or Columbus. They came the same week Bill sent the orders. Dad remarked on this fast service; Mother wanted to know what was in them.

We had never received a package in our own names before, except for the ones we got from Aunt Willie, and her return address on them reassured Mother. The return addresses on these two packages did not. She asked a second time what was in them.

When she finally pinned Bill down and he had to tell her, she said a flat no. She said to send them back without even unwrapping them, but Dad came in on our side. He said it was time we learned something about business and money and earning it.

Mother said, "For heaven's sake, Buddy, you are pitting three boys against some of the slickest business people in the world."

"It all came through their Sunday school class," Dad answered, "it's bound to be all right."

"The Devil was once in heaven," Mother replied, "and now I believe he's moved into our churches. And right here in my front room too," she added, glaring at Dad.

At last Mother surrendered. We were allowed to keep the collars and bluing and Mother retired completely from the scene. She didn't even say I told you so when it was all over.

Bill, free to go ahead now, organized our campaign to start the following Saturday, which was two days off. Jack and I were both in school and our time would not be available until Saturday.

Saturday morning we set out but not exactly as Bill had planned it. Bill and I went alone. Jack had tonsillitis and it was drizzly that day, so Mother wouldn't let him out of the house. He was operated on later on and had them removed, on our kitchen table, for we had no hospitals in those days, and he almost bled to death.

Bill and I started out. It wasn't quite drizzling then but it looked like it might. We would be close to black cabins all during our campaign and Mother told us to stop in one of them if it got to raining hard.

Our first stop was, of course, at Jessie's house. It was the first cabin we came to. Cora didn't think she needed bluing, but when she looked she found she was out for Monday so she bought a pack.

This bluing was something new. The bluing we were familiar with came in sticks, sort of like chalk. You simply broke off or shaved some of it into the water as it was needed and waited for it to dissolve. Our product came in handy sheets, twelve to the pack. You simply tore off a piece of the sheet (easier than breaking a piece of chalk) or snipped a portion off with scissors (easier than shaving) and dropped it in the water, where it dissolved almost instantly. That was one of the things about this bluing; it dissolved so quickly. It was on flimsy paper about like Kleenex and so soluble that even to touch it with a damp finger could cause it to melt and run. We sold Cora a package for a dime and went on to the next house.

By the time we finished Negro Hollow, I had sold five packages of bluing, but Bill had sold only one collar. There were not many preachers in the Hollow. We decided they must live over on the north side of town, so to the north side we went, out past where the white folks lived.

We had just got to this area when it began raining hard enough to remind us that Mother had told us to go to the nearest cabin if it did. We ran for the nearest cabin but got rained on some getting there. I got wet enough for some of my bluing to run but Bill managed to keep his collars dry.

The black woman who lived in the cabin told us to come inside by the fire and dry out as soon as she found out who we were and what we were doing on her front porch. I tried to sell her some bluing and that's when we found out it had run. She clucked her tongue over my bad luck and just then I heard some puppies whining on her back porch. I went to see about them but Bill stayed in by the fire. About that time the woman's husband came home. He looked over my bluing and came out to where I was on my knees beside the straw-filled box of puppies. We soon made a trade. I swapped him what was left of my bluing for his whole boxful of puppies. He even threw in a tow sack for me to take the puppies home in. The rain had now slacked off to a drizzle so Bill and I started out again.

We lived clear across town from where we were. It was close to a mile. Though the rain had stopped there were puddles all along the way. The going was heavy, and Bill had to help me every now and then with my load of puppies. When he took the puppies I carried the collars. It was while we were making such an exchange that we dropped the collars in a puddle. We rescued them as quickly as we could but until we got home we didn't realize that some of the water had seeped in and stained them brown in spots. It had melted out the starch in those spots too.

As soon as we walked in we found out about puppies. Dad was there. He took one look in my sack and yelled for Jessie. Jessie was out at the barn unharnessing, but he came running. The other blacks there came too to see what Dad was yelling about. Dad told Jessie to take the puppies out and drown them. I could have cried, but I was scared to. I don't believe I ever saw Dad so mad about anything.

I stood there without a word as Jessie took away my sack of puppies. Mother just stood there too. She looked at Dad, but she didn't open her mouth either. This was not her problem, she simply wanted to be left completely out of it.

Of course I never saw my puppies again. I don't know whether Jessie really drowned them or not. After he left with the sack in his hand, Dad turned to me to find out exactly how I had come by them. When I told him, he wanted to know who the black was who swapped them to me.

I didn't know his name. Dad said he wished to God he did. All I knew about the black was what a good friend he had turned out to be for swapping me six fine little puppies for what was left of my bluing after I got it so wet that even I knew I could never sell another sheet of it. In fact, he was even nicer than that. As I remembered it, I now believed he was the one who first mentioned the swap. And even after he had seen what a gooey mess the rain had made of my bluing. He must have been even nicer than I thought.

Although Bill had helped me to get my puppies home, he had taken no part in the trading. That's what Dad got after him about now. He said that even if I was too little to know any better, Bill should have. Bill was standing there with his box of collars in his hand while Dad was giving him what for, and he dropped them. The package burst open and that was the first time either of us realized the muddy water had got in to them.

We all examined them. Jack was in the room by then, having come from his bed, where he had spent most of the day with books and toys to keep him entertained. We were all there, Mammy too.

Dad decided the collars could be sent to our Chinese laundry-man and made like new. He would then send them back to the company, the eleven of them, and pay for the other one that Bill had sold. And the bluing—he would simply pay for that. And he would himself write to both companies warning them never to send Bill anything again.

So the episode was closed out except for one thing. When Mother sent the collars to the laundryman she forgot to tell him not to put our mark in them. He put it there, with India ink and a brush, in Chinese. When Dad saw it he was fit to be tied. He said he'd be damned if he ever saw such boys in his life. He paid the bill in full, to both companies. There was nothing else he could do.

The last I saw of those collars, we had them up for sale in our store that next summer. All the children in our neighborhood, and in all the other neighborhoods too, used to have stores in the summertime. Some group would put up one, others would see or hear about it, and soon they would spring up in every yard.

All our yards had fences around them, some wooden picket and others iron. Ours was wood. We put two barrels against the inside of the fence, laid one-by-twelve planks across the tops, and we had a store. Then we ransacked our homes for things to sell. Some of us would find old shoes, worn out or outgrown, old dresses, shirts, hats, old anything we could find. These we would stack on our counters and we were in business. We also always sold lemonade from a zinc bucket at one penny a glass.

That summer, in getting up merchandise for our store, Mother found the eleven collars and gave them to us. We put them out on the counter, but whether we sold them or not I don't remember. The main thing I remember about them is our name printed in them in Chinese, before Hum Wo sent them back.

Chapter 7

DAMUDDY HAD BEEN DEAD FOR OVER A YEAR NOW. Granny, Grandfather's wife, had died the year before that.

Granny's was the first death we had ever looked upon. We stood in the hall and looked at her, on her bier, and we did not believe she was anything more than sleeping on her quiet table. She seemed neat, precise, dusty-rose permanent as always. We could not believe we would never see her again. We went out in the yard and played.

Damuddy had showed the ravages of her disease. Cancer had worn her till only patience and kindness were left. She had even seemed to shrink during her last few years. Bill and Jack and I have never spoken of her as anything except small, and patient and kind with us.

The next of our kinspeople to die was Cousin Iola. Her parents lived across the street from us. She married Cousin Word Falkuer (about Dad's age), had two sons by him, Brown and Eugene, contracted consumption, and then Cousin Word brought her home to die from where they had been living in Arkansas.

None of us remembers much about her except seeing Cousin Word help her from the hack the day he brought her home, and up to the porch where old man John F. Brown and his wife, Aunt Kate, waited. We stood almost on tiptoe, big-eyed, quiet. We had been told, or maybe we had only overheard, that she was being brought home to die and we wanted to see what someone dying looked like.

I will always remember how thin she was, how weak. Cousin Word had almost to carry her to the porch but that couldn't have been much of a job. I've never seen anyone so thin, so wasted away. She must not have weighed ninety pounds and her eyes were the biggest things I ever saw. We tried to do our faces like hers later and play we were dying.

Cousin Iola did not last long. After Cousin Word helped her into the house we never saw her again. I don't know as we would have remembered her at all, if it hadn't been for that death mask of a face she brought home with her, but even at that we all remembered her as young (she was not old) and pretty.

The two little boys they brought home with them became a part of our lives. We played together every day, mostly in our yard so that the noise we made would not disturb Cousin Iola.

I remember Cousin Iola's funeral. Dad's livery stable furnished the hearse. One of his drivers brought it down to old man John F.'s house to carry Cousin Iola to the cemetery, and when they brought her body out Bill and Jack and I were on the driver's box waiting. Dad snatched us off and sent us over in our own yard, so we watched them take her away from there.

Of course Cousin Iola was nothing more than a memory to us. She had never been more than that. We had never heard her speak. The one time we saw her she could not even move by herself. But Damuddy and Granny were something else.

They had been a part of our daily lives, particularly Damuddy. She lived with us. We went to them both with our troubles, and whatever their own happened to be at the moment, they always gave their whole attention to us. So they were actually with us a long time after we never saw them again.

I think maybe Mammy, in a strong measure, took their places. Perhaps in a stronger measure than they, for Mammy was never averse to scolding and had a good deal sharper tongue. On more than one occasion I can remember her making any one of the three of us, or all three of us, "hump it" when we were a little slow in minding her. However stern her hand was toward us, it was even sterner toward anyone who was against us. We were more than her children; we were her trust, her charges.

We had always gone to Grandfather's for Christmas dinner. Now that Granny was gone, he wanted his family around him more and more. The same feeling drew us to him too. A part of us was gone, and we were in that measure lonesome. Now he began sending for us on Thanksgiving and Easter and on no special occasion, simply because he wanted us around him.

Auntie had taken over the housekeeping duties at Grandfather's after Granny died. Her own daughter, Sallie Murry, was Jack's age and the four of us were together like we were one family. And Auntie treated us as such. No one could have been better to us than she was. She spoiled us. And of course we loved her and Bill would fight you about her. She was the Miss Jenny, the Granny Millard, all the women in *The Unvanquished* that Bill wrote about.

Whatever we children wanted we told her and she saw that we had it right there. I remember one time she took all Grandfather's horses and carriages and buggies and blacks, and took us all for a summer trip to Lafayette Springs and left him to walk home from his bank in the rain, and how the towns-people heard him cussing every step of the way and never using the same word twice from the corner of the Square to his own side gate. Once we set up a store in his yard and she gave us a box of his fifty-cent cigars that we sold for two and a half cents each. There was a steady stream of men from uptown coming to our store till the cigars gave out. She bought us boxes of pep-permint-stick candy (the only kind you could get in Oxford in the summertime) that she paid two and a half cents apiece for and we sold for a penny till Grandfather finally put a stop to that also.

But Grandfather was good to us too. Every now and then he would gather up Bill and Jack and me and take us to town and outfit us in shoes or suits or overcoats. And every fall, after frost, he used to take us persimmon hunting. He made persimmon beer himself and I loved it, especially with peas and cornbread. And Bill was not far behind me for he was a good eater too until he fell in love with Estelle, whom he later married, and, for a while, went on a diet. All at once he wouldn't eat anything for breakfast except dry toast and black coffee, because Estelle did. I remember how flabbergasted Mother was. Bill was still in his mid-teens.

When time would come to gather the persimmons Grandfather would send word to us. This was always on a Sunday. We would rush through dinner to be ready. Everyone would go. Auntie and Sallie Murry would go with Grandfather, with old Gate or Paul or Chess or one of his blacks driving, and we would all go in the surrey with Dad. I can remember Mammy going and taking Dean after he was big enough to be taken.

After frost hits persimmons, they become mealy and sweet. They almost drop off the tree when you look at them. We would throw pieces of dead limbs, or I would shin up the tree and shake it. The ripe fruit would come tumbling down, enough to nearly cover the ground. Everyone would help at picking except Grandfather and he would come close and watch.

Grandfather made the beer himself. I can remember him, with two or three blacks to help, squeezing and measuring juice and sugar into his keg in the kitchen. He kept a special keg for the occasion, a five-gallon charred-oak keg.

Each season after the beer was gone he had one of his blacks store the keg in his basement. Then along about the last week in October he had it brought up to the kitchen and set against the wall, so it would be absorbing room temperature against his beer making.

It took a week or more to make the beer if I remember right. Then when it was ready, he would call us to a special dinner of mashed-up peas and cornbread with which we drank the malty-flavored brew.

The trips for persimmons were not the only ones Grandfather took us on. He had a farm out north of town, about three miles. A tenant ran it for him. I can remember us going out there in season for sacks of apples, potatoes, peanuts and such. And I can remember trips there in the early spring, through the lazy summer, but most of all I remember the ones in the fall.

It would be hot, shirt-sleeve weather when we left home, but by the time Grandfather had got through conferring with his tenant and we had been called in from what we were doing, it would have become nippy. I can remember the hazy blue of the hills as they unfolded on our way home and scrounging down behind the front seat where Grandfather and a black sat, and smelling the spicy apples, glad we were going home because it was getting dark. It was the time of year to talk about hunting, too early to go yet, but time to begin thinking about it.

That must have been what Bill talked to the black blacksmith about, when we would go out there. Jack and Sallie Murry and I always headed for the apple orchard or the peanut patch, but I can remember Bill hearing away from us as soon as we got in the gate, if he could hear the hammer ringing in the shed. He would be the last one back when Grandfather rounded us up to go home, and years later, when I read "The Bear," there was a scene that I had looked at too.

I remember one Thanksgiving dinner we went to at Grandfather's because we took the whooping cough with us. At least Bill and Jack and I did; Sallie Murry was already there with hers. Nobody knew any one of the four of us had it till after dinner.

After Granny died Grandfather wanted us around him more and more. It was not that Auntie did not take care of him; it was simply that he missed Granny so. A tremendous part of him died with her. He lost interest in a great many things that had occupied him before. With less and less to fill his time, he had all the more time in which to miss her.

In one or two stores on the Square, he kept a chair that he would move out on the walk and sit in. I've seen him sitting there writing her name, Sallie, in the air with his walking stick, completely oblivious of where he was or of anyone around him. He died when I had just turned twenty years old. He was, I think, the loneliest man I've ever known.

Auntie always set a heavy table at Grandfather's. Mother said Auntie didn't have anything to do with it. She just told the cook to cook everything in sight, and went on about something else. Her special meals were something. They were Thanksgiving, Christmas, Easter and the Fourth of July.

The Thanksgiving we had the whooping cough we didn't know it, for you couldn't tell at first. You might be coughing up a storm only because you had an extra-bad cold. The only way you could be sure it was whooping cough was when you coughed so hard you shot your lunch. All four of us did that day, lined up on the balusters of Grandfather's front steps. I'll never forget how he laughed. He thought it was the funniest sight he ever saw. We had finished dinner—soup, red snapper, turkey, fresh ham, beef roast, vegetables, ambrosia, cakes, pies—and started from the dining room. Grandfather was ahead, headed for his chair on the front porch. Mother and Dad, Uncle John and Aunt Sue were behind Grandfather and Auntie had gone back to the kitchen with some last-minute instruction for the cook.

It hit Jack first. Things always did. He broke into a run for the front door with his hand over his mouth. Sallie Murry saw Jack and started running. Grandfather had got to the porch by now and was sitting there. He saw Jack run out on the baluster with Sallie Murry right behind him, then Bill and me. I guess we were a funny sight.

It was after Christmas of that year, the late winter of 1909-10, that Dad decided to put us on an allowance. I was eight, Jack was ten and Bill was twelve. We were to have fifty cents a month apiece. Dean, of course, was left out. He was only two.

Mother tried to make Dad leave us all out, or at least take mine and Jack's and Bill's ages into consideration as he had Dean's. She said if he must give us money, then give Bill the fifty cents, Jack a quarter, and me two nickels. Dad was adamant. He said no. We were all three his sons, and we should have equal amounts. Mother said Dean was his son too, but he was being left out. Dad said Dean was a baby and that settled that.

So he gave us fifty cents apiece.

Jack and I didn't have a thing in the world in mind to spend our half dollars on. However, we went to town at once to find something. Our minds did not run much toward money in any of its usefulnesses; to keep, to spend, to have. We were furnished with money to buy Christmas presents for each other and birthday presents, but other than that it really had no meaning to us. Thus the fifty cents apiece at this odd time of the year seemed enormous. It simply laid a proposition before us: how to get rid of it? That's the reason we went to town.

Bill did different. He pocketed his money and watched Jack and me start for town.

We shopped the town that day with our hard money, Jack and me. I soon found a way to spend mine—candy. But Mother had singled me out in particular and forbidden this. She was afraid fifty cents' worth of candy might kill me. In going through a drugstore Jack found what he wanted—a baseball mask. Jack liked to catch. The catcher's mask was for him. But it cost a dollar and a quarter and the drugstore didn't have a cheaper one. That was the cheapest one they had. We went home when the stores closed with our money still in our pockets.

Bill was there waiting for us. He had not gone to town at all. He knew even before Dad gave us the fifty-cent pieces what he would do with a dollar and a half if he had it. Now he had it. He borrowed mine and Jack's and added it to his. He had seen something in the *American Boy* several issues back that he wanted and now with my and Jack's half dollars he had the amount necessary to order it.

When it arrived it was an electric gadget run on flashlight batteries. The thing was flat, in a cardboard box, with pegs of metal sticking up through it. There were sheets of paper, with holes that fitted over the pegs. The sheets were divided down the middle with questions on one side and answers on the other. One sheet was geography, another arithmetic and so on. The wires to the batteries had metal tips on them. If you touched one tip to a "question post" and the other to the right "answer post," a light came on.

Bill was pretty accurate the first time he tried it. He had had four years of school by then. Jack and I learned a trick though that made us even surer in our answers than Bill. We found you could hold one tip on a question and simply slide the other along the pegs until the light came on and you had the answer. We went even further than that. Experimenting one day, we found to our surprise that you could flash the light without a paper of any kind on the board.

We lost interest in Bill's gadget then. We found out he wasn't near as smart as we had at first thought either, in spite of his four years of schooling. It was the board that knew the right answers all the time, not him.

Bill used to "squirrel away" things, as Mammy called it. He saved that board for several years. I can remember him getting it out every so often to test his memory on those pegs.

All of us had special storage places for our possessions. Jack's and mine were never very interesting. We broke our toys or forgot them. But Bill's was always neat and seemed to have everything in it he had ever owned. He was still that way about saving curious mementos up until he died. His study had more objects stashed about in it, and most of us wondered why in the world he kept them.

Chapter 8

TO HIS SCHEME TO BORROW JACK'S AND MY allowances Bill added a further proposition: that the next month Jack was to get Bill's and mine and the third month I was to get theirs.

That next month Jack got Bill's and mine and bought his mask. Bee Woodward stepped on it within a week, when he was crossing home plate one day, and mashed it flat. We got the wire mesh rounded back in place enough so that Jack could get his face in it, but we never could get the eye holes bent back as small as they had been. Mr. Henry Faser, who lived across the street from us, ran a drugstore in town and played baseball with us, threw a ball clear through the eye piece one day so Jack threw the mask away. It had knocked him flat, but aside from a black eye it had not really hurt him.

Before the time came for me to get the dollar and a half, Dad had cut out our allowance, and I never did get any. However, like Mother had told Dad at first, we didn't need money for our pleasures in those days. They came free. We simply manufactured them.

Money was not so important to grown people then either. Each family was nearly self-sustaining, and we all found our pleasures at home or visiting in the homes of our neighbors. And as far as Jack was concerned, he simply moved back a step or two from the catcher's box and began catching the pitched balls on the first bounce, as he had before, so the mask really wasn't missed. Bill had by then put his electrical gadget away. And I was deprived of a dollar-and-a-half stomach-ache.

Home was never measured by the amount of income its members could bring in each month. Its value was according to the amount of living each member put into it each day. Each of us had tasks that were necessary to that day's well being. There was no excuse for not having done them. So dusk each evening saw the three of us coming into the yard from wherever we might have been to dispatch the chores.

Now my job was bringing in the kindling. I inherited that job from Jack, who now brought in the coal, in scuttles. He had taken it over from Bill, who now slopped the hogs. I finally graduated to milking the cow.

There was a family in town named Leavell. There were eighteen children in the group, one girl and seventeen boys. Dad used to hold them up to us as models. One time, when Bill was milking, and wanted to know when it would be Jack's turn, Dad told him again about the Leavell boys. He told him how all seventeen of them took the job in turn without complaining. Bill asked him how many cows they wore out.

Everyone bought stove wood already cut, by the cord. A cord of wood is four feet wide, four feet high and eight feet long. Stove wood was cut fourteen or eighteen inches long, and about as big around as your wrist. It took a lot of pieces to make a cord.

Grandfather didn't buy his wood like we did. He bought pole lengths, ten or twelve feet long, rail-fence size, and had Mr. Reynolds saw the poles up for him.

Mr. Reynolds had a gasoline sawmill. The engine was one cylinder. The blade, a circular one, was about two feet in diameter. You mounted a pole sideways on the carriage, which had a slot in it for the saw, and swung it back and forth. You could hear that one-lung engine coughing all over the neighborhood when Grandfather was having his winter wood cut. The saw going through the poles whined almost like a siren sounds now.

A regular part of each fall we used to be hearing that old engine and the whine of the saw. We would hear it from the Square and run all the way home so we could watch Mr. Reynolds swing the carriage back and forth. We were sure that every time, or the next time positively, he would slice his hands off. I can remember Bill and Jack and Sallie Murry and me standing there for hours as blue dusk came on and a chill bit the air, waiting for next time, when the saw would get Mr. Reynolds for sure.

One time when Bill's job was bringing in the coal, Mother noticed that Fritz McElroy came home with him every evening. Children were always coming home with us or we were going home with them, but for the same one to come with Bill every evening was odd. She began watching Bill and Fritz to see what they were doing. She found out.

It took several buckets of coal to keep a fire going until bedtime and still leave enough for starting the fire again the next morning. At two buckets a trip it took several trips to get in enough for all the fireplaces.

Mother watched the two of them go straight to the coal shed. Bill stood around while Fritz loaded two buckets and carried them into the house. Bill walked along beside him, never touching the buckets. Fritz made several trips with Bill walking back and forth beside him. Mother moved closer when they passed and found that Bill was telling Fritz stories while he toted in coal.

She didn't say anything about what they were doing. She wanted to see why Fritz kept coming back every day. Finally she found that Bill was telling Fritz continued stories, breaking off each day just at the point where Fritz would be sure to come back next day to find out what happened.

Some of the stories Bill had read, but many he made up as he went along. Mother told me about that again not too many years ago when we were talking about Bill one day. She never told Dad.

Fritz carried coal for Bill for the rest of that winter. By the next year Bill was milking and Fritz didn't have time for that. He had his own cow to milk.

Dad had blacks about to do these chores but we never thought of someone else doing them. They were for us to do. It our part of in a family enterprise that made for a better living. Though we did not think this at the time, of course, I believe it gave us a pride and a warmth toward our home that we could feel. Home was more than a sanctuary, a shelter. There was a good stout comfortableness about it and we helped create it.

If we wanted to throw another lump of coal on the fire, we threw it. We brought it in and would have to go for more if it gave out. And since we had to have our chores done by dark, we were always right there handy when the supper bell rang. And that was a comfortable time too. I can remember the good fresh sausage and hot buttered biscuits Nancy Snowball used to make, with gobs of homemade jelly to dab on each bite, and fresh ham with spicy relish. We were allowed coffee too, if it could be called that. Mother measured each cup and the younger we were the more cream and sugar went it. I remember a mix Dean used to drink not too many years after this that had five spoons of sugar in it, a lot of water and almost no coffee. He said he didn't like cream so Mother put in butter instead.

It was the sort of life we grew up to and it made Bill like he was and made him think like he did. At that it was about like life in any small town. Oxford, then, had about twelve hundred souls.

We didn't know much about organized sports and certainly not directed play. Usually we made up as we went along and Bill was particularly good at that. He was small in size but always the number-one man on his side. Picture shows had not come to Oxford yet, so we hadn't them to pattern on. Even our baseball was modeled on how many were available at the time. We played fox in war, hide and seek, of course, follow the leader, paper chase, follow the arrow, leapfrog, whipcracker and unnumbered other games.

We lived under strict discipline at home, even stricter than those around us, with the exception of the preacher's family who lived next door. I can remember our study periods at home. During school session we sat down to a table in the hall after supper and got our homework up every night. There was no time limit on the performance. We simply sat there until our assigned work was done-correctly. If we got a licking at school we got a worse one when we got home.

It was about this time that Mother put braces on Bill. For some reason he got stoop-shouldered all at once. Mother was afraid it might be his lungs. She took Bill to the doctor and braces were ordered for him. They were sort of like a corset without a front. There were two padded armholes for Bill's arms and the back was stiffened with whalebone and laced crossways with a heavy white cord.

At first Mother laced Bill into it, with the knot in the cord about at his belt line in back. But Bill could reach that. So she put the lace in from the bottom and tied the knot between his shoulder blades. I remember he complained about the thing being too tight each morning when Mother laced him into it (of course, Jack and I stood there and watched and laughed) but tight or not, it sure cured his stoop.

Most little men rear back and take long strides, but with the exception of Grandfather, I've never seen a man with a straighter back or firmer stride than Bill's. It lasted him all his life too, so I guess Mother knew what she was doing.

We were not poor folks. It was simply that you did not waste. I still believe it to be some sort of sin and I'm not sure at all we will be forgiven for it.

All children wore long underwear in winter. We wore long black stockings too, both boys and girls. Girls might wear white ones in summer but not in winter. Winter weather was black stocking weather.

Every other spring Mother would cut off the arms of our long underwear at the elbow and the legs at the knees. These would do us for the transitional weather between winter and summer. In summer we didn't wear any underclothes at all.

We didn't wear shirts then. At least little boys didn't. We wore blouses. They were kind of like shirts but made real full and had waistbands that fitted tight. The blousy part was the best carrying pocket of all. You could carry a geography book there and geography books were about the size of typewriter paper.

You could carry other things there besides schoolbooks. We used the space for live pets, green apples and peaches and almost anything else.

After Dad sold the oil mill and ice plant, the new owner piped the overflow water from the plant well over into Bailey's Woods. Those woods were one of our main playgrounds. One day we got the idea to dig a swimming hole at the end of the overflow pipe. When we got through we had a pond a little larger than a nine-by-twelve rug and neck deep in the middle. It was good enough for us. We spent most of our afternoons in summer, after that, out there swimming.

As soon as we would gobble down our dinner we would streak off for Bailey's Woods. The heat would be ninety or better in the shade as we loped off through the dust of South Street. We'd cut over to Second South, cross behind Miss Ellen Bailey's and stop long enough to raid her orchard, filling our blouses with green apples or peaches.

That's the swimming hole Bill wrote about in *Soldier's Pay*, where the girl was walking home through the woods after seeing the soldier off on the train and her brother accused her of spying on him and his friends, naked, in the water. Bill and I both learned to swim in that pond. Jack almost never did. He just couldn't get the hang of it.

Mother and Dad never seemed to worry about our daily programs in vacation time. Dad had taught us woodlore well. We knew how to fish, hunt, take care of ourselves, and about the only rule we had was to be home at mealtimes unless we told them beforehand where we'd be. Naturally, Bill, being oldest, was leader. Jack and I obeyed him, but either one of us was as well qualified. The worst injuries any of us ever got didn't come out of the woods, they came from progress or organized sports.

All we ever got in the woods was chestnut burrs in our feet, chiggers, of course, or Jack turning up with a dose of poison ivy every year. But Jack and I both got our arms broken cranking automobiles, and Bill broke his nose playing football (which accounts for the hump in it). I also broke my ankle hook-sliding in baseball.

We all got barefooted each year as early as Dad would let us. He went by the old saying that the cold was never out of the ground till after Easter. So whatever the weather, when we got home from Sunday school on Easter we'd strip our shoes and stockings off. We never caught cold from going barefoot too soon, so I guess the old folks were right.

I think he got that idea from Grandfather. Grandfather always changed from heavy to light or light to heavy clothes by the date. He said he couldn't outguess the weather, but he could read the calendar. I've seen him uptown in a white linen suit with an overcoat and a cap with earmuffs. He could read the calendar, but I guess he wanted to be sure and keep warm too.

Some of the other boys we knew were not held to the calendar as we were. Every year, long before Easter, a few of them would begin going barefoot. We wondered about it until Bull discovered that those other boys weren't supposed to be barefooted yet any more than we were. They simply took their shoes and stockings off on the way to school, hid them and put them back on before they got home in the evening.

We tried it, but it caused us to get caught. I crawled in bed without washing my feet one night, just as Mother came in. One look at the bottoms of my feet, and our secret was out. From then on, we waited our regular date to shuck our footwear.

Chapter 9

THE OLDHAMS LIVED TWO DOORS DOWN THE
street from us. There were three girls and a boy in their family.
The boy was Dean's age and as yet too little to play with us. His
nurse was named Missy, and she and Mammy were very friendly. They would stand to one side with Ned and Dean while the
rest of us played whatever game we were interested in at the
moment.

Dot was about my age and Victoria—Tochie, we called
her—about Jack's. Tochie was a tomboy. I would rather have
her on my side than almost any boy in our gang. Estelle was
older than Tochie and she was a doll.

Small, petite, dainty, like a fairy. She never did get into our
games. She did not like to get mussed up or dirty. Even at my
age I could tell she was a girl. All the rest of our gang, boys and
girls, were just playmates, but I think we all recognized Estelle
as different. She caught Bill's eye, I think, the first time he ever
saw her.

Bill tried to attract her attention by being the loudest one,
the daringest. But the more he tried the more mussed he got, and
sweaty, and dirtier, and Estelle simply wasn't interested. She
liked to look at something pretty. And in our play, none of us
were. The other girls in the crowd, of course, tried to make fun
of her for, of all things, being a sissy. The boys all showed off.

The only time I ever remember her essaying into our world
at all was one afternoon when, for some reason, she decided to
ride Tochie's Shetland pony to town and back. She didn't know
anything about riding. The rest of us had ponies and riding was
an everyday affair, but Estelle never seemed to want to. This
day she decided to ride to town and back on Lady. That was the
name of Tochie's pony.

Miss Lida (that was Mrs. Oldham) had the pony saddled and brought around front and their boy (that was Magnolia's, their cook's son) helped Estelle on. She took the reins and the little pony began walking sedately out the drive.

We were playing in the Oldham's yard at the time, and didn't pay any attention as Estelle guided him toward town. About fifteen minutes later they came back. Lady was running away and Estelle was screaming and crying, her hat blown off and held by its ribbons, and her curls streaming. Lady ran into the yard and stopped beside the house. 'Nolia ran out and grabbed Estelle from the saddle and holding her in her arms took her into the house.

We all stood with our mouths open and our eyes popping. We saw nothing in the world for Estelle to get scared about. That was about the way we rode most of the time. We never took Lady to be running away. We thought it must have been something Estelle saw uptown. We only found out later that it was Lady's running so fast that scared her.

Estelle became Bill's sweetheart when he was in his teens. He lost her again when he was twenty, but she came back to him. The time that they were apart was an unhappy, tragic interlude for both of them.

I remember another happening in the Oldhams' yard. We were playing down there one day and Tochie whipped both Bill and Buddy King with a canna stalk.

Every front yard was kept neat and orderly in those days, for every home had a "yard boy," usually the cook's son. Servants lived on the place in cabins built for them in our back yards. The "boy" was always handy for jobs about the place and usually tended the lawns in summer, whenever he was not playing with us. And anyhow, neatness in a front yard took second place to its use to us as a playground. Each yard on the street was ours to play in except Mrs. Plant's. She lived on the corner above us and didn't like us or anybody else I ever heard of.

All of our yards had fences around them, mostly picket. The first thing a man did when he bought a piece of ground was to fence it in. Inside the fence was his, and ours too, for the chances were he had children who also claimed our yard as a playground. It was a sort of good-neighbor policy in the early Nineteen Hundreds, I guess.

The Kings lived next door to us. Mr. King was the Cumberland Presbyterian minister. He had five children, three boys and two girls. Buddy was the youngest. He was about Bill's age.

The Oldhams lived just beyond the Kings.

The Oldhams' front yard happened to be our playground that morning. Their yard was a little more formal than ours or the Kings'. I guess we had too many boys in our families to keep anything in place for very long. Mrs. Oldham had flower beds arranged in symmetry at measured spots along the half-circle walk and at the sides of the house. Just at the foot of the frontporch steps she had two canna beds, one on either side. At a certain time each year she had the canna stalks cut. They were green when she cut them, and full of juice. They were almost the size of corn stalks and were great to fight with.

That morning she had just had the canna stalks cut. When you hit someone across the legs with them, like a switch, they were tough enough to break the skin, yet brittle enough to mash juice out. The juice stung like fire.

I don't remember what Buddy and Bill were doing to Tochie, but I do remember her beating them to the pile of canna stalks. As soon as they saw she had beat them there and had a stalk in her hand, they lit out for home.

Buddy was the smallest and the closest, so Tochie concentrated on him. She whipped him clear across her yard and over his fence. Then she took out after Bill. Bill had gained some time while Tochie was finishing off Buddy, but it wasn't quite enough. She caught him just as he reached the corner of our yard.

Of course, we had all run out front to watch, and I'll never forget Bill's legs, trying to climb our fence and dodge Tochie's switch at the same time. When he finally got out of reach she turned back toward us. She was still mad. We stood real quiet as she drew near and raised the stalk as if to switch us, but she had beaten the stiffness all out of it on Buddy and Bill. It hung from her fist like a piece of string. She looked down at it and grinned, and then we grinned too.

We all learned to ride a bicycle in the Oldhams' front yard. It was Tochie's bike. She was the first one of us to have one.

Major Oldham was federal court clerk, at six thousand dollars a year, an almost unheard of salary in our town. The Oldham family had almost everything you could dream of, any toy the children wanted. The Major even had a set of golf sticks. So Tochie had a bicycle, and we all learned to ride it.

It was a girl's bicycle. There was no horizontal bar between the handlebar post and the seat. The frame swept right down to the sprocket. You simply stepped on the pedal instead of throwing your leg over the seat.

The Oldhams were the first family in Oxford to take their yard fence down. Their lawn sloped down to the sidewalk, then sharply down from there to the street. We would take turns on the bicycle with someone to push us to the slant, where we picked up speed and sailed out into the street. Our momentum would fail there and we'd wobble and fall, until we learned the knack of peddling.

I remember how quickly Bill learned. He was the first of us who did. I think it was his sense of balance that helped him live through flying Camels in the First War, for there never was a more tricky airplane built than a Sopwith Camel.

We used our unpaved streets for more than learning to ride a bicycle. We played baseball there and football, and it was in front of our house that Dad taught us to play shinny. Tochie nearly cut off Buddy King's ear with a midiron and left a scar on Bill's shin that was still there when he died. She didn't do it on purpose. She was simply playing shinny. She was the captain of one side and Bill was the captain of the other. We played for several days with homemade sticks, then Tochie remembered about Major Oldham's golf clubs and got out his midiron.

The way we would play the game, we would draw two lines across the street in the dust, about a hundred yards apart. They were the goal lines. A block of wood would be placed halfway between the goals, and each team would get behind its goal line. Then someone would count to three, and we would all run for the block of wood and come in swinging. Tochie and Bill met at the block of wood that day and Tochie's first swing scraped up Bill's shin and sent him hopping to the sidelines. Her second caught Buddy right where his ear joined his cheek. He ran home holding his ear clamped to the side of his head and then the Major took his midiron away from Tochie. We continued to play shinny but golf sticks were barred from then on.

That was in the fall of the year, I think. Dad took us walking in the woods almost every pretty fall Sunday. He loved the woods and hunting and that's where we got our taste for it. It was during these walks that he would remember hunts he had been on and tell us about them. Dad was a good storyteller. We all remembered the stories he told us on those walks, perhaps Bill best of all, for a number of them, or parts of them, appeared in his stories of the woods and hunting in later years. Each time I read those stories the picture comes back to me of Dad walking through the fall woods with three little boys trudging along beside him.

All this had a part in forming Bill's love for the woods and hunting. He was a tenderhearted someone, with a very real feeling for those creatures he killed for food. I never knew him to kill needlessly. One of his outstanding hunting traits was that he would never go off and leave a cripple. I've been with him when he would down a bird, maybe with a broken wing, and we would hunt no more till that bird was found and put out of its misery. One afternoon he crippled a bird not long before dark. We could not find it and the next morning Bill came back to try and find it.

The best hunting story I know of is Bill's "The Bear." He knew the Big Woods well, for he went there every fall to hunt. But it took a lifetime of training in woodlore to be able to see them as he did, and that training started in those autumn walks with Dad.

Dad had mementos of his hunts he kept in a collection at home. There was a panther claw from a big cat he killed in Tippah County, where we all came from, and an eagle feather from the wing of the last eagle ever seen in this part of the country. He shot it at the request of a farmer friend whose flocks and herds were being raided by it. Dad lay in wait and shot it in the air as it came in over a newborn lamb on a spring hillside, and he saved the feather as a souvenir. He also told us about the last wolf ever seen in our own river bottom, Tallahatchie, which was the name given the same river in Bill's Yoknapatawpha County.

The time Dad met the wolf was down at old man Bob Cain's place, down in the bottom. He used to hunt there a lot and this time he was squirrel hunting. He crossed a log over the neck of a slough and just as he stepped up on one end of the log the wolf stepped up on the other. Dad raised his gun as quickly as he could on the slippery log but before he could draw a bead on the wolf it whisked from sight. It was a big gray wolf, the last one ever seen in our bottom.

Our river bottoms were full of virgin timber then, tall soaring gum and oak and cypress, just like in "The Bear." By the time Bill was grown and began deer hunting, our timber had mostly been cut. That's why he had to go to the "Big Bottom" for his story, but he saw its beginnings on the banks of our own Tallahatchie.

The first timber cutters we knew were small bands of Slavic stave cutters who traveled the country for whiskey makers, cutting special hardwoods for whiskey barrels. Dad belonged to a group who had a clubhouse at the mouth of Tippah River where it runs into Tallahatchie and he began taking us down there almost as far back as I can remember. We would see groups of stave cutters camped there in the bottom, cutting staves. They only felled special trees and we hardly missed them.

But then hardwood mills began coming in and after them mills that cut almost anything that would make a board. And our wildlife retreated farther and farther into the Big Woods, the still virgin tracts of timber that cloaked the Mississippi Delta. The Delta begins thirty miles to the west of us. The bluffs drop a sheer fifty feet to the flat plain that stretches for over fifty miles to the river. It was here, just beyond Batesville at General Stone's cabin, that Bill first went on his deer and bear hunts and wild-turkey shoots.

It was through these woods that the single-line logging road ran. It was here that the half-grown bear, scared by the train's whistle, climbed the tree and stayed up there while the line's only locomotive made the trip to the end of the line and back and was halted to wait until the young bear finally got up nerve to come down. This was the road over which Bill and Mr. Buster Callicot made the first and last part of their journey to Memphis for more whiskey (both incidents appear in "The Bear") when the camp supply ran out, and Mr. Buster got back with the partially wrapped corset he had bought as a present for his wife trailing under his arm. This was the Big Woods that was cut back and back until only the triangle was left that Bill wrote about in "Delta Autumn."

We began our lessons in hunting food for the pot by hunting rabbits. For this Dad bought us beagle hounds. He had got us two of them. Bill went hunting with them one day and killed one of them. He dropped his gun and forgot it and brought the dog home in his arms. When he got there he laid the little dog on the porch and went to his room and locked himself in and cried. He was about fourteen then, I think, and did not take up another gun until he was grown and went on the deer hunt below Batesville.

At the time Bill killed the dog our family doctor was Dr. Linder. He had come to us from Panola County, where he owned wide farming acres. His wife had died, and he brought four children with him, an girl and three boys. He bought a place on the south edge of town in the area where we played and that's how we came to know them.

The boys were about our ages, the sister a little older and she served as a sort of mother to the three Linder boys, and to us too, I expect, on occasion. I can remember her making us mind when we played down there just as Mother did when we were at home.

Jack never cared for hunting or the woods, for he was too prone to take poison oak. But Bill and I began hunting early and did a great deal of our first hunting on the Linder place with the Linder boys. Bill's particular favorite was Dewey, the second boy. Dewey was with Bill the day he killed the dog.

Friday night was our only free night a week. Even after picture shows came we were only allowed to go on Fridays. That is during school term. The other nights we stayed home and studied. Friday nights were the nights Bill and Dewey swapped with each other. One Friday night Dewey would spend at our house and the next one Bill would spend down there. They would see each other in school every day too, and usually what they did they did together. So of course when Dad got us the two beagles, Bill and Dewey planned a hunt.

On his way home from school that day Bill stopped by and left his books and got his gun and the dogs while Dewey waited, then they went on down to the Linders'. Dewey got his gun and they began hunting and as soon as they crossed the road from Dewey's house the dogs struck a rabbit.

Bill and Dewey scrambled to the nearest high ground to follow the chase. They saw, from where they were, that it was only a short ways to a ditch up which the hounds were bringing the rabbit. They ran and took position. Almost at once there came the dogs with the rabbit before them.

He jumped out of the ditch on Bill's side, but on seeing him darted back down. Dewey came running and the dogs surged up out of the ditch and whirled back as the rabbit had done. They chased him on up the shady way about fifty feet, with Bill and Dewey running along the side.

"Watch for him when he jumps out," Dewey yelled at Bill, who was in the lead.

Just then the rabbit jumped up on the far edge of the bank. Bill slid to a stop and leveled his gun. Just as he brought it to bear on the scurrying rabbit and pressed the trigger, the lead beagle surged up from the ditch right into the blast. It didn't even yelp. The load took it right in the back of the head.

Bill dropped his gun and gathered the dog up and began running home. Dewey did not follow then. He didn't hunt any more that day either. He simply watched Bill from sight, then picked up his dropped gun and went home himself. The next day, on his way to school, he stopped by our house and left Bill's gun.

That was Bill's first shotgun. Dad had given it to him the day he was twelve. It was Dad's own gun, a double-barreled, hammerless Ithaca with twenty-eight-inch twin Damascus-steel barrels. It was a beauty in its day. I doubt if it would stand up under today's loads. Bill did not use it after that and I fell heir to it. By the time it became mine the barrels were two inches shorter, for Jobie, one of Uncle John's blacks, had blown the ends of them and his big toe off one day, and when the gun-smith finished dressing them they were exactly twenty-six inches. It was the best bird gun I ever owned.

After Bill set the gun aside it remained in our closet for over a year until that day Uncle John borrowed it for Jobie.

Jobie had aspired to wider horizons than trimming a lawn, working in a garden or toting stovewood and such. So he got a job on the railroad. It wasn't long before he got his arm caught in one of the old link-and-pin couplings, which tore it off above the elbow. That happened in Memphis. Of course, he got in touch with Uncle John and Uncle John brought him home.

Between them they rigged up a sort of harness to take the place of Jobie's missing arm, so he could handle what tools were necessary in tending his old chores about the place. He could use the harness to hold one handle of a wheelbarrow and push the barrow well enough. He could use a hoe, a shovel, an ax. He began bootlegging on the side and could do this as well one-handed as he could with two; besides, everybody felt sorry for him on account of his losing his arm, and when they caught him with whiskey they always turned him loose. Then he wanted to go hunting, so Uncle John borrowed Bill's gun, and took him. And Jobie blew his toe off, with Uncle John telling him not to do what he was doing at the time.

It was Jobie's left arm that was gone. He had to carry the gun in his right hand, and he'd never handled a hammerless one before. Uncle John explained that it was cocked all the time once it was loaded and showed Jobie about the safety. You could work it with your thumb while at the same time you held your finger ready to pull off a shot.

Uncle John told Jobie to keep his fingers off the trigger until he got ready to shoot and to leave the safety alone till he got ready to pull the trigger. Jobie said, "Yassuh." He immediately tried the safety and Uncle John got after him several times until he finally got Jobie to leave the thing alone.

They were hunting on horseback and had dismounted while the dogs worked some singles. Uncle John looked over at Jobie. Jobie had the end of the barrel of the gun resting on his toe, his thumb sliding the safety back and forth, his finger on the trigger.

"Jobie, I told you to let that safety alone."

"Yassuh."

"And take the end of that barrel off your toe."

"Yassuh."

And Jobie lifted the gun and shot his big toe off.

Uncle John got him on his horse and he mounted his and they headed for town. They were out about six miles at the time. Uncle John would ask Jobie every now and then how his foot felt. For several miles he said it was still numb, but before they got to town it was "th'obbin' right along."

Jobie used that gun again after the gunsmith cut the end of the barrel off smooth. He was a right good quail shot. The gun was light and he could handle it easy. But from then on he sure let that safety alone.

Bill used Jobie in several of his stories, in one as a bootlegger. Jobie got after Bill about it too. He said Bill accused him of selling bad whiskey. He didn't like that.

Chapter 10

IT WAS THE NEXT SPRING THAT WE BUILT THE airplane. We built it in the old barn on South Street, where we moved across the street from Grandfather's. We couldn't get it out the door, and we had to tear it down and reassemble it outside in the shed.

Bill got the idea out of his *American Boy*. There was a picture of a plane in there and instructions on how to build it. We followed these instructions and built our plane and Bill flew it as far as Mink and Dooley could throw it off the sand-ditch bank in our back lot.

I don't know as we would ever have gone so far as to actually build an airplane if it hadn't been for Mother's bean stickers. The article had come out in Bill's magazine several months before and he had read it and put it aside. It was seeing the bean stickers that brought it back to mind.

They were of a uniform thickness but varied in length from six to about eight feet. All of them were an inch square. Mother took good care of them from year to year and made us store them carefully in the old barn after each bean season. It was the uniform size, the careful stacking, the plentiful supply, I think, that caused us to build the airplane. That many of anything in a neat pile was a challenge.

Dad kept tools handy for repair work about the house and barn and we quickly procured a hammer, saw, nails and the like and took them to the barn. Bill found his copy of the *American Boy* with the airplane in it and we were ready to begin.

This old barn was the one already on the place when we moved there. As soon as we arrived, Dad built a new one and the old one was used only for storage. Mainly, as I've said, it was a playground for us when the weather was bad.

That airplane was actually almost full-sized. It was scaled down only enough to fit the length of the bean stickers. We sawed and hammered and built the frame just like in the picture Bill had. When the time came to cover it, we used old newspapers stuck on with flour paste. We had used that covering many a time on kites that flew, so why not an airplane? You mixed flour and water to make the paste. It dried quickly and hardened and after our kites had been flown a time or two in the sun, the paper tightened, and they flew better than ever. It seemed ideal stuff for airplane wings.

This all took place in the barn, and it was not till our plane was finished and we tried to carry it outside that we found we couldn't get it through the door.

Sallie Murry helped us build the plane. She was in it from the start.

More than once we found four of us to be a handy number in building an airplane. For one thing, it took all four of us to lift and carry it. Then for the lengthy members, such as wing spars and main fuselage pieces, we found two necessary to hold the ends in place while a third nailed them secure. Bill, of course, stood to one side with his *American Boy* and read the directions to us.

Dad's blacks got awfully interested after our plane began to take shape as we reassembled it in the shed, and they found out what it was we were building. Each evening, as soon as they would bring the wagons in from town and feed and care for the teams, they would come to the shed and lean over the rail to watch us and admire what we had accomplished that day. I remember them well. Many of them appeared later in Bill's stories.

There were Mink and Jessie Hayes, who lived in our pasture, and Mallory, who died later of drinking wood alcohol by mistake, and Dooley. The blacks called him "Right-now-for-bear" Dooley. Most white people called him that too. It was his favorite expression.

We had picked a place to fly our craft even before we finished it. At least, Bill had picked the spot and explained to us why. It was the lip of a bluff in the back of our lot. The bluff itself dropped about ten sheer feet to the sand ditch below.

Bill said he needed that drop to dive a little to pick up speed for maneuverability, so he could guide the airplane. We agreed. He had the book with the directions in it. The blacks would throw the plane off the bluff with Bill in it. He claimed first ride as inventor, and we agreed. The blacks promised to throw him off the cliff.

When the time came, Mallory and Dooley carried the airplane to the back of the lot by the wing tips and Mink walked along behind steadying the tail. Bill, Jack, Sallie Murry and I ran along beside them and all the other blacks followed.

When we got to the lip of the bluff, Bill had them set the airplane down, and he explained to us again just what he proposed to do. He pointed out his pattern of flight. After the blacks threw him off he would nose down, pick up speed, follow the course of the sand ditch and circle back and land where he had started. Then it would be Jack's turn, for he was next oldest.

Sallie Murry's turn would come third; even though she was a girl, she was older than I. Then me.

Bill took his seat in the airplane, braced his feet and grabbed two struts. He was ready. Mallory and Dooley lifted the craft gingerly by the wing tips and began swinging it to and fro. To make sure they were in time, they began to count:

"One."

"Two."

"Three." And Dooley added, "Right now for bear."

In unison the two blacks heaved the machine out over the ditch. It went up for several feet and did the first part of a loop, minus the wing tips Mallory and Dooley had used for hand-holds, which remained in their hands. We saw Bill against the skyline, upside down, and then the ship began to come to pieces in the air. Stiff tatters of paper fluttered loose. The bean stickers began coming apart. And Bill fell in a shower of torn paper and scraps of kindling wood and landed on the back of his head in a pile of sand at the bottom of the ditch.

I can still see Jessie, craning over the lip of the cliff, peering down at Bill. "Is you hurt, Memmie?"

Of course he wasn't. A ten-foot drop into a pile of sand never hurt anybody. He disentangled himself from the wrecked airplane and climbed glumly back up to where we were. The four of us stood there looking down at our wrecked airplane for a while, then turned and wended our way across the lot toward home. It was about suppertime anyway. The blacks left right after we did.

That bare back lot was an important place in our lives. We flew kites out there, and for some reason bats found it a good hunting ground. I suppose it was the insects that collected above the horse droppings that brought them. Most any late afternoon in spring and summer you could find them in numbers, swooping about. We spent many an hour out there trying to hit them with cobs and handy clods of dirt. We never did hit one, and I tried later with a shotgun and couldn't. Their flight is too erratic.

Bill never had many fights. I only remember about four. Two he had with Buddy King, in our back lot, and I can't even recall what they were about. One, I think, was because Buddy jumped on me, and since I was little Bill took my side. He won that one. I remember Buddy going home in the dusk and climbing the fence over into his own pasture. I remember Bill going home after the next one, so I suppose Buddy won that one. None of our fights interfered for long with our friendship. Buddy and Bill were on the same side the day Tochie whipped them with the canna stalk and that was right after they had their two fights.

Fritz McElroy whipped Bill once, and Bill got even the next time and then Dewey whipped him. Dewey took him by surprise. Leo Callaway had just finished whipping Dewey and because Bill was standing there watching, Dewey got up and whipped him. I guess he had to get even with somebody, and Bill was just handy. That didn't interfere with their friendship either, for later on Bill and Dewey teamed up on Henry Hiler and knocked him clear off the top of the Linders' barn with a wet corn cob. But that one came later.

It was not long after this that the Kings moved away and a new preacher came in to take Mr. King's place. His name was Atkinson and his family consisted of Mrs. Atkinson, a meek, mild little woman, and two boys and a girl. The boys were Robert and Curtis and the girl was named Margaret. Mammy called her Margaret Action, in fact called the whole family Action. It was close enough; we knew who she was talking about.

Mr. Atkinson was big and good and lumbering and always dressed in black, except when we would see him about the house at some piddling task in his shirt sleeves and without his collar and tie. He was looking over our back fence the evening Bill and I put up an acting bar.

We had acting bars at school, a big one and a little one. They were homemade and all the playground equipment we had. Heavy posts were sunk in the ground and iron pipe was run through them. We learned to do the little and big drop on them, and the elbow grind.

For the little drop you swung by your knees, back and forth, till you got high enough to let loose, flip and land on your feet. For the big drop you sat on the bar, fell backward, caught and swung under by your knees, let loose when you were straight out and flipped and landed. The elbow grind was different. You never let loose from the bar at all. You hung down with your elbows crooked behind you and locked over the pipe, then swung until you could go all the way over backward in a complete circle. Some of us could keep it up for minutes, going round and round and round. Bill was better than most of us and liked it. I did too. So we decided to build an acting bar at home.

We didn't have a piece of pipe for the bar so one evening after school Bill and I took the ax and went to the woods to find one. We cut a sapling and skinned it and brought it home. There were some fence posts stored in the barn shed and we got one of those and set it in the ground about five feet out from the crotch in a cedar tree, not too far from the back porch. We placed one end of our pole in the cedar crotch and I held the other end in place on top of the fence post while Bill nailed it down. Mr. Atkinson was standing there in his shirt sleeves, his arms folded on top of the yard fence, watching us.

It was getting on toward dusk when we finished and Bill got ready to try it out. He decided to do a little drop first. He chinned the bar a couple of times, then sort of bounced his weight on it to test it. It seemed all right, so he swung his legs over it and let down head first.

Gently he began swinging back and forth. The pole still held. He went higher and higher. Now he was almost leveled out on his back swing and ready to make his final swoop and let go and flip. But Bill never had a chance to let go. Just before that instant came the fence post pulled out of the ground, and Bill plowed across our bare back yard on his chin and chest. He gave an awful "Whuff" and lay there.

It scared me. I thought he was dead. He didn't move.

I remember Mr. Atkinson in the dusk, on the other side of the fence, lumbering back and forth trying to remember where the gate was. He finally found it, and running over to where Bill still lay, he picked him up and carried him into our house, with me trailing along behind, still too scared to say anything.

Bill wasn't really knocked out, he'd just knocked the breath out of himself, which was the reason he lay so still and couldn't move. He came to on the way into the house and I guess Mother must have heard something of what was going on, for she met us at the door and held it open for Mr. Atkinson. As soon as Mr. Atkinson put Bill down on the bed he got up. He had his breath back by then.

I think Mr. Atkinson was as scared, at first, as I was. When we got in the house he was white as a sheet. Mother thanked him for bringing Bill in, of course, and I remember she was baking a cake. She sat Mr. Atkinson down in the dining room and cut him a piece of hot cake and brought him a glass of milk. And of course Bill and I had a piece of cake just out of the oven too.

Jack was not at home at the time. He was spending most of his spare time at Mr. John Buffalo's gunshop, watching him build an automobile. Though Bill wasn't interested in automobiles, he was in guns, and he used to hang around the gunshop too. He put Mr. John in one of his books as a dreamy-eyed monk who built an auto and invented parts and machined them as the need arose.

When he finished the automobile Jack watched him build, it ran. Jack and I went riding in it with him and Dad whipped us because it scared him so. He thought Mr. John would get himself killed along with anybody that rode with him. Then Grandfather had a law passed against running it or any other auto within the city limits of Oxford, because Mr. John's car made all the horses run away. The ordinance is still on the books, for the simple reason that it has never been rescinded.

When the people in Oxford first started buying cars, Grandfather wouldn't loan his bank's money to anyone who owned one. Then he bought one, a 1912 Buick, and hired Chess Carruthers to drive it for him. From then on owning a car looked different to him.

There's another thing I remember about Bill and Mr. Atkinson. After he carried Bill into the house that day after the acting pole broke, Mr. Atkinson seemed to take a kind of special interest in him. When we would play in our front yard, he would come over to the fence and watch us. He even invited

Bill to join the Sunday school at his church but we were regular goers at our own. Then one Sunday afternoon he invited Bill to go walking with him and his children.

I don't remember where the rest of us were that afternoon, or why Bill was home alone. Very probably we had gone riding and for some reason he had not wanted to go. Anyhow, he told us about it when we got home.

Bill said he was in the yard when Mr. Atkinson came out his door with Robert and Curtis and Margaret, and seeing him in our yard by himself, he asked him to go walking with them. They walked down Lake Street and turned off at the Chilton place toward Burney Branch. Burney Branch was a small spring-fed stream, maybe half a foot deep and four or five feet wide.

When they got to it Curtis couldn't jump it. The rest got across easily. Bill and Robert jumped over and Mr. Atkinson took Margaret in his arms and stepped over with her. Then for some reason he insisted on Curtis jumping it.

Curtis told him he couldn't, but Mr. Atkinson insisted. He believed Curtis could jump it if he would, but he was afraid to try. So he decided to give Curtis a little boost.

He had a walking stick with him. It was one of the kind with a crooked handle. He took the cane by the tip and extended the crook to Curtis, telling him to catch on. Curtis did. Then Mr. Atkinson told Curtis to back up one step, step toward the creek and jump, and he would boost him across. Curtis did as he was told but when he took the step, instead of jumping, he balked. Mr. Atkinson jerked the stick out of his hand.

Bill said Mr. Atkinson said, "Pshaw," and stood there thinking awhile and looking at Curtis. Presently he leaned across the creek and hooked the stick around Curtis' neck and told him to jump, setting his feet to snatch Curtis across as soon as he got off the ground. Curtis balked again. Then Mr. Atkinson told Bill to hop back over the branch and throw Curtis in the air and he would snatch him across. He did.

Bill said that as soon as he pitched Curtis, Mr. Atkinson jerked. He jerked Curtis out flat and the stick slipped over his head and he did a belly buster into Burney Branch. It was fall and coolish and they had to come right home to get Curtis some dry clothes lest he take cold in the chill air.

Bill was sitting on the front steps when we came in. He told us about his walk with the Atkinsons and what Mr. Atkinson had done. Mother asked if he hadn't been afraid they might break Curtis' neck. Bill said, no, he didn't guess so, or they wouldn't have tried it. Mother told him he ought to have had sense enough to put a stop to it even if Mr. Atkinson didn't. Bill said he didn't want to. He wanted to see what would happen when Mr. Atkinson jerked the stick.

Chapter II

IN THE FALL WE HAD OUR COUNTY FAIRS. They were held on the Square, which was dirt then. We hadn't thought of paving. We'd just got our first concrete walks. Concrete was new. Some called it formed stone. The sand and cement and gravel was mixed by hand.

Old man Cullen, who lived just south of town, was the first one to learn about it and our only concrete man for a long time. He built our first sidewalks in 1909. You can still see his signature in some places on them: A. B. Cullen 1909. Two of his sons learned the business and later the signature became A. B. Cullen & Sons.

Jenks and John learned about concrete by working right along with Old man Cullen's blacks. They shoveled sand and gravel and mixed and toted the wet mass right along with the best of them. They were good stout boys and learned to finish concrete themselves and became concrete contractors on their own later on.

The sand was piled on the job to be screened and of course old man Cullen let us play in it. All the Cullen boys (there were two more of them, Hal and Malcolm) were particular friends of ours. They passed our house on their way to and from school every day and always stopped to speak to us, or to invite us out to their place to hunt and fish. John was later one of Bill's hunting companions on his trips to the Big Woods and the Delta.

Our town was nicer in those days than now. At least I liked it better. Our Square in particular was nicer. Every store was two storied, with an upstairs porch reaching out over the sidewalk, making an awning for it. At the edge of the walkway were spaced elm trees, whose limbs made shade for us in summer. The courthouse, old Gothic, sat in the middle of an octagonal lawn with an iron picket fence around it. Just outside the fence were posts with chains to hitch teams to.

Our courthouse has had wings added now, and the iron fence is gone. The hitching chain has long since been done away with, and the Square itself is paved. Some of the buildings have narrow aluminum awnings, and most of the stores are glass-fronted. The elm trees have long since been chopped down and the concrete watering troughs are no longer there. It has been changed a great deal. I liked it better the other way.

Mr. Cullen built those two watering troughs that used to be on the Square. The county had them placed there for the farmers who came to town by wagon on Saturdays. Pigeons flourished on the spilled feed they brought to feed their teams and we used to trap them in wooden boxes, propped on a stick with a long string tied to it. We would set these traps over the spilled feed, pay out the string till we were far enough away not to disturb the pigeons, then lie in wait. When any of them fed under our trap we would jerk the stick with the string, the box would fall on the pigeons and we'd gather them in and run home to put them in our cage. The Cullen boys were good at it and so was Dewey Linder.

We had a neighbor willing to pay two bits apiece for squabs, but we never raised any. We were told that if we penned the pigeons for two weeks they would stay there, but ours never would. They always went straight back to town as soon as the first flock from there flew over. We never quit trying though.

When fair time came the county pitched canvas display booths where our farmers could show their prize produce. These tents were backed against the hitch chain around the courtyard. Here the farmers placed their best ears of corn and biggest potatoes, and their wives displayed cakes and jars of jelly and preserves. The merchants believed carnivals were good for business. They would bring crowds to town with fall money in their pockets. The carnival pitched their tents with their backs to the line of elm trees at the edge of the sidewalk. There was always a lady snake charmer, and a wild man from Borneo, that some English explorer had caught in a net. The scene of his capture was always depicted on the front of his tent. We stared at it and believed and paid our dimes to go inside and stare at the wild man, seated in a cane-bottomed chair with one leg chained to the stand on which he sat, and gnawing at the bones scattered about him.

There were games too, where you won things by pitching rings over numbered pegs, or covering a painted circle with five disks you got for ten cents. The man who ran the booth could easily fan the disks out and cover the circle. We tried but couldn't. Jack and I tried several times. Bill tried once. I did win a dollar watch by fishing for toy fishes in a canvas trough, though. It didn't run good, but then time didn't mean much to us, at least the time we kept ourselves. Mother saw to it that we got off to school on time and we knew better than to be after dark getting home to do our chores.

Anyhow, I broke the crystal on my watch on the acting bar at school the first day I carried it, and twisted the hands together trying to get it out of my pocket. I was disappointed for a while but not for long. Time didn't make that much difference.

Bill didn't go in all the side shows and try every game like Jack and I did. He would listen to the barkers and try a game every now and then, but that was about all. Dad gave us money for the carnival, but Bill always had something else to do with his. Whatever he came by, he always saved some. I never knew him not to have a hoard tucked away somewhere when he came across something he really wanted.

They always had a special children's day, usually on Wednesday, and school would close. Then we'd go back to school for two days until Saturday came, when we had a whole day for the fair's closing. Saturday was the highlight of the whole week—the balloon ascension. We called the man a "balloonitic" and wanted to be sure to be there if he fell.

All airmen of that day were looked on as lunatics. Our papers always pictured them with Death riding by their sides. We knew one of them would fall and be killed sooner or later, and many of them were. We believed any man was a fool if he got both feet off the ground at the same time. If he insisted on being a fool, we wanted to be there and see him when he got what was coming to him.

About eight o'clock in the morning the balloonist and his helper, a black, would appear with a great pile of dirty canvas loaded in a wagon. With curses and grunts they would dump this into the widest part of the midway at one of the corners. A frame would be erected and the mouth of the great bag would be draped over it and pulled down close to the ground. Then the black would bring the man a five-gallon can of coal oil, a dipper and an iron skillet full of hot coals. Soon we would see a tiny flame in there, then a gush of flame as the balloonist would fling coal oil on the coals.

Throughout the day he would feed the fire and the bag would begin to swell with hot air. During those hours we would stand there and watch, Bill most steadfast of all. Other children would come by to watch with us. Their pet dogs would be with them. Most of us would wander off, to come back later, but not Bill. The only time I remember him leaving was to hurry home to dinner so he could come right back.

Although it would take nearly all day to fill the bag with enough hot air and smoke to whisk the man aloft, by about ten o'clock it would begin to take a flabby, wrinkled shape above the framework. Soon he would step out from under the frame, dirty and smoke-grimed and with his eyes reddened from the fumes, and pitch us ropes to hold. These were mooring ropes, attached to the reinforced top of the bag, and there were about a dozen of them. We would spread out in a circle around the inflating balloon. Each of us would take an end as they were pitched to us and stand there till three-thirty or four in the afternoon, watching the bag swell, grow taut and sway above us.

Along about noon, with the bag swelled enough for the man to stand erect within the smoothing canvas, we would see him in the glare of each flung dipper of coal oil. He would stand back against the canvas wall and we'd see him raise a bottle to his lips. As time wore on and the moment of ascent came closer and closer, we would see him raising the bottle more and more often. Usually one bottle wasn't enough. He'd emerge from his canvas igloo and send his black for another one. And soon he would have drunk that one too.

By three or four o'clock in the afternoon the bag would be tugging at our hands. It was time to go. The man would come out from under the bag for the last time. He'd be almost black from oil fumes and smoke and his eyes would be red and streaming. But he would be as coldly sober and as steady as anyone I had ever seen. Glaring at us, he would say, "Move in a little now," and wave us closer with his hands.

We would step forward slowly, moving in toward the balloon, and as we advanced it would rise until a bar, like a trapeze bar, fastened by two ropes to the bottom of the bag, would rise from the ground to knee height. At that point he would stop us. "Hold it now." Tensely we would hold, staring at him, readying our muscles to be sure and let go when he said so.

As we watched he would fasten his parachute harness on, flexing his legs and arms to seat the straps. The parachute itself was packed in a crokersack, tied end-down to the horizontal bar on which he would sit to go aloft. The sack was laced with grocer's string so it would rip out as he fell away from the balloon. Trailing the risers behind him, he would seat himself carefully on the bar, making sure the risers were free. He would settle himself, reach up and grab the ropes leading to the balloon with clenched hands and, with his feet placed firmly upon the ground, stare at us with the fever-ridden eyes of Old Nick and say, with the most tragic voice in the world, "Let her go, boys."

We would release our grip and jump back, craning our necks upward to follow the smoke-filled bag's flight, to see which way the wind would drift the balloon as soon as it cleared the elm trees. As soon as we did, we would begin running, to be near where the man jumped, to see him land in his parachute or to watch him fall if his chute failed to open.

Bill always gave us the signal to start and though we could see as well as he could which way the balloon was drifting, we always waited for him to tell us which direction to run. He knew more about aircraft than we did. He had read about them in the *American Boy*.

We never got there in time to see the man actually land in his parachute, nor did we ever see one fail to open, though we chased the balloonitic each year. The bag rose swiftly. It didn't take it long to get high enough for the man to tumble backward from his roost and jerk the chute from its bag and float down to earth. We would watch as we ran, and shout and point as the gas-filled bag swept away, then a small dot would appear below it and a long white ribbon would flower out behind the dot and we would shriek again. There would be fifty to a hundred of us in the pack, all running toward the descending toadstool.

The balloon, free of the man's weight, would turn upside down and trail a long black smear of oily smoke across our autumn sky. The bag itself would always land not too far from where the man came down.

We watched this too as we ran, but we kept our eye on the man. We never did beat him to the spot where he landed. He always got there first. Yet we usually arrived while he was still in his harness, staggering around, cursing, trying to free himself from the straps. By then he would be too drunk to know what he was doing. Once back on the ground, the liquor seemed to hit him all at once. He would be higher than the balloon from which he had just jumped.

I remember Bill leading us into a thicket in which he had landed one day, and trying to help him free from his straps, but he flailed us away with his hands. Always, soon after we got there, there would come some carnival men in a buggy with the black helper. They would gallop up and subdue him, get his harness off and him into the buggy and away before the law came and arrested them for disturbing the peace. The black helper would be left to gather up the parachute and roll the balloon, so they could be picked up later after the balloonitic had been taken somewhere and sobered up.

One day the parachutist came down in our lot and the balloon fell on our chicken house. It caved the roof in on our chickens, who had already gone to roost, and caused Dad to shoot a pig right between the eyes.

It had been still that day when the balloon left the Square. There was almost no wind, and the sky was gray and overcast. It took several seconds to tell which way the balloon was going to drift and then we took off. It seemed to be drifting toward South Street, toward our house. We saw the man had come down in our lot and the balloon not far behind. As soon as he had left it, it had turned bottom side up and plummeted to earth.

By the time we began pouring over our fence he was already on the ground, staggering around and cursing. It was almost dark. The balloon had hit the hen-house roof and caved it in and our chickens were squawking indignantly and running around every which way. We never did find some of them. Others were two or three days getting over their fright enough to come back home.

Where the man had landed was right in our pig lot. It was fenced off from the rest of the property, and we had several shoats in there waiting for first frost to be butchered. They ran and squealed and bunched up in the far corner.

Dad had just come home from work when he heard the disturbance out back. He ran out the kitchen door in time to see the thirty or forty of us swarming over the fence and knotting up against the hog pen, where the man was stomping around trying to get himself out of his harness. The hens were sailing around, screeching, and the pigs were squealing and the man was cursing. Dad shouted at him to stop, so loudly that Mother could hear him from inside the house. The man paid no attention. So Dad turned and ran back to the house and came out this time with his pistol.

It was a silver-plated Colt, a .41 single-action, and with the longest barrel 1 ever saw on a hand gun. It was dusk by then, but you could see the pistol shining in Dad's hand as he strode across the back yard and into the lot. A man from the carnival had got there by then and was stripping the harness off the balloonist and trying to calm him down. He went to Dad to try to pacify him while the black, now that the parachutist was free of his harness, tried to lead him away to the wagon. Of the boys there, all of us stood still at the sight of Dad with his pistol, watching the carnival man talking to him.

In the carnival buggy the balloonist quietly went to sleep. By that time Dad had sort of calmed down, especially since the man talking to him promised to pay damages if Dad would agree to let the matter rest there.

The black helper hung around outside the gate. He didn't like the look of Dad with his pistol. Now he came in and began working at the balloon, trying to get the one corner off the chicken house so he could fold it. The rest of the balloon was spread over the hog lot but that one corner was caught on the roof. Finally Dad called one or two of our blacks to help and they got the balloon rolled up and loaded in the wagon and hauled it away.

All the other boys who had chased the balloon with us left then and in our darkening lot was left only Bill and Jack and me and Dad. Dad was standing there with his arm hung down, the pistol in it and cocked. He stood there glaring about the lot, at the caved-in chicken house, a few white feathers strewn over the ground, and the pigs huddled in the far corner of the pen. Bill and Jack and I sort of huddled together, quiet, looking.

Just then one of our smaller pigs came up behind Dad and raised his snout and said, "Unh!" Dad whirled, and leveling his pistol, shot that pig right between the eyes. He stood there looking down at the pig a few moments, then told us to go get Jessie. He wanted Jessie to come dress the pig out before it spoiled. Then he turned and strode off toward the house, the pistol still swinging from his hand.

I'll always remember three little boys standing there wide-eyed in the deserted gloom of that empty autumn lot, watching Dad with that long shiny pistol in his hand, cocked, his anger at the boiling point, and nothing to shoot at. When that pig grunted right behind him, it was more than he could stand. He simply raised his gun and shot it between the eyes.

Chapter 12

IT WASN'T LONG AFTER THIS THAT THE LINDERS moved to town. Dr. Linder bought a place up on Second North Street and they moved away from their home at the edge of town.

Across the street from the Linders' new house lived the Hilers. The Hiler home faced North Street, but their land ran back to just across Second North from the Linders' lot. The Hilers had two boys, both mean. As soon as the Linders moved to their new home they began fighting with the Hiler boys. Most of their fights were from one side of the street to the other, like strange dogs trying each other out. Then one day Van Hiler threw a piece of pipe over the fence at the Linders. Dewey climbed his fence and ran Van clear into his own kitchen.

Both the Hilers talked big. Henry was always talking about his gun and how Van carried a knife. Both of them fought dirty. They would use any sort of underhand tricks, like Van throwing the pipe, or hitting you in the back with a brick and then running. Henry wasn't as underhanded as Van but a lot meaner. Bill had a fight or two with him and Dewey was tired of the way he fought.

The Linders had a big barn with a tin roof, sharp-peaked in the middle, and with sheds on either side. It was an ideal place for corncob battles like we used to have at the old Linder place and cobs were plentiful about the stalls and lot. We used to go down there Sunday evenings and choose sides and have cob fights, and we did the same now, usually with the Hilers on one side and us on the other.

One day they found out that Henry and Van had left some cobs soaking in a bucket of water to use for the next fight. So Bill and Dewey naturally laid for them. Van didn't know that

Dewey had seen the wet cobs. The bucket was in the corner of a back stall and Van thought he had slipped into the barn without being seen.

As soon as Dewey made out what he was doing, he told Bill. They got buckets of water of their own and put in cobs to soak too.

In a corncob fight, the use of wet cobs is dirty fighting. Getting hit with one of them is about like getting hit with a wet brickbat. The next time we fought, Bill and Dewey got there first and hid their wet cobs. They let Henry and Van go ahead with theirs, without letting on they knew anything about it. They had already laid out their strategy.

Our cobfights took place on top of the barn. Each side would stand on top of a shed. The roofs there were almost flat. The center roof was high and peaked. Each side would stand prepared on its shed roof out of sight of the other, and at a signal each side would run as hard as it could, so as to get as high as it could on the sharp peak. As heads would pop against the opposite skyline you threw your cobs and then had to turn quickly and run back down the slant. The pitched roof was too sharp to stand on. You'd brake to a stop on your own flat shed, get more cobs and charge again.

The way Bill and Dewey had worked it out, Bill did not wait with us on the shed roof for the signal. Instead he went to the edge of the peak and climbed to just below the top on hands and knees, clinging by the overhang. From here he could peer around the corner of the peak without being seen by the other side, as they wouldn't be expecting anyone that near the edge of the roof.

The secret of cob fighting on a roof was quickness of reflex. With each gang charging up its own side, there was such a racket you couldn't tell exactly how high up the other side was. A head would pop up in front of you, and you had to adjust your aim and let fly quickly. You had better be right too, for after your shot you were out of ammunition and your momentum had given out. For the moment you were a sitting duck for the other fellow, just before you whirled to run back down. At that moment the other guy was armed and cocked, and you had come to a complete stop right in front of him.

The captains always charged in the middle of the line, so Bill and Dewey knew where Henry would appear. If they could know the instant his head would pop up, it would take away the element of surprise. It worked too. At the signal to charge, both sides went thundering up the roof. Just before Henry got to the top Bill yelled, "Now, Dewey. Now."

Dewey drew back and just as Henry's head popped up on the horizon, Dewey let him have it with the wet cob. It caught Henry right between the eyes. It sounded like Dewey had hit him with a log. He went limp and fell backward down the roof, his cob still in his hand. He rolled clear off the shed on his side and lay on the ground, out cold.

Van began crying and screaming and we all scrambled down off our side of the roof to run around and see just what Dewey's cob had done to Henry. Van pulled a knife and Dewey lit out after him and ran him clear out into the road. Van stood there with his knife, cursing, and finally Dewey came on back to where we were. By then Henry had come to and was on his feet. He was dazed and mad. But with Van gone, we were too many for him and what was left of his side and they drew away muttering.

We had other cob fights after that, on occasion, but I don't ever remember Henry and Van joining in.

There was another boy, named McElroy, whom Bill outsmarted. Fritz was about Bill's age. They were in the same grade. Fritz was about the toughest boy we knew and bragged about being tough. He would fight anybody to prove it. He fought Bill and whipped him. Bill was smaller but that didn't make any difference to Fritz. He would fight anybody, bigger, littler, his size, or two or three at a time. When he whipped the rest of us we started ganging him, and he would whip us in gangs. He was a good boy but he just liked to fight. What really made us mad was that he would brag he could whip us and then do it. Bill never fought him a second time. Once was enough for him. He simply laid for Fritz and outsmarted him without laying a hand on him.

On the Saturday that Bill fooled Fritz, we had gone down to Fritz' house to play. He lived on Second South, way below where we used to live. He lived almost down to the Bailey place that Bill bought later and lived out his life in.

That morning Bill and Jack and I started down there and picked up Ed Lowe on the way. By the time we got there, there were already several boys in his yard. We joined them. I don't remember exactly how many of us there were but I would think at least a dozen. Some of the Linders were there. They lived not too far on past Fritz.

We decided to play hide and seek. The way we played it covered a lot of ground, several front and back yards. Some of us would hide as far as two houses from where home base was. It not only took in front yards, it took in back yards too, and barn lots and barns.

All of us raised pigs then for our own meat. Most of us had separate pens for them inside our barn lots but the McElroys didn't. They let their pigs run loose and they had made a wallow right in front of the barn, just to one side of the entrance door. Right over the main doors to the barn was the door in the hayloft, through which hay was thrown in season to feed the stock through the winter. The hayloft doors were open. That's how Bill tricked Fritz into diving into the hog wallow.

I don't remember who "it" was the first game but I know it wasn't long till Fritz got caught first and had to take his place. Fritz was easy to catch. He was sort of lumbering and clumsy and didn't know how to hide very well. He was always getting caught and usually had to be "it" for several games in a row.

Bill made it up with Fritz to let himself be caught so he could help Fritz catch the rest of us. Fritz agreed wholeheartedly. He had already been "it" four or five games and he was tired of it. Besides, Bill explained, not only would Fritz be getting even with the rest of us, he would play a good practical joke on us too. Fritz liked that. He was a great one for practical jokes, the rougher the better.

Bill told Fritz that all of us were hidden in a bunch, just beyond the far corner of the barn. He directed Fritz to go up in the loft and tiptoe up to the hay door, real quiet, taking up a position one step back from the opening, so we couldn't see him from below, and wait for his signal. Bill would go around the barn the other way and flush us out and signal Fritz just the moment to jump. That way Fritz would catch us all just passing the hog wallow on the narrow path and could push us all in.

Fritz fell for it. He climbed up in the loft and slipped up to the hay door and waited. Bill went around the barn and when he got to the corner where he'd told Fritz we were, he began yelling like he had seen us. Of course we weren't there at all. Bill had just told Fritz that. He stamped his feet on the ground to sound like running and yelled for Fritz to jump. He dived out that door and went nearly out of sight in the mud. We were hid not far away and saw the whole thing.

We began running to get home free but Bill called us to stop. It took all of us to drag Fritz out of the wallow. He was covered with mud all over, even his face. We had to lead him to the back door and call Mrs. McElroy to come get him. We didn't offer to stay around to help. We were afraid of what Fritz would do to us when he realized what sort of trick Bill had played on him.

But in spite of Fritz wanting to be tough, he was a good-natured somebody. After that he became sort of fascinated with Bill. All that following winter Bill used to bring Fritz home with him, and he would bring in Bill's coal, like I said, while Bill walked along beside him and told him stories.

That was about the end of Bill's boyhood. It was about time for it to come to an end anyhow. That winter Mother discovered he was becoming stoop-shouldered and put the braces on him. That put an abrupt end to it for, he could not engage in rough-and-tumble play with his upper body in a corset. He found he could stay neat all day and didn't necessarily have to get dirty and mussed just to have a good time. He learned to entertain himself other ways, like reading and painting. He found that Estelle liked him better neat and with her listening, Bill found he could talk. From then on he spent more and more time down at her house, being with her and talking to her and listening to her play. She was an accomplished pianist even then, for Miss Lida was a music teacher and taught all her daughters to play, Estelle best of all.

Chapter 13

OUR TALENT TO DRAW AND PAINT CAME FROM Damuddy. Mother inherited it and passed it on to Bill and me and Dean. Jack missed out somehow. Bill's writing ability probably came from our great-grandfather, the Old Colonel, who was a novelist in his own right. He wrote a novel called *The White Rose of Memphis*, which was a best seller in its day. He also wrote *The Little Brick Church* and *Rapid Ramblings in Europe* and a play that had a short run on Broadway. In 1851 he had his first book of poems published.

Damuddy came from Arkansas. She was born Lelia Dean Swift, a cousin of the man who founded the Swift Packing Company. Damuddy was a Baptist and her father was evidently of the hard-shell variety, for he thought that any creation which came out of thin air, like a painting, was the work of the Devil. When he caught her painting one day he took her paints and brushes away and told her never to touch them again.

Damuddy had her own private black, like all children did then. She got hold of more painting materials and would make her black row her out in the middle of a lake that was near her home. She would sit there in the boat and paint, far enough from shore, so that no one could tell what she was doing.

She won a scholarship to Italy to study sculpture in 1890 but would not go because she said she had to stay at home and look after Mother. Actually Mother was taking care of her. Mother's brother, Uncle Sherwood, was married and had his own wife to look after, and Mother's father had walked out on Damuddy. So Mother had had to quit school at Mississippi State College for Women, where she was studying art, and take a quick business course to learn stenography in order to support Damuddy.

We have a picture or two that Damuddy painted, and a small statue of a black boy fishing that she molded out of kitchen soap. They were living in Texarkana at the time, where Mother had a job working as secretary. Damuddy was supposed to keep house for the two of them. But Mother left for work one morning, leaving Damuddy at the kitchen sink to wash the dishes, and when she came home at noon for dinner there was Damuddy sitting at the sink making the statue of the little black boy. No dinner was ready and the breakfast dishes hadn't been washed. Damuddy had started to wash them, and when she put the soap in the water and it began to get soft, she simply sat down and began making the statue. She hadn't moved since Mother left that morning.

Among her paintings we still have is a tiny one on a piece of velvet that someone commissioned for seventy-five cents and never came to claim.

Some of Bill's black-and-white sketches appeared in the Ole Miss yearbooks in the late Teens. My youngest brother, Dean, was also an artist. He began a course in commercial art, but his bent turned to flying when Bill bought his first airplane after the First War and Dean went to Memphis and learned to fly it. He never took the time to draw again. A student spun him in and killed him in 1935, so we don't know how far his talent might have carried him.

Dad had married Mother in 1896. Since she was Damuddy's sole support, she told Dad that if she married him he would have to take Damuddy too. He agreed and she lived with us the rest of her life. And died with us too, though Bill and Jack and I did not know that was what was happening to her. She never let us see her suffering. All we knew was that for the last day or so we were not allowed in her room, and then she was taken to the cemetery.

Dean was not born until after she died, so he did not know her or remember her but Bill and Jack-Jack especially-and I remembered her tenderness and patience with us. I can see her now, small and dressed in black and hurrying to church on Sundays. She never missed a Sunday and always walked. Dad would have sent her in a buggy, but for some reason she would not let him. I don't know whether walking fitted in with her religious convictions, or whether she felt that with Dad supporting her she should do all she could to relieve him of his burden. Knowing Damuddy, I suspect it was the latter.

It was during Bill's shoulder-brace-and-eyeglass period that he developed a neatness about his personal appearance that won him a nickname and lasted throughout his life. The only exception was the coats that he grew fond of and would not throw away. He would wear them patched with leather and with strings of yarn hanging from worn places. I don't think he ever threw one away or stopped wearing it.

I remember a trick he pulled on Jack and me during the early part of this neatness period. It was another time he used his flair for words and got a day's work out of Jack and me, and we didn't realize until it was all over that he hadn't raised a hand.

We were still living on South Street, but we had moved across to the other side, the same side Grandfather was on and next door to him. Dad had a hardware store now. It had a huge warehouse attached to it, but for some reason Dad decided to store a load of sewer pipe in our lot. It was a railroad carload. He had a one-horse delivery wagon that Elam drove. Elam made trip after trip down home with pipe until he had it stacked head high all along one wall of our barn. Then Dad decided it should be moved across the lot and stacked against the fence. He told Bill and Jack and me to move it.

It took us the biggest part of a day. When we finally got through and went in the house Mother called our attention to Jack and me. She said to just look at us. We looked like we had crawled through every piece of pipe we had moved. And just look at Billie. He was neat as a pin, not a dirty streak on him, and he wasn't even sweating. For a minute Jack and I wondered why. Then It came to us. He hadn't done a lick of work. He hadn't touched a single pipe. We had done it all. There was nothing much we could do about it then. It was too late.

Bill had picked up a new friend just before this, a Ralph Market from Water Valley, whose father was a railroad engineer. Dad had sold his livery business and had got the Standard Oil agency. At that time the only market for coal oil was what people burned in their lamps, but there was enough of that to support an oil agency in Oxford. Dad got it. Every grocery store in the county sold oil, so Dad had to have a delivery wagon of some kind. It was a tank on a wagon bed. The tank held about five hundred gallons of oil, and one of his blacks made weekly trips all over the county. We used to take time about going with them, carrying our lunches, for each trip was an all-day affair.

The oil came into Oxford by railroad so Dad's office was beside the tracks at the depot with huge storage tanks behind it. Dad knew some of the men who ran the trains through Oxford from his railroading days and one in particular was Mr. John Market (Marquette). Of course he used to let us go to work with him. Trains fascinate all boys and they did us. Then one day Mr. John brought his boy, Ralph, from Water Valley on the train with him. Ralph rode in the cab. He and Bill met at the depot and Mr. John let them take time about running the engine while it switched.

Ralph spent the night with us that night, and when he went back home the next day Bill went with him. It was Mr. John's return trip, and they both rode in the cab with him and he let them run the engine all the way to Water Valley. From then on, every now and then, Ralph would come to see Bill and they would go back to Water Valley on the train, running it. This went on for several years. Sometimes Jack and I would go down to the depot, and Mr. John, finding out who we were, used to let us ride about the yards in the cab with him. I don't remember him ever letting either of us run his engine though, like he did Bill and Ralph. Dad did not have the oil agency but a year or two before he bought the hardware store. He traded our house in on it and that's when we moved across the street to a rented house.

It was about this time, 1912 or '13, that the Merchants and Farmers Bank went broke and Grandfather put in his bank, the First National. It still operates in Oxford. It's the bank where Bill worked for a while.

General Stone was the guiding genius of the Bank of Oxford, our other bank, and he and Grandfather had been life-time rivals about almost everything. For that reason Grandfather patronized the Merchants and Farmers. After it went broke he still refused to put his money in General Stone's bank, so he put up his own.

He put up most of the money, sold some stock and opened his bank. That's where he was voted out of his presidency because he was deaf and everybody heard whoever tried to borrow money from him, and it was bad for business so they went to General Stone instead. Grandfather got madder at his own bank, after that, than he stayed at General Stone, so he took his money out of the First National and put it in the Bank of Oxford. He never forgave the First National, and when he died his money was still in the Bank of Oxford.

Bill was in high school by then. He did well in school through about the tenth grade, then he simply lost interest in school and a formal education. It was the end of his formal training. He simply quit going to school.

During Bill's first two years in high school he was a pretty good athlete. He played football and baseball both. In later years he was a good tennis player (we had a court in our front yard) and even later he was a crackajack golfer. He played par golf on the old University course and had one hole in one to his credit.

In his high school days he pitched on the baseball team and played quarterback at football.

We were playing Holly Springs once when Bill was quarterback. A family named McDaniel had moved to town from Pontotoc County, so their children could go to our school and the University. The oldest boy was named Benjamin. He came to town nicknamed Benny, but we soon changed that to Possum because he looked like one. His younger brothers fell heir to the same nickname, but Benny was the original Possum.

Possum was a good old country boy, stringy and tough from working spare time and summers on his father's farm. He wasn't tall, but he had the longest arms I ever saw on a man. He had tremendous ambition too. He later studied medicine at Ole Miss.

Possum played end in high school and at Ole Miss too. He couldn't catch a pass even though his arms were so awfully long. Somehow when you threw him a pass he simply could not get his arms away from his sides. It was like throwing a pass to somebody holding two sticks of stovewood out from his belt. Even if you hit his hands the ball simply bounced off.

We didn't throw him passes in high school or at Ole Miss. But when the other side tried to run a play over him, I've seen him run into a whole backfield with his arms stretched wide and down all four men, including the one with the ball. The other side simply could not get past him. Although we couldn't throw him a pass, the other side, after one try, usually let his side of the line alone.

I never knew Possum to catch but one pass. It was at Holly Springs, that same day I'm talking about. Bill didn't throw the pass to him. It was one Holly Springs threw and he intercepted.

Possum saw the play developing, and the Holly Springs end racing downfield, so he simply took out after him and outran him. Possum was deep in the other end and running the same way when the pass came sailing over the Holly Springs man's head and fell into Possum's arms. That was fine, except Possum was running toward the Holly Springs goal at the time and he just kept right on going.

All of our team began shouting at Possum to turn around and run back toward his own goal. Possum didn't hear them. I guess he was too excited over having at last caught a pass. Bill, playing safety, was the only man between Possum and the Holly Springs goal. He tackled him just before he could carry the ball over for the other side.

We won that game and they gave Bill credit for it for tackling Possum. That's where Bill got his nose broken, the reason for the hump in it.

It was after Bill's sophomore year in high school that he just sort of quit. Mother and Dad didn't like Bill's refusing to go to school, but they didn't force him to go back. They knew it would do no good if he had made up his mind not to study. So Phil Stone guided his reading for the next two years.

Phil was a Yale graduate, the only "up East" man in our community. He was a lawyer in his father's firm, James Stone and Sons. There was another brother, Jack, who was in Charleston, near the Delta, whom Bill visited frequently later on.

The Stones had a big old Studebaker touring car, a seven-passenger affair. Phil loaded it with books for Bill to read and turned the car over to him. Bill would go out on some country road, a side road where it was quiet, and park the car and spend the day reading. He taught himself French out there and later he actually taught French at the University. Phil's guidance was good, for it put the finishing touches on the reading program that Mother had established in all of us. I think that's the reason she didn't object any more than she did over Bill's quitting school. What Phil picked for Bill to read was pretty much what she would have chosen. Bill read Plato, Socrates, the Greek poets, all the good Romans and Shakespeare. He also read the other good English writers and the French and German classics.

The next year, 1916, Bill was nineteen and Dad went to Grandfather about him. Grandfather put him to work in his bank. Bill was happy throughout that year. He sort of settled into his job. He was going regular with Estelle, and maybe he figured this was his future—a job and her, and a home.

It was about this time that Bill began to develop an almost foppish taste in clothes. He now had a regular monthly income and he spent most of it adorning himself. If pants were tight, he had his tighter. If coats were short, he had his shorter. He began going to the University dances because Estelle was always there.

He even bought himself a dress suit. A great many of the students rented theirs from Ed Beanland's tailor shop. But not Bill. He owned his. That's when Bill picked up the nickname "The Count."

That dress suit cost twenty-five dollars. It was a Styleplus. There were only two makes of ready-made clothes we knew anything about—Styleplus and Hart, Schaffner & Marx. Styleplus suits were seventeen-fifty, their dress clothes twenty-five dollars. Hart, Schaffner & Marx suits were twenty-five dollars, I think, so most of us wore Styleplus.

Bill would get Mother to alter his clothes for him, and when she got through they looked like they were tailor-made. It was about this time that he opened a charge account with Phil A. Halle's in Memphis and until his death bought most of his clothes from them.

Back in his bank days he bought a pair of shoes from them. They were Johnston & Murphys, and he paid twelve dollars and a half for them, an unheard-of price for a pair of shoes in those days. Most of us paid three dollars. When he left for the First War I inherited those shoes and finally wore them out.

Bill used to lend me his dress suit every now and then, and the rest of his clothes too, on occasion. We were about the same size then. I finally outgrew him and couldn't wear his clothes any more. I was sorry too. I never had as good clothes as Bill did. But I don't think clothes are worth the money he spent for his, except for shoes. He taught me about shoes. The best ones you can buy are the most expensive.

I remember one suit Bill had about this time. As soon as he bought it, he brought it home for Mother to make the legs tighter. She altered them. They were not tight enough. She did them over. Finally they fit him so tightly he couldn't get his pants on over his shoes. He had to take them off. But they still weren't tight enough. She had to narrow them some more.

When Bill was finally satisfied, he could hardly bend his knees when he had them on. The bottoms of these pants hit him way above his shoes, and they were high-top shoes too. We all wore high-top shoes in the winter. You couldn't even see the crease, they fit so tight around his leg, and the cuffs stuck out before and aft like little spurs.

Seemie, one of the blacks who hung around us, thought the way Bill dressed was the last word in elegance. Whatever Bill wore Seemie had to have as soon as Bill wore it out or got tired of it. He began pestering Bill for that suit as soon as he saw it on Bill.

Bill finally did sell that suit to Seemie. Then Seemie wanted to return it and get his money back. He couldn't get his feet through the legs, even without his shoes on. Bill refused to reverse their deal. Later on Seemie told Bill he had sold the suit to Eskimay. Eskimay could get his feet through the legs, but he never could get them back out. He simply wore the pants till he wore them out.

I remember one time when Bill still had that suit. He got to drinking one day with Charlie Crouch. Charlie was our town drunk. He was harmless and everybody liked him, but he would get drunk. That night Bill didn't get home at all. The next morning when Jack and I were on our way to school we met him coming home. He was in a foul humor and had on Charlie's hat. They had swapped during the night.

Bill's hat had a narrow brim, to go with his suit. Charlie always wore sort of a cowboy hat, a black one with the crown creased fore and aft and a big wide brim. Bill sure looked funny in that suit and Charlie's cowboy hat. Jack and I stepped off the walk and bowed as he passed. Without looking at us he said, "God damn it!"

When we got to town, there was Charlie in Bill's hat. He was going around the Square on the outside of the sidewalk looking down in the gutter. We knew what he was looking for—his teeth. Every time Charlie got drunk he got sick and lost his teeth. So the next morning, you would see him walking along the edge of the sidewalk looking for them.

As usual Charlie had a sign pinned to the tail of his coat saying *Kick Me Please*. Some of the boys had found him looking for his teeth and slipped up and pinned it there. Somebody always did. Jack and I sniggered and passed on.

Charlie was a good old soul. We were always playing tricks on him, but he never got mad at us for it. I guess he figured a drunk was worth whatever you had to pay for it. He never stopped getting drunk as long as we knew him. He's dead now, but I do hope wherever he is he finds enough to get drunk on every now and then. And that the next morning, that he always manages to find his teeth. If I were there I would help him.

We had one or two other town drunks then. I look on all of them with a great deal of affection, for they were a part of the nicest town I ever knew—Oxford, before the First World War. I know this is the way Bill felt about Oxford. He told me so more than once. And this is the way he felt about old Charlie too. He liked him for more than just a drinking partner.

It was about this time that Bill's talent for drawing cropped up. He did a series of black-and-white sketches that were used in the Ole Miss year book. There were about a dozen of them in all. And it was about this time that Estelle got engaged to someone else. Bill never drew again; his world went to pieces.

In his later life, every so often, he would get the urge to paint and he'd buy water colors, but he never used them. He would keep them around for a while and then bring them by Mother's and give them to her.

It was in the spring of 1918, the early spring, that Estelle announced her engagement to Cornell Franklin. His people were from Columbus, Mississippi, but they were well established in business in the Philippines. The wedding was set for June, right after Cornell graduated from Ole Miss. After the wedding, he was going to take her to Manila for their honeymoon and go into business out there with his uncle.

Bill left town. He wouldn't stay around to see someone else claim Estelle. There were not too many of us in Oxford who could drive a car at that time. The Oldhams had a Cole Eight, and when Major Oldham asked me to drive the car in the wedding, I did. I drove Estelle to the church and brought her and Cornell back to her house afterward for the reception. I also drove them to the train that night, on the first stage of their journey to Manila.

Phil got Bill a job in a bookstore in New Haven. The shop was run by a friend of his, a Miss Rawls or Miss Rawlings, I forget which. That's where Bill went, so as to get as far away as possible when he found he'd lost Estelle. He must have gone through torment in that strange land with his whole world gone to pot. He counted the days as Estelle's wedding approached, and when that deed was accomplished, he joined the Royal Flying Corps.

Bill always had loved airplanes. All of us did. He tried the U.S. Signal Corps first. Our flying arm was a branch of that service then. Flyers wore crossed signal flags on their collars. But the Signal Corps turned Bill down. They said he didn't have two years of college.

Bill went to the British next. They needed men, and badly. He applied for training with the RFC, the land branch of the British flying service, and they turned him down too. He wasn't tall enough. Bill got mad and told them he was going to fly for someone, and he guessed if they didn't need him the Germans would take him. They needed flyers too. He asked them the way to the German embassy and the RFC man said, "Wait, hold on a minute." Bill waited and the man went inside an office, and pretty soon he came back and told Bill they could use him.

They sent Bill to primary training in Toronto on Canucks, ships about like the Jennies we used to train our pilots. He graduated from them and went on to fighter training on Sopwith Camels, the orneriest airplane ever built. They had rotary engines and were placarded against a left-hand spin at anything less than three thousand feet. It took that long to get one out once it got in.

The whole engine turned. The prop was bolted onto it. The back end of the crankshaft was fastened to the first station of the fuselage frame and a mixture of gasoline and castor oil was fed into the engine through a hollow crankshaft and hollow piston rods. Immediately you landed one of them you headed lickety-split for the bathroom.

The war ended before Bill could finish his training. But the British government told him and some others that if they wanted to stay and finish their course, they'd get their wings and commission. Bill and a few others stayed. They lacked only a few weeks.

He received his commission as a lieutenant in His Majesty's Royal Flying Corps. His commission was signed by George R.I. He had it framed and kept it on his wall when we lived out on the campus. It hung above the mantle over the fireplace.

Chapter 14

WHILE BILL WAS IN NEW HAVEN, JACK HAD JOINED the Marines. When the British signed Bill up, they gave him leave to come home and see his folks before he reported for duty. As soon as school was out I had gone to Muscle Shoals to work in a powder plant, and when Bill got home Dad and Mother and Dean drove him over there so he could see me.

Before either Bill or Jack had got in service, I'd run off and joined the Army. I lied about my age. I was sixteen, but told them I was eighteen and that I had my parents' consent. When Dad and Mother missed me, Dad phoned every recruiting station around Oxford until he found me. He told them how old I really was and to put me in jail and hold me till he could get there.

They put me in jail in Jackson and Uncle John called a friend of his, Major General Hairston, who came and got me out and sent me home. When Mother and Dad let Bill and Jack go, I raised so much Cain that when I asked to go to Muscle Shoals to work in the powder plant, they were glad to get rid of me.

A lot of boys from Oxford went there that summer. Roy Donaldson, a son of our high school superintendent, was on the police force there. Dad got hold of him when they arrived at the plant and Roy helped them find me.

I was a time checker, and one day when I looked up, there came Roy leading Bill into the plant. Bill grinned when he saw me. We went out to the car where Mother and Dad and Dean were waiting, and visited for a while. Then I told Bill good-bye.

He wrote me every now and then from Canada, about the funny things that happened in flying school. He told me how they washed their greatcoats, putting them on under a shower and scrubbed each other with soap and brushes. Bill said it got the coats clean all right, but it took them two or three weeks to dry. He sent me a picture of himself in cadet uniform. There was not too much difference between cadets' and officers' uniform, except the cadets wore white bands on their caps. I wanted one of the bands and Bill sent it to me. I still have it.

He wrote me about a sergeant they had, who was forever giving them a hard time. So one night they slipped in on him while he was asleep, wrapped him in his blanket, and before he could wake up threw him in the lake.

Bill got home before Christmas, but by then I think Mother and Dad were both about crazy. Bill's flying was bad enough but now Jack was missing. We didn't hear from him till the following April, a letter dated the last of October. He had been at Saint Mihiel, with the Second Engineers in Champagne, where he was badly gassed, and now he was going in the Argonne. He was wounded there on the first of November, and we next heard from him in April.

That Christmas Mother hung a stocking for him as usual and would not take it down or let us touch it. Jack himself emptied it when he came home late that next spring, in May. Dad sort of went to pieces, but Mother kept telling him, "Hush, Buddy. He'll be back."

Dad kept a picture of Bill on his desk at the hardware store. He had a small British flag fastened to it. There was a picture of Jack beside it with an American flag. Grandfather got mad about Bill joining the British Army. He said he'd rather have him join the Germans. Grandfather hated the British because his great-grandfather had fought them at Cowpens and Kings Mountain. He still considered them our enemies. He wanted Dad to take Bill's picture and the British flag off his desk, which of course Dad wouldn't do.

Bill came home one morning in December. He came in on No.23, a passenger train that ran through Oxford, southbound, about eleven o'clock in the morning. Mother and Dad and Mammy and Dean and I went down to meet him in our Model T.

Bill got off the train in his British officer's uniform-slacks, a Sam Browne belt, and wings on his tunic. He had on what we called an overseas cap, a monkey cap that was only issued to our men if they had served overseas. A part of the British uniform was a swagger stick and Bill had one, and across his arm a trench coat.

He had that coat until he wore it out, and then he bought another as near like it as he could find. For the rest of his life he wore trench coats. I don't know how many he bought and wore out. It must have run to half a dozen or more.

Dad drove us down to the depot that morning. He usually drove whenever he was in the car. We parked against the side of the spur track and when we heard the whistle blow, got out and waited for Bill. When he got off, we saw that he was limping. As soon as we greeted him and got him in the car, he told us that some of the graduating class had gone up to celebrate getting their wings, and he had flown his Camel halfway through the top of a hangar. The tail of his ship was still outside, and they got Bill down from inside the hangar with a ladder.

All of our own returned soldiers saluted Bill in his Sam Browne belt and monkey cap. To them it meant he had been overseas, and they saluted an overseas man. They turned up their noses at our own officers who had not been over and refused to acknowledge them in any way.

I liked to walk around the Square with Bill on account of all the salutes he received. I was only seventeen at the time.

Bill wore his uniform for some time after he got home. He liked it; besides, I had worn out all the clothes he left when he went in service. I had worn out Jack's too. Bill and I went to several victory dances at towns around Oxford and Bill did all right in his British officer's uniform, his slacks and RFC wings. He lent it to me several times. I liked it too.

We heard from Jack in April. He was in a convalescent hospital in Hyères, France. He got home in May and opened his Christmas presents and emptied his stocking. It had become a part of our lives. Along with Mother's conviction that he was coming home, it became a constant symbol that Jack would be back. It was on the mantle in the living room, where we saw it every day. We all stood around and grinned as Jack opened his packages and emptied his stocking that hot May morning.

Bill and Jack and I were together more the next few years than we had been for the last few. We were no closer, for we had always been close. It was simply that we were together more.

Bill's first writings were published along about then, the winter of 1918-19. He wrote stories about flying school for the Oxford *Eagle*, our local paper, and they printed them on the front page. I remember how much I liked them. I would ask Bill when he was going to write another one. I wanted to read it. He would grin and say, "Sometime."

You could talk to Bill about writing then. I used to talk to him about his later stories, up in his room. That was when we were living on the campus, and he was being published now and then in the magazines. He used to call me to his room and show me his stories when he had written one of the kind he knew I liked. I don't know whether the *Eagle* paid him anything for those stories he did for them, but anyhow they published them on their front page and he was in print.

It was about this time that Bill bought his first civilian clothes after getting home from service. He went to Memphis and bought a sport coat at Halle's. It was one of the first sport coats I had ever seen and the best-looking garment I ever saw. It was one thing he never let me wear. He never took it off.

It was a heather tweed, sort of smoky-looking, with raglan shoulders and pleats behind each arm, and leather buttons. Bill wore it for everything. He used to play golf in it. His golfing outfit was that coat, his British Army breeks, with leather patches inside the knees, and green golf stockings Mother knitted for him. They were heavy wool and came to just below the knee, after the tops were folded over.

The University golf course was new then. It had sand greens, all square and all the same size. They were flat and a ridge of dirt was thrown around them so rain water wouldn't wash the sand away.

Bill figured out that the main thing in a good golf shot was to keep the left elbow stiff, so he rigged up a piece of tin stovepipe with a strap on it to hold it over his elbow. He practiced with that till he cut a hole in the sleeve of his jacket.

He must have learned by that time to keep his elbow stiff for I've seen him take a pail of practice balls and hit one after another through a space in a tree limb. He was as accurate a golfer as I ever saw.

One day he made a hole in one, only we didn't know he had till we got to the green and found the ball in the cup. This particular hole was on top of a ridge 132 yards long, and you couldn't see the green from the tee, only the flag. You hit your ball toward the flag, and, if it rolled over the ridge, you did not know where it was till you got up to the green.

Bill teed up his ball and hit it and we watched it go straight, drop short of the green, and disappear over the ridge. The rest of us shot and then walked toward the green. No one else was over the green and when we got close enough to see the ridge we couldn't locate Bill's ball. Then we walked on the green and there was Bill's ball in the hole.

We all signed his card and Bill sent it in, and then the presents began arriving. He got a dozen golf balls, a pipe with "Hole in One" inlaid in the bowl, and I don't remember what all else.

We played golf regularly through that summer and if Bill did any writing I don't remember it. The next fall both he and Jack entered the University.

After the First War was over the government set up a vocational training program for veterans. It was sort of like our later GI Bill. Because a great many of our veterans had gone into service from high school, they waived entrance credits. Though neither Bill nor Jack had finished high school, they both qualified and signed up at the University in the fall of 1919.

Jack entered law school and Bill the school of liberal arts. Bill wouldn't take a regular course, only the things that interested him. One was French and he must have learned a lot, for a year or so later he took a walking tour through Europe and lived in Paris for a while. He even had a job on a French newspaper.

Jack spoke French, too but his was doughboy French, and he and Bill never could understand each other.

I don't remember what else Bill took at the University. He didn't graduate. As I remember it he only went two or three semesters.

Not long before he won his Nobel Prize the faculty brought up the subject of awarding him an honorary degree, but it was voted down. Then, after he received the award, it was brought up again by those who had voted it down the first time. But the others said, "For shame. We can't afford to give him one now. It's too late."

Dad was business manager and secretary of the University at that time and Bill had several jobs during the summer. He was a carpenter's helper and later Dad put him on the University painting force. They were painting the law building, which had a steeple. No one else would paint the steeple so Bill did. He tied himself to it with ropes and painted it from top to bottom. After that Mother told Dad not to get Bill any more jobs without talking it over with her first.

It was the fall of 1920, I think, that Bill was appointed postmaster. The University had its own post office, a small one for professors and students. There were only six hundred students in Ole Miss at the time and about thirty-five or forty professors. All the professors and most of the students had boxes, though a few got their mail by general delivery.

There really wasn't much to keeping the University post office, but Bill didn't attend to that little bit very well. If he was sitting in his chair reading he wouldn't get up to wait on anyone at the window. He said he didn't intend to be beholden to every son-of-a-bitch who had two cents to buy a stamp.

We used to go out there at night and play red dog with George Healy, now editor of the New Orleans *Times-Picayune*, and Charlie Townsend. I had a flat-backed mandolin that Bill had lent me eleven dollars to buy, and Brahnam Hume, son of the University's chancellor, had a ukulele. We kept our musical instruments at the post office and practiced there. Brahnam and I also played in a Sunday school baseball league, and when we played during the week Bill would close up the post office and come watch us.

It wasn't too long before they fired Bill. A paragraph from the bill of complaint, signed by a professor, said that the only way he ever got his mail was by digging it out of the trash can at the back door. He said Bill took the sacks as they came in and dumped them there rather than take the time to distribute the letters. One student said that Bill so seldom disturbed his box he had to blow the dust out of it each time he opened the door.

Bill didn't care about gambling. He never did. He simply liked the company and enjoyed the playing. We liked the post office the way he ran it.

In the spring of 1920, they caught the SAE's running *sub rosa*. Bill and Jack were both members. They, along with several others, let themselves be turned in to save the degrees of two other members.

When Lee Russell, then governor of Mississippi, had walked in from Tula, a village about thirteen miles from Oxford, to go to school, he had had to wait on tables to pay his way through. He did not get a bid to a fraternity, and it had riled him. He said that because he had had to work his way through school no fraternity would look at him, and that one day he would be elected governor of Mississippi, and when he was he'd abolish fraternities in every college in the state.

Now he was governor and carrying out his promise. Most of the fraternities and sororities turned in their charters when they were outlawed, but KA and SAE kept running. They went *sub rosa.*

We had always been SAE's, so of course Bill and Jack had joined. They met at houses of alumni members around town: at Uncle John's and Grandfather's, at Major Oldham's, and Jim Stone's, Phil's brother. That's where they got caught.

J. N. Powers was chancellor at the time. It was the year before Chancellor Hume took over. The chancellor knew the SAE's were running, and he set out to catch them. He got a student to spy on a meeting they held at Jim Stone's, then to report to him who was there, and, word for word, what was said. Then Chancellor Powers let it be known that he had evidence to expel the entire group but would not do so until it was better substantiated. He said that if any SAE would turn the rest in, he would pardon him.

The group held a meeting and came up with a plan. Two of the members, Spencer Wood and Charlie Townsend, were senior medical students with two weeks to go before graduation. If they were expelled, they would have to start all over again. The others were in law or arts school and could transfer what credits they already had. So they made it up for Spencer and Charlie to turn the rest in, and while they were doing it the others withdrew from school. Bill and Jack were among those who did. Charlie and Spencer remained in school and graduated that June.

The next year Bill started his Bluebird Insurance Company, which insured students against failing classes. The *Mississippian,* the school paper, came to Bill for an idea of how to liven it up and he came up with the insurance company. He, and Sonny Bell, and Louis Jiggetts were all presidents. They were all there was to the company.

The way they figured their rates was on how tough each professor was. We had one awfully tough English professor, and the rate per dollar under him was ninety cents. The rates scaled on down to ten cents under Judge Hemingway, who was dean of the law school, and if you were an athlete, five cents.

Judge Hemingway was an outstanding faculty supporter of Ole Miss athletics. He wasn't too tough on any of his students, but if you were an athlete, all you had to do was get to class and keep awake and you had it made. All the athletes took law.

Bill's company lasted about two weeks before the faculty outlawed it, threatening even to shut down the *Mississippian*. The school paper over at Mississippi A. and M. had sent in an application for a charter to be established there, but the A. and M. faculty heard about it and outlawed it before they could get going.

Up until this time Dad and Judge Hemingway had been close friends, but Bill's estimate of his teaching brought on a strain in their relationship. It might have ended it altogether had not Mother and Mrs. Hemingway been bridge-playing partners. They smoothed things over so as not to break up their Wednesday-afternoon bridge game.

It was during Bill's postmastership that he bought his first car, a Model T Ford. He bought the chassis and built a racer body on it and painted it yellow. Time payments hadn't been invented then, so Bill borrowed the money from Grandfather's bank and pledged his salary against it. The car didn't cost him but about three hundred dollars.

I remember one night we were sitting on the porch after supper (Bill had had the car for a couple of months by then), and Bill asked Dad to loan him a hundred and twenty-five dollars to reduce his note at the bank. Dad let him have it. I think the reason was that he was proud of Bill for sticking to his salaried job as long as he had.

That was the last salaried job Bill ever had, except when he wrote for the movies.

Bill was playing a lot of golf at that time, and after he got the car he began going over to Jack Stone's, at Charleston, almost every weekend. He would load a suitcase and his golf clubs in his stripped-down racer and take off for Mr. Jack's, mainly because of the country club there. It was a better course than ours and Mr. Jack had given Bill a guest card there, so Bill stayed at his house.

There was a girl there, I think she was Mr. Jack's secretary, who fell for Bill. He used to take her presents and every Christmas she would send him some handkerchiefs. The top one or two in the box would have his initials worked in them, but the rest would be blank. She always sent half a dozen and never did get his initials worked in all six of them. Bill used to begin worrying to Mother, several weeks before Christmas, about the girl laboring over his initials. And sure enough, when Christmas came there would come the box of handkerchiefs.

Bill made a book of poems for her. The book had a dozen pages in it, hand lettered, and a design sketched in it around the edges. He got a piece of purple leather and bound the volume. When he showed it to me, I liked it so much I did one for my girl too.

Bill kept his Ford till Dad got ready to trade in his Buick for a bigger one, then he swapped with Dad and Dad traded in Bill's Ford. The Buick was a roadster, about like a modern convertible, four-cylinder, and painted dark green. Bill painted it white. He painted it himself. Even if he never got around to painting any pictures, he always loved fooling around with paints.

I remember one day that Albert drove the University truck over to our house. The University had only the one truck at the time, and Albert drove it. Dad told him to bring it over and Bill would paint UNIVERSITY OF MISSISSIPPI on both cab doors.

Bill didn't even measure or sketch in the letters. He just squatted beside the truck and took a small pot of gilt paint and one of Mother's brushes and painted the name on each door. It looked like a regular sign painter had done it when he got through.

Dad was sitting on the porch watching him. It took only a short while. When Bill finished and Albert drove off, Dad said, "I'll be damned."

It was after Bill acquired the Buick that he got up his scout troop. There wasn't one in Oxford at the time, so Bill organized one. He had been a scout, and he knew what the boys who hadn't known scouting were missing.

He spent a great deal of time with his scouts. He had no trouble getting an appointment as scoutmaster and quickly organized his troop. He held weekly meetings, teaching them scouting from the handbook, and he took them on hikes in the woods to teach them woodlore.

One of our professors, Dr. Hedleston, lived at College Hill, about three miles from Oxford and had a big farm out there. There was a pond on the property, and Dr. Hedleston offered it to Bill for a camping site. Bill used to take the scouts out there in his Buick and whatever other transportation he could arrange. Dad used to tote some of them in his new Buick. But if Bill couldn't get anyone else to help him, he'd make as many trips as it took in his car to get the whole troop out to Hedleston's Pond.

Some of those who were scouts under him (they are grown men now) told me not long ago that the highlight of those camping trips was after supper when Bill told them stories around the campfire. They said it was the way he made them behave. If they broke some rule he made them go to their tents after supper, and they'd miss listening to his stories.

Bill bought a scoutmaster's uniform, and when the boys asked him to, he sewed his wings over the pocket. He did it because they asked him.

Then one of our ministers began a tirade from his pulpit against Bill about his drinking. Bill never did do as much drinking as he got credit for. He never tried to hide it, but he did do most of it at home. Whatever stories got out about it, he never did deny. He simply paid them no mind. He passed on no stories about anybody else and asked only that they accord him the same courtesy. But people talk, and their stories grow, and that's the way it was about Bill's drinking.

I have drunk with Bill, more than once. He never was the nuisance about his drinking that I am when I get started. I drink around town. Bill stayed at home. Any writer has spare time on his hands. He finishes a story or a book, and he has time on his hands.

Bill did a lot of play acting about his drunks. He wasn't really drunk at all. Anyone who writes spends a lot of his time in an imaginary world. During the time he is there, that world is more real to him than his own world can ever be. He lives with his characters and becomes one of them. It's easy enough for him to become someone he is not. Bill was about the best at it I ever saw.

I think that a lot of times, after Bill learned how well he could act a part, he would play drunk simply to get waited on. For the time being, he had got tired of waiting on himself. Several times, after I went to the farm, Mother would come get me to help sober "Billie" up. I would go in and I noticed how little liquor he had drunk to be as drunk as he was supposed to be.

He would take two or three drinks to begin with, then flop on the bed and stare wall-eyed at the ceiling and everybody would come to sober him up. He would have special meals fixed for him and would eat as long as anybody would feed him. As soon as they quit, he would begin staring at the ceiling again.

When his everyday world got boring, he would slip off into his land of make-believe. Sometimes, he would take a drink or two and play drunk simply to get out of work. Writing is a chore, an onerous one. A writer will do almost anything to get out of it. It takes as much out of you as a bad spell of sickness.

I think that if a man's characters didn't force him to write, he would not do it at all. They begin raging around you and give you no peace till you sit down and tell what they are doing. No man can drink and write. So Bill would take a drink or two and excuse himself from going to work for a while.

One time Estelle called Mother that Bill was drunk and she could do nothing with him, so Mother went down there to see what she could do. For two days she fed Bill iced tea, first with a little whiskey in it and then less and less till he was drinking straight iced tea. For twelve hours Bill didn't have anything but tea. Mother knew that by then he ought to be sober enough to talk, anyhow. She drew a chair up beside his bed.

"Billie, don't you think it's about time you got up and went to work?" she asked.

"I can't," Bill mumbled. "I'm drunk."

"If you are, you're drunk on iced tea," Mother said. "That's all you've had for the last twelve hours."

Bill shifted his eyes from the ceiling to her, then sat up on the edge of the bed. He said, as pleasant as you please, "Well, I believe I'll get up and go to work then."

And he did.

I don't mean Bill never got drunk. He liked a drink as much as the next one and sometimes he took too many. You might say he went on tears every now and then. But no man could turn out the amount of work Bill did and drink as much as people claimed he did.

Bill did one funny thing about whiskey one night. It was in January, and the thermometer was hovering in the mid-thirties. A drizzly rain was falling.

Felix Linder, Bill's doctor and close friend, said he heard someone knocking at his front door that night. It waked him. His house was cold, for he had cut the fires down for the night, and cold as it was in his bedroom, he knew it must be late. He looked at his bedside clock. It was two-thirty.

He pulled the covers back tight around him and decided he would not get up. The knocking continued. Finally he did get up and went to the front door. When he opened it, Bill was standing there. He had on only a pair of shorts. He was dripping wet, having walked through the rain to Felix's from his house, about a quarter of a mile.

"Felix, have you got any whiskey?" Bill asked.

Felix thought a minute. "Yes, Bill, I have," he said. "I've got about half a bottle."

"Will you let me have it?"

"Sure. Come on in."

"I'm wet," Bill said. "I might drip on the floor."

Felix left the door open with Bill standing there and went and got the whiskey. He brought it back and handed it to Bill. "Don't you want an umbrella or a coat or something?"

"No," Bill answered. "I'm already wet now."

Bill turned then and Felix watched him walk away across the yard, headed toward home. He went back into his bedroom and crawled back into bed.

But a few minutes later, knocking started again at his front door. He got up again and went to the door and there was Bill again, wetter than before, standing there with the whiskey in his hand. "Have you got a sack you can lend me to carry it home in?" Bill asked.

Felix got him a sack and Bill put the whiskey in it and left, this time for good.

Another time, Bill was up at the airport in Memphis one day with Dean. It was summertime. He had flown some that day, and Dean had tended his regular flying business—instruction and field hops and such. Now it was sundown and time to shut up shop for the day.

They pushed the airplanes into the hangar and then went out and sat down on the grass strip, about three feet wide, that ran between the ramp and hangar line. A cyclone fence separated the two areas and ran just to the rear of the strip. They leaned back against the fence. They had a bottle of whiskey between them.

After a few drinks Dean got barefooted. He always did, at almost any opportunity. He played baseball for Ole Miss, and on the Oxford town team in summer, and on the teams of the towns around us, and on country teams too. Always, as soon as the game got well started, he took off his shoes. Sometimes he played in his sock feet. Usually he took them off too. He played golf barefooted when the weather was warm and nearly always went about home without shoes or socks.

When he got barefooted that day at the airport, Bill did too. It was now about time for the American Airlines early-evening flight to come in, and they sat there watching for it. Finally, it approached and landed.

By now they were hungry, and they decided to go to town for something to eat. They took the bottle of whiskey with them. When they got to town, they left their car at a parking lot on Second Street, near the Peabody Hotel, where they intended eating. Getting out of the car, holding the whiskey bottle, they started, still barefoot and in their shirt sleeves, down the street. They turned off Second at Union, down which, about half a block away, was the Peabody.

Suddenly Dean said, coming to a stop on the sidewalk, "They won't let us in the Peabody with this bottle of whiskey."

"We'll have to hide it before we go in then," Bill answered.

They looked about for some place to hide the whiskey.

There were several likely places at hand, in the shadowy corners of door entrances and behind posts along the street, but Bill objected. He said they were too dark. They might put the whiskey there and not be able to find it themselves when they came back out. So they hid it under the stoplight in the middle of the intersection of Second and Union.

It was well lighted there. The bottle could be seen from half a block away and, Bill figured, was safe from traffic as no traffic ever passed directly under the light; it flowed to either side. They went on into the Peabody to supper.

They ate supper there too. I don't know how they managed it, dressed as they were. I guess they knew Bill.

I do know of another time, in Memphis too, when Bill went to a gambling place to the south of town, barefoot and without a coat. He was stopped at the door for lack of a coat and tie. The owner was called, and when he saw who it was he lent Bill his coat and tie, so he could get into the dining room.

But he went in barefoot. There was no rule that said you had to have on shoes and socks to get in.

Anyhow, the preacher collected all the stories he could about Bill's drinking and told them from his pulpit. He said Bill was unfit to be a scout leader and that the troop should be taken away from him. It was about this time that Bill had got up a boy-scout day at our Episcopal church. His troop had asked him to read the lesson to them. He did. His boys all came that day and Bill donned robes and read them that Sunday's lesson from the pulpit. Some of the preacher's Sunday school children were in Bill's troop and went to hear him. Perhaps that's the reason the preacher was so bitter.

Bill gave up the troop, and the preacher let it go too. He had taken it away from Bill and that was what he considered his duty. He made no effort to find another leader, and the boy scouts disappeared from our town for the next several years.

It was not long after this that Bill got fired from the post office and began writing in earnest. His first book was a collection of poems, *The Marble Faun*. Phil Stone put up the money for its publication. A thousand copies were printed and I doubt if they sold fifty. Phil stored the rest, in the cartons they were shipped in, in his attic. That was the old Stone home, just across the railroad on the road to College Hill.

After Bill's other writings began to be published and appreciated, people began to ask what else he had written. They found out about *The Marble Faun* and began to search for copies. When it was found that so few were available they began to bid for them. The price had gone to seventy dollars a copy when the old Stone house burned down, along with the copies of the book still in the attic. Phil lost somewhere around nine hundred and fifty copies in that fire. He did save a few, a dozen or so. Recently, a copy brought six hundred dollars at a New York auction.

Phil Stone and Mother were the first ones to believe in Bill. No one could have helped him more than Phil did. If he ever wants to sell those dozen copies he still has, I hope he makes a fortune on them.

Maud Falkner (wife of Murry, Sr.) holding her third son, John Wesley Thompson Falkner III, nicknamed Johncy, in early 1902.

William Cuthbert (Bill), left, and Murry Charles (Jack) Falkner, right, around 1903.

From left to right: Bill, Jack, and John, on ponies in front of their first home in Oxford on South Second Street, 1905.

Jack, John, and Bill, from left to right, pose for a studio portrait, around 1905.

The four Falkner boys, about 1910. Left to right: Jack, Bill, and John; standing in front of them, Dean.

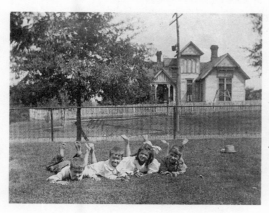

Bill, John, Sallie Murry Wilkins (their first cousin), and John, from left to right, at play in Oxford, 1907.

A group photograph taken in front of John Falkner's home in 1941 included much of the family. Left to right, first row: Chooky, Dean, and Jimmy; second row: Holland Falkner Wilkins, Maud Falkner, J. W. T. Falkner, Jr., his wife Sue; third row: Lucille Falkner, her husband John, Dean's widow, Louise; also shown are servants Minnie Bell and Gene Harkins.

John and William Faulkner in 1949, a few months before William learned he had won the Nobel Prize for Literature. Phil Mullen took this photograph, the only one of the two together as grown men, on the occasion of William picking up a lawnmower he had lent his brother.

John Faulkner, in 1950, at the Old Rebel Bookstore in Oxford celebrating the release of his new book Chooky.

John (middle) reading from Chooky *to his two sons, James Murry Faulkner (Jimmy) on the left and Murry Cuthbert Falkner (Chooky) on the right, around 1950. Jimmy chose to restore the "u" to the family name, following the example set by William and John. Chooky kept the name "Falkner."*

Jimmy, John, and Chooky strolling in Oxford, around 1950.

John, Lucille (Dolly), and Chooky around 1950, from left to right. The painting is a portrait of Chooky by his grandmother Maud.

John and Dolly behind their home in Oxford, 1956.

John Faulkner at a show of his series of paintings, "The Vanishing South," Jackson, Mississippi, 1956.

From left to right: James Murry Faulkner Jr. (Rusty) in swing, William Faulkner, Sallie Murry Williams, Maud, and Estelle Faulkner at Rowan Oak, 1955.

John and his grandson Thomas Wesley Faulkner (Buddy) sharing a love for airplanes, 1958.

Chapter 15

AFTER BILL GOT FIRED FROM THE POST OFFICE, Dad began getting him more odd jobs around the campus. One of them was firing the boiler nights at the power plant. Bill said he wrote his best book there, *As I Lay Dying*. He told me it was a good place to write; it was warm and quiet and he was never disturbed. The hum of the big old dynamo was soothing, and he wrote between the times he had to stop and shovel coal into the furnace.

Bill went to New Orleans soon after that, where he wrote *Mosquitoes*. It was not supposed to be very good, but it contained the biggest whopper since Mark Twain, the part about the sheep and the empty whiskey kegs.

Roark Bradford was feature editor for the *Times-Picayune* when Bill was down there, and the paper allowed him ten dollars a week to buy a free-lance story for that page. He turned the money over to Bill each week, to live on while Bill wrote his book.

Bill wrote stories for Brad, and one was one of the best things he ever wrote. It was about a black trying to get home to Africa and mistaking the Mississippi River for the Atlantic Ocean. He crossed the river in a rowboat and was killed by a farmer because he had killed the farmer's cow, thinking he was in Africa and it was some kind of dangerous wild beast.

Next Bill sold *Sartoris* to Harcourt, Brace. It was a story taken mostly from our family history. He took the Harcourt advance and went on a walking tour of Europe. At New Orleans he got a job as cabin boy on a tramp steamer that landed him in Italy, then walked up through the Alps and into France. He lived in Paris and worked for the French newspaper. When he got word that he had sold another book with the same advance, he came home by way of London, where he stayed for several more weeks.

Bill didn't work his way back across the Atlantic, but he did come home steerage with a beard. He smelled like steerage too. When he came in Mother said, "For heaven's sake, Billie, take a bath."

When Bill came back from Europe we were living on the campus, in the house the University furnished Dad. I was married by then and going to school and living with Dad and Mother, with my wife and first son, Jimmy. I'd planned to go to Dallas, Texas, with a friend of mine to work in a wholesale-grocery house. But Dad couldn't stand to see his first grandson get out of his sight, so he persuaded me to stay in Oxford and go to the University.

We lived upstairs in a room across the hall from Bill's. Jack was away from home with the Federal Bureau of Investigation and had been for several years. Dean was still home and going to school too.

During that next year or so, Bill wrote mostly short stories. He knew I'd liked *Sartoris* and his flying stories, so any time he would write one he'd call me into his room and let me read it. Two of the ones I remember best I read while he sat and smoked his pipe and waited to see what I would say about them: one was about the Scotsman named MacWriglingthbeath (or some such name that no one could pronounce) who soloed himself in a fighter so he could qualify for pilot's wings and flight pay, and the other was "Turn About."

One time Bill called me in. He was standing in front of his opened closet door writing something on a sheet of paper he had tacked there. I walked over and looked over his shoulder to see what he was doing. He was keeping track of the short stories he had sent out and to whom he had sent them.

He had a piece of typewriter paper tacked up on the back of the closet door. On it were ruled columns, with lines drawn across them like the pages of a ledger. In a wide column to the left were the names of various stories. The rest of the page was double columns. At the top of each double column was the name of a magazine—the *Post, Collier's, Atlantic Monthly, Scribner's*, etc. When he would send a story to the *Post*, he would mark the date down in the first half of the column, then when they'd return it he would mark down that date alongside it. He said he kept a record like that so he wouldn't send the same story to the same magazine twice.

The page was almost full. Bill must have written and sent out fifty or sixty stories up to that time. After *Sanctuary* came out the *Post* wrote Bill and said they wanted to apologize for having turned his stories down, and if he would send them back they would put him in a preferred bracket and buy them at a thousand dollars apiece.

Bill sent them sixty!

During the time that Bill was living at home and writing short stories, he took up hunting again. He was invited to go on General Stone's deer-and-bear hunt, at his lodge below Batesville in the virgin bottom lands of the Mississippi Delta. Batesville is only thirty miles from Oxford, but you had to travel about a hundred and fifty miles and change trains twice to get there by rail. We had no paving then, and in winter you couldn't get there in a car.

The hunters went by train and had a wagon meet them in Batesville to take them and the supplies from there to the lodge. They always loaded the wagon and sent it a week ahead of time. Old Add, the cook, and his helper, Curtis, made the trip in the wagon. It would take them most of a week to get from Oxford to the camp, fix it up and then get back to Batesville in time to meet the train with the hunters on it.

Dean always loved hunting more than any of us. Even in high school he'd hurry home in the evenings during quail season and get his gun and dogs to hunt during the hour and a half or two hours left until dusk. I've seen him shoot quail on the wing with a .22. He never shot a squirrel. He simply "barked" him, that is, shot the limb under him to stun the squirrel so he'd fall out of the tree. Then Dean would break his neck with his rifle barrel. That way no meat was spoiled by a bullet.

Of course, Dean was awfully interested in this bear-and-deer hunt that Bill was going on. He pestered Bill about what sort of rifle he'd use. Bill told him which rifle he'd use to kill a deer. When Dean asked him what he'd use to kill a bear, Bill said he didn't intend taking a rifle. He said if he met a bear in the woods, he didn't want to have to take the time to throw away a gun before he could start running.

Some of Bill's best short stories came out of those trips. "The Bear" was one. I remember also the one about the Indian named John Basket and the boy with the hiccups that was Bill. They had to bring him into Batesville to get them stopped.

Bill went on those hunting trips almost every year he was home from then on. He followed the cutting of the big timber and made his last trip down there into the triangle left near Yazoo City, just as Uncle Ike McCaslin did in "Delta Autumn."

Bill served his apprenticeship well. He killed his buck and was blooded, and he also killed a bear. Because he was a writer, the town had already begun to look on him as a little queer, and at first the other hunters didn't know whether they'd get along with him or not. They soon found different.

Bill asked no favors, just to be allowed to hunt with them and be one of them. They assigned him the most remote and least likely stand of all because, as a novice, that was all he rated. He took it without a word and stood fast till they came for him each evening. Before his hunting days were over, Bill could find his way around in any woods. He became one of the old men of the hunt, and one year was its captain.

Another of Bill's better stories was "Spotted Horses." The incident actually happened, in Pittsboro, a small place in Calhoun County. Uncle John was running for circuit judge at the time, and Bill drove him around campaigning in a Model T Ford Uncle John bought for the occasion. Uncle John had filled an unexpired term as an appointive judge, and he decided to run for the next term. He wasn't elected. He never was elected to any office for which he ran, but no one could get elected in north Mississippi unless they had him for their campaign manager. It was the way of politics.

One day Uncle John was scheduled in Pittsboro, so they decided to spend the night there. There was no hotel, so they got rooms in a boardinghouse. Bill was sitting on the front porch of the boardinghouse late that evening when some men brought in a string of calico ponies wired together with barbed wire. They put them in a lot just across the road from the boardinghouse and the next morning auctioned them off, at prices ranging from about five dollars apiece on up.

Just like in Bill's story, the men sold all the horses, put the money in their pockets, and left. When the buyers went in to get their purchases, someone left the gate open and those ponies spread like colored confetti over the countryside.

Bill sat there on the porch of the boardinghouse and saw it all. One of them ran the length of the porch and he had to dive back into the hallway to get out of its path. He and Uncle John told us about it the next day when they got home.

Bill was invited to and went to a great many country dances around Oxford in those days. He never danced at them. He simply sat by the tub of whiskey, taking a drink from a tin cup every now and then and watching and listening.

On a great many occasions, the reason for the dance was simply that some whiskey maker had turned up with an over-supply of whiskey—more than he could use or sell—and he invited the neighbors over to help him drink it up. It was poured in a washtub set on a bench against the wall and tin cups were placed around it. The occasion was used for a dance.

I've heard people talk about Bill at those dances. They say he simply sat by the tub with a tin cup in his hand, smiling pleasantly at everyone around him. No one remembers him dipping into the tub too much. He never got into any fights either, and one or more usually broke out before the whiskey got used up.

One man told me that he hit at a man once and knocked Bill out of his chair, and he never was so sorry for anything in his life. He and the other fellow quit fighting long enough to pick Bill up off the floor and set him aside in another chair where they wouldn't knock him over again by mistake.

What Bill heard and saw there turned up in a good many of his books in later years. Most of the folks who were at those dances began to look sideways at each other and at Bill after those books came out. They recognized or thought they recognized themselves and each other in the pages. They never were quite sure which one of the characters was which one of them. They never realized that no one character in a book is just one somebody. Each is a composite of a hundred or more people the writer has known. No wonder they still aren't sure which one of them he was talking about.

This was getting toward the end of the 1920's, and Bill's books were beginning to sell. He was married by then, too, in 1929. Estelle had divorced her first husband and came home, and she and Bill began going together again. Shortly after that, they went out to College Hill and Dr. Hedleston married them, in an old church out there with a slave balcony and private pews with individual gates.

Estelle's first marriage hadn't been a success. She came back from the Far East with two children and a Chinese amah.

Cornell remained in the Orient, in Hong Kong, where he had moved from Manila. He was mayor of the international settlement there when the Japs took over and came home to Virginia, I think, after the Second War. He died there not too many years ago.

One of Estelle's two children was a boy, the other a girl. The amah had corrupted the girl's name—Victoria, for Estelle's sister—to Cho-Cho. It reminded us of Tochie and we liked it. The boy was called Malcolm. Bill took them into his home after he and Estelle were married and raised them as his own, along with his own daughter, Jill.

I never thought Cornell was Estelle's choice to start with. I think she always loved Bill, but with Bill's prospects so poor, Miss Lida and the Major felt compelled to step in. Bill wouldn't even finish high school. Cornell was a graduate of Ole Miss, his future seemed assured in his family's business. I guess you can't blame them for feeling as they did.

After Estelle and Bill were married they rented an apartment from Miss Elmer Meek, who first called the University of Mississippi "Ole Miss." That was the name the mistress of a plantation was known as to those who belonged to it. It connoted alma mater. Like most diminutives, it embraces love and affection, as well as respect and awe. It stuck. The University is known to all of us who went there and to most others too as Ole Miss.

Miss Elmer still has some of Bill's handwritten manuscript pages of his earlier novels. One he used for a dart-game target one day when he was playing with Malcolm. Bill tacked it to a tree and it is punched full of holes where they threw darts at it. I saw it not long ago with Bill's tiny writing on it. It is in our local museum. Miss Elmer had saved it and gave it to the city as part of Bill's memorial collection.

One day Bill was in the bank, the one Grandfather used to own, and Joe Parks, its president, asked Bill why he wrote so tiny. Bill told him he had only so many miles of ink left and he aimed to make as many words out of them as he could.

Bill and Estelle lived at Miss Elmer's for only a short while. Then Bill got another advance on a book and bought a home of his own. It was the old Bailey place, where we used to raid the orchard on our way to our swimming hole. It is just to the southwest corner of Oxford on the old Taylor road.

There is only a short distance between where I now sit and Bill's place, about a quarter of a mile. Nothing is between us but my pasture and Ross Brown's. With the leaves gone I can see his rooftop. I used to have a regular path beat through our pastures from going back and forth visiting him.

That house is the only one Bill ever owned in Oxford. He never wanted another. At first it had about fourteen acres, but he bought the land adjacent to it and added on. He had his stables there and kept a saddle horse or two handy. That's where he lived until he died, from where he was buried.

It's an old colonial house, two-storied, with columns across the center section in front. It was built before the War Between the States, and at the time Bill bought it had neither electric lights nor running water. Bill helped put these in himself.

After Miss Ellen Bailey died, her kin people in Coffeeville inherited the house and rented it to a man and his wife from College Hill, a Mr. and Mrs. Claude Anderson. They truck-farmed it, raised chickens, and Mr. Anderson milked several cows and sold their milk and butter, along with eggs and such. When Bill went to Coffeeville, made a down payment, and secured deed to the place, they didn't like it, as they didn't want to give it up. But Bill was adamant. He wanted that place to live in.

Besides electricity and water, the house needed a lot of repair. Bill didn't have the money then to hire such as that done, so he got a helper and did the jobs himself. He jacked up the house first and put new beams under it. For the wiring and plumbing he had to have men who had the tools and know-how, but he hired himself to them as apprentice. He helped with the roofing too, for the house needed a new roof. Bill himself did a great deal of the painting.

One of Bill's helpers was Rusty Patterson. Rusty was a house painter. He always came to work with some whiskey, some in him and some still in a bottle he had in his hip pocket. As they painted along, he and Bill nipped out of Rusty's bottle till it was gone, then Bill went in the house and got a bottle of his.

They finished what painting they had to do, and then Bill went back under the house to work on the beams some more. Rusty went along with him and helped. They stopped working after a while and sat there under the house drinking. Rusty wouldn't charge Bill for the time they spent under the house putting in the beams. He said he had too much fun; it wasn't like working at all. He told Bill that any time he wanted him to help in any sort of work, just to let him know.

Bill added to the house in later years-more rooms, another bath or two, a back parlor. And though he continued to do little odd jobs around the house, like setting birdbaths and laying brick in a wall he built across one end of his porch, he didn't do any of the major work any more. He didn't have to. He could afford to pay to have it done now.

It was before Bill sold *Sanctuary* to the movies and got into his first real money that I used to visit him so often through the woods. He was quiet then, worried about money, I reckon. He had wood fireplaces in the house and used to saw his own wood. I would come up out of the big sand ditch, just to the rear of his place, and he'd be out in his pasture with a tree down, sawing it up in firewood lengths. I'd take a hand at the saw and then help him split the bolts and tote the wood to the house. He'd always thank me for helping but didn't have much else to say. I guess he had just too many other things on his mind.

After *Sanctuary* came out, and sold like it did, and the movies bought it, he was never really faced with money worries again. He would be out of money at times but never far away from another good-size batch. Bill made several fortunes and spent them and left one when he died. I never saw anyone who could spend as much money as he could. I think the reason he left as much as he did was because he finally got to where he was making more than he could possibly get rid of.

In his later years he bought whatever he happened to see and decided he wanted—an airplane (the one Dean was killed in), a sailboat, a race horse named Big John (after Bill had the horse for a while he changed his name to Iron Mouth).

The reason the man sold Big John to Bill so cheaply was on account of his mouth. It was so tough, once you started him you couldn't stop him, even make him change directions. Pulling on the bit was like sawing on a concrete post. Of course, the owner didn't tell Bill about that when he sold him the horse. He left it to Bill to find out for himself.

When Bill decided to get Big John, he bought a riding outfit from Abercrombie & Fitch. He also bought an English saddle with kick-out stirrups.

I'll never forget the first ride Bill took on Big John, in all his saucy riding clothes. He saddled him up and mounted, with Big John facing out his driveway. It took him a while to get Big John started, but when he did that horse lit out just the way he was pointed. He ran clear to Taylor, seventeen miles, before he gave out and Bill could get him turned around again.

Chapter 16

THE FIRST BOOK OF BILL'S THAT REALLY SOLD was *Sanctuary*. He told me he couldn't get people to read his other books, so he decided to write one they would. He sat down one day to think of what would be the most horrible thing he could put in a book and came up with the idea of a man using a corncob on a girl.

When the movies bought it they offered Bill a job turning it into a screenplay. He decided to accept and made his preparations to go out there. He bought a Model A Ford touring car so that he could take Estelle and Jill and Jill's mammy and Jack Oliver, his houseboy. They packed the car one day and made ready to leave early the next morning. Bill called me and asked me to come over and spend that night at his house. I went.

I don't know exactly why he called me except that it was his first trip to California to work for the movies, and maybe he was a little uneasy about what he was getting himself into. We sat up all that night, playing checkers most of the time. He didn't do much talking about anything. I think he just wanted the company of some of his own folks before he left. We ate breakfast early the next morning, and they left right after that. His first contract was at six hundred a week for six weeks, with a renewal clause and a raise to eight hundred after that. Bill stayed out there for about a year and came back without Jack and Jill's mammy. They stayed in California and are still out there. Neither ever came back to Oxford.

Jack Oliver was taken with the idea of becoming a writer himself after he had been with Bill for a while. He used to bring what he wrote to Bill to get Bill to help him with it. He couldn't write. I don't know why Bill fooled with him but he did.

When Jack and Mammy (Jill's mammy, not Mammy Callie) decided to stay in California, Bill saw to it that they had good jobs before he left. He got Jack a job as houseboy with some family he knew out there and Mammy another job tending children. Her name was McEwin, and Jill used to call her Mammy MaTewin. She always called Bill "Pappy," so she took to calling him Pappy MaTewin. She used to eat breakfast in the kitchen with Mammy, fat back and turnip greens with molasses poured over them and cornbread. Jill wore her teeth off clear to the gums, she ate so much.

Bill spent a big part of the next ten years in California. He was out there when Dad died in 1932. We couldn't get hold of him for several days. He was on Catalina Island with Clark Gable and Doug Shearer on a mountain-lion hunt, and there was no way to reach him. He came home as soon as we got in touch with him, but that was after Dad had already been buried.

Bill took another hunt with those two, in the desert. He told me about the morning they got to the desert and stopped at some old fellow's cabin to get him to act as guide. Bill said that when they walked in, the old man had the best coffee boiling on the stove he ever smelled. They were offered some and drank several cups.

Before they left Bill complimented the old man on the coffee and told him it was the best he'd ever tasted. He wanted to know how it was made, and the old fellow told Bill it wasn't any trouble to make good coffee. All you had to do was use a double handful of grounds per cup and let it boil good.

When Bill got back, in 1933, he bought his airplane, a Cabin Waco, fast for its day. There was no field in Oxford big enough to get it in and out of, so he kept it at Memphis Municipal Airport, at Mid-South Airways. Vernon Omlie was owner and manager of Mid-South, and Bill thought a lot of him. He was a topnotch pilot, having learned to fly in the First World War and never done anything else since.

After Bill left his airplane with Vernon, Dean decided he wanted to learn to fly, and Bill sent him to Memphis to live with Vernon while learning how. All four of us had the flying bug and all four of us flew. Bill and Jack flew for pleasure, Dean and I made our living at it.

Bill had never lost his interest in or got out of touch with aviation since he got his wings in 1918. There were not too many pilots in the 1930's, and those you didn't know you knew about. When some stray would come into Oxford, he'd always look Bill up and stay with him while he was in town. Most of them were broke and needed a few meals and a bed to sleep in. Bill always went out to the field when one came in, and picked him up in his car, and carried him on home.

Right after the First War, you could buy a Jenny for five thousand dollars. You could get twenty-five dollars per passenger for a five-minute hop and haul two passengers at a time. Instruction was fifty dollars an hour. A parachute jumper got as high as five hundred dollars for a jump, and both planes and jumpers were in heavy demand at county fairs. You could make good money just barnstorming around the country.

But that didn't last long. Soon jumps were down to fifty dollars and a Jenny was worth only five hundred dollars. During the depression, if you flew, you flew for peanuts. Most of us who flew, flew because we loved it and wouldn't do anything else.

Bill was bound to have been a good pilot with the RFC, else he would never have got by flying Camels. But in the 1930's, when I knew him as a pilot, he had lost his touch. He said so himself, in those days, that he was not much good. But he was the best navigator I ever saw. When he would fly with Dean or me, we would tell him where we wanted to go and hand him the map. He could tell us where we were every inch of the way.

Bill did learn this much about flying—he never had a crash he couldn't walk away from. He did pretty good flying 0X5 stuff, but every time he was out in his Waco by himself and went into some strange field he did something to it. Usually, it never amounted to more than wiping off a wing tip or blowing a tire, but he did it nearly every time.

Dean was a crackajack pilot and never had but one crash, the one that killed him. That wasn't Dean's fault. He was doing something he shouldn't have, letting a student have the controls with passengers aboard. Dean's luck just ran out. Mine, Bill's, and Jack's never did.

Bill didn't fly the Waco much unless Dean or Vernon was along. After they both got killed and I took over Mid-South, Bill used to come up and fly our Waco (we sold them), but he always wanted me along. He never took it out by himself.

The number of Bill's Waco was 13413. Mother was afraid of that number from the start. She said it had too many 13's in it. Dean poo-pooed the idea, and Bill told her the number had nothing to do with how the airplane flew. Yet Dean spun to his death in it.

When we used to go to Oxford, Dean or I, we would fly over Mother's and buzz the house for her to come pick us up at the field, which was several miles south of town and big enough now to accommodate the Waco. After Dean's crash, Mother told me not to fly over the house again. For several years I didn't, until she finally told me it would be all right. I would go in around the edge of town, and land, and catch a ride in. When I'd go to see her, she'd know how I got to Oxford, but we would not mention airplanes. Then she said she'd been foolish, for me to go ahead and buzz the house so she could come pick me up, that she realized we were always going to fly, and she had rather know where we were.

Jack was flying then too. He was with the FBI and bought a Monocoupe that he used to travel around the country in. Bill was still flying too, in an 0X5 Commandaire. He flew out of the airport at Oxford.

Bill always felt more at home in something like a World War I airplane. The one he flew was like the Canuck he trained on. It was powered by an 0X5 engine too.

The 0X5 had ninety horsepower. The government had contracts for them that outlasted the war. Stacks were built and stored in hangars and finally auctioned off to the highest bidders. A great many of our airplane companies were started on those engines, which they bid in cheap, like Waco and Travelaires, Commandaires and Eagle Rocks.

They were all about alike, the same engines of course, and to fly one was to be able to fly the others. They took off and landed at about fifty miles an hour and flew at eighty or ninety. They had no brakes, but metal tail skids. A man in Oxford owned a Commandaire, and Bill used to fly that.

Bill had a partner in his flying, a big black named George McEwin, a kinsman of Jill's mammy. He took up as Bill's houseboy when Jack Oliver did not come back from California. George was not interested in writing, but he was sure interested in flying. Bill bought him a helmet and some goggles and took George with him everywhere he went.

George wore the helmet and goggles all the time, whether they were going anywhere or not. Bill said he used to come to work in them just to remind Bill that they could go flying instead of doing whatever Bill had laid out for him to do that day.

Those old airplanes didn't have self-starters. You cranked them from in front, by the prop. They usually took a good twist, especially on cold mornings, and I've never seen anyone who could throw a prop farther through than George. He would give it a yank and it would spin for, it looked like, five minutes. Bill always said George could throw it through, get in the cockpit and fly halfway to Memphis before it gave out.

Bill used to fly to Memphis every now and then in that Commandaire. A Mr. Holmes was airport manager there at the time. He made Bill stop landing at Municipal because his airplane was so old-fashioned. He said Bill and George were always coming in with weeds or sometimes cornstalks hanging from the landing gear from where they had landed in some field on the way in.

The Memphis airport was new then, and Mr. Holmes said that Bill and George and their old airplane ruined the looks of his airport, which was built for modern airplanes. Bill told Mr. Holmes O.K., and from then on he and George went into Park Field, a World War I primary training station. Charlie Fast, a World War I mechanic, had a repair station out there. The whole airport was nothing but one hangar and a grass landing strip, so Charlie didn't care what came in.

George left Bill around '39 or '40 to go work in a war plant in Detroit.

Sanctuary, even though it made Bill money and brought him recognition, distressed Dad a great deal. He did not go for that kind of writing. In fact he tried to suppress the book and have it withdrawn from the market. He said that if Bill was going to write, he should write Western stories. That was about the only kind of reading Dad did. He had a complete library of Zane Grey and James Oliver Curwood and writers like that.

Mother said, "Let him alone, Buddy. He writes what he has to."

Bill's recognition finally came to Oxford when they found out how much money he was making. Everyone here went looking for his books. Most of them wanted Bill to give them copies. You cannot convince most people that writers only get ten copies, and your agent sends about half of them abroad. They think that because you wrote the book you can have all you want for free. Some of them get mad when you tell them you have to buy your copies like anyone else. They think you're lying and just don't want to give them one.

Of course, Mother was proud of Bill's writings, just as she was of mine when I started. She always kept copies of our books on a special table in the front room to show them off. Then she began missing them, even the ones in foreign languages. Someone even took one of Bill's in Japanese. That's when Mother stopped keeping them where visitors could lay their hands on them. After that she moved my and Bill's books to a closet in her bedroom and kept them locked up.

Bill was a tender man. He wore his heart on the outside of his sleeve. The shell he placed around himself was to protect his own feelings. When a man creates a piece of writing, it is even more his than the child he begets. It takes two to make the child.

His writing is his alone. A criticism of it is a criticism of him. Bill could not stand the hurt of adverse criticism. He simply refused to hear it. Except on rare occasions, he wouldn't even talk to anyone about his writing. He was simply protecting himself from hurt. When I first started writing, he told me never to read a review. He did not explain why. I know now.

A great many of the stories about himself Bill started, pulling someone's leg. He usually told Mother and me about it beforehand. I used to go down to Mother's every morning and have coffee with her and frequently Bill would be there. I think that was where he first told me the most important requirement for any writer was a good thick skin. That was why he put up the shell he retired into as far as his public was concerned. His skin was too tender to withstand the barbs fired at him.

When Bill sent anything out, he washed his hands of it. He was through with it. He told me never to rewrite anything, I would be wasting my time. He said to spend my time writing something new. Once finished, Bill would never go back to a thing he had written. He had told his story and he refused any comment on it from himself or anyone else.

He did get a kick out of what was happening to him though, and sometimes he played some funny tricks back on people. As soon as his books began to be talked about and his name began appearing in print, he started getting fan mail. Requests for photographs, autographed ones, began coming in too. He invented a secretary for himself and named him Earnest Trueheart. He had some photographs made and borrowed the scratchiest pen he could find from the post office and signed *Earnest True-heart* across his face in the photograph. He sent them to people who requested a picture, and he would bring them by to show Mother and me too, if I was there. Earnest Trueheart became almost a living character among the three of us. That was one of the things no one else thought was funny.

One day a reporter came down to interview Bill, and during it Bill jokingly told him that he was a cross between a black slave and a crocodile. The reporter printed it in his paper, in quotes. After that Bill didn't pay any attention to what the papers or anybody else said about him.

The only trip Bill carried Estelle and Jill to California was his first one. They stayed about a year that time. After that he made the trips by himself because of the expense. That first time he went he thought he could deduct his expenses in California from his state income tax. He not only couldn't, he found, but both California and Mississippi levied on him. Bill fought the Mississippi levy because California had already taken its cut from his pay check. But Mississippi refused his claim. They said he maintained a residence here and must pay income tax on whatever he made, wherever he made it.

With the kind of money he was making (Hollywood was paying him twelve hundred a week now), I didn't see why he couldn't save money somehow. It was hard for me to even think of money like that, let alone how to spend it. Bill explained that his house rent out there was $550 a month. I said, "Good Lord, why don't you live in a tent?" Bill said the movie people wouldn't allow it, that if a director bragged about how much he was spending on a movie, people wanted proof before they would believe it. The number of writers a director had who could afford $550 a month rent was a gauge of how much he had to spend on the picture they were making.

I asked Bill where in the world the people that worked in filling stations and grocery stores lived. He said right next to him. When I asked what sort of salaries they paid clerks out there, he answered about like they do here. I wanted to know how they could pay that kind of rent and Bill said they didn't. The reason he paid so much was because he worked for the movies. No one would rent you a house in California till they found where you were working so they would know how much rent to charge.

Bill never came back from California with very much money. He didn't like it out there, or the movies either. Everything was overblown and all for show. He said the flowers were all too big and had no odor, and the houses were all picture windows in front and two-room sheds behind.

Although he did not want to, Bill had to go back to California time after time because of the money he could make out there. His books never did sell very well until after he won the Nobel Prize. More people talked about them than read them. He would get back from California with enough money to last him a while, then go in debt when that was gone. Then he'd have to go back to California long enough to get himself out of debt again.

One day he asked me how my books sold, and when I told him he said his had never done that well. He had a steady market for about five or six thousand and that was about it. At the time he won the Nobel Prize he was virtually out of print. There was not a single copy of most of his books on the market.

Until Bill's last ten years or so, he lived on credit like I do. The people in Oxford have been good to us about that. We explain to them, before we open an account, that we can't pay every thirty days. Maybe sometimes we can, but our money doesn't come in like that. At times we won't have any for six months or even longer. When we don't have money, we have nothing to pay bills with. There's nothing we can do about it until our next royalty check comes.

We told them if they were willing to trade like that, fine, but we didn't want our unpaid balance to worry them, and the Lord knew we didn't want them worrying us about it. The people here believe we will always have another check coming. Bill always did and so far I have. Sometimes our accounts have run as long as a year, and no one here ever bothers us about them. They say we are as good as gold, but slow.

Bill didn't have to live like that after 1950. He had plenty of money from then on. In fact, one time after a hailstorm, the insurance company sent Bill a check for hail damage to his roof and he sent the check back. He wrote saying he didn't think the hail had damaged it that bad.

When Bill would get back from California, the first thing he would always do would be to get out all his old bills and mail checks to cover them. One time he emptied the pigeonholes in his desk, where he had stuck his bills, unopened, and began slitting them open and writing checks.

He came across one from the Elliott Lumber Company for $194 with a note at the bottom asking him to please pay it if he could. So Bill wrote a check and mailed it. A few days later Baxter Elliott sent his check back, with the note: "For God's sake, Bill. You paid this four years ago!"

I got wounded in the Second War and was in the hospital for over two years. A part of that time I was an outpatient, living at home and reporting in to Memphis one day a week. I ran into Bill one day during this time, and he offered me a job in California working for him but I refused it. I told him I had rather dig ditches in Oxford than live anywhere else. He said he didn't blame me; he felt exactly the same and wouldn't go back out there if he didn't have to.

It was not long after this that I began painting. Bill offered me five hundred dollars to execute two scenes from his books on the wall of his study. I did the water colors for him but never got around to reproducing them, life size, on his wall. I still have the water colors in my studio, one from "The Bear" and one of Doom in "Red Leaves," sitting with his dogs on the foredeck of the steamboat as his people and his slaves pull it the twelve miles through the bottom.

Chapter 17

DEAN WAS KILLED IN NOVEMBER AND Vernon Omile the following summer, so I was given charge of Mid-South Airways, where they had worked. At the time I was flying out of Clarksdale with a cotton-dusting outfit. Because of Bill's influence at Mid-South, I was given first consideration as Vernon's successor. We offered student flying instruction, charter work, in fact, most any kind of flying. We also had the agency for Waco airplanes.

Bill was a frequent visitor. He always stopped by when he came to Memphis and sometimes made special trips up there to the airport to visit.

Some time later, he came in one day and showed me a check. He had just sold *The Unvanquished* to the movies and said he wanted to buy a farm. The check was for twenty-five thousand dollars. Bill said he had always wanted a farm and asked me whether, if he bought one, I would come home and run it for him.

I told Bill I didn't know anything about farming. He said together we could learn how. What he wanted to do was raise mules and enough grain to feed them. I told him I was ready. It was in the Depression and people just didn't have the money to fly. There wasn't even a living in flying any more.

We moved back to Oxford then and I began looking for a farm. I finally found what I thought would do. The place was in Beat Two; the Free State of Beat Two, the residents called it. It was seventeen miles from town, part bottom land and part hills, with a creek running for half a mile across it. It seemed to me like a good place to stock-farm. Bill came out and looked at it with me and agreed. He bought it.

Bill found more than just a farm out there. He found the kind of people he wrote about, hill people. They made their own whiskey from their own corn and didn't see why that could be anybody else's business. They fought over elections and settled their own disputes. We had a killing just across the creek from us, over redistricting a school zone.

Dean's wife had come from out in that area. Her sister's husband left there and went to Jackson after his first election. He said he fought from daylight that morning till past nine o'clock that night, and he swore then he would never spend another election in Beat Two.

I tried to persuade Bill to raise cows instead of mules. Uncle John did too. Mississippi is no place to raise mules. We have no lime in our soil and it takes limy soil to grow bones. If we raise a good mule, he is too small to be any account. If he's big he's too logy and lazy to be any good. Bill wouldn't listen. He said he had no feeling for cows. He wanted brood mares and a tack room with riding equipment in it. So we raised mules.

Bill bought his brood mares, twelve of them, and a big Spanish jack named John. He stood fourteen hands high and the blacks immediately nicknamed him Big Shot. They were all afraid of him, but actually he was as gentle as a dog. Bill directed us to build him a pen with solid walls eight feet high, so he couldn't look out and see something that might excite him. We built the wall.

We had a lot of flat bottom land for a place the size of ours and Bill bought a tractor to farm it. He didn't want the mares to do heavy work for fear it might make them strain and slip a colt. We bought a second-hand Fordson in real good shape and began planting corn to feed our stock through the next winter.

The fields were grown up in button willow, and we had to clear that out first. We ripped them out of the rich bottom land with middle busters on the tractor. Some of them came up with root systems as big as a bushel basket. As soon as we cleared each field we planted it "to" corn, as Bill called it.

I began living on the farm as soon as we bought it. Bill stayed in town but came back and forth every day. Some days he would take an airplane and fly over the farm to get a better picture of just what we had and how to develop it. He was having the time of his life.

Estelle never came with Bill very often, but Jill did every chance she got. Bill would leave her at the house with Dolly and head for wherever I was working with the hands.

Until Jill was in her teens, I never saw her when she wasn't ready to eat. She would spend her time out there fooling around in the kitchen with Dolly. And she was a good cook too. She joined the Four-H Club later on and won ribbons for her preserves and such.

When Bill put me in charge, he left the running of the farm up to me. He told me in a general way what he wanted, then left it up to me to carry out his plans however I thought best. The main thing he wanted was to take good care of his brood mares. We broke all our land with the tractor and only used blacks and mules to cultivate the crops. That was light plowing and the exercise was good for the stock.

After the first of June, it was hot and close in the bottom where we planted our corn. From eleven in the morning until about three in the afternoon it was too hot there for our mares, especially in belly-high corn. The blacks did not work too well through that part of the day either. No one could. It was stifling.

So we set up a schedule to take advantage of the coolest parts of the day. We would get up at two-thirty in the morning and I would go out on the front porch and blow a boy scout bugle Chooky, my youngest son, had. It would wake the blacks and we would all meet at the barn and feed the stock. While the horses were eating, we would return to our houses and get our breakfast. By the time we got back to the barn, the horses would be ready to harness and we'd go to the field and be ready to start plowing as soon as it was light enough to see the rows.

We would knock off at eleven and go in and hole up through the hottest part of the day. Then at three we would go back to the fields and work till it got too dark to see.

We were getting a lot of work done that way and had good crops and it suited Bill. In fact, I think he sort of liked doing different from his neighbors, trying out something new.

One day we had come in early. We had finished out a field we were working in and about then someone brought a mare to our jack and we had to go in to service her. I decided not to go to that new field till that evening, so we all turned in to rest out the middle of the day.

When Dolly saw us coming she put on dinner. Just as she was serving it, Bill drove up with Jill in his car. "Come in to dinner, Bill," Dolly called, as Bill stopped at the gate.

"Dinner?" Bill said. "Good God, I just ate breakfast. Don't you know what time it is?"

"No," Dolly answered.

Bill said, "It's not yet nine o'clock."

Bill didn't eat anything but Jill did. While we were eating, he went out on the front porch. When we had finished, he called Dolly out there.

"Look here," he said.

Our house faced the sun at that time of year, and it shone in across the floor about halfway to the wall. The porch was screened, and the screen was tacked to two-by-four uprights, spaced about three feet apart. Bill had taken the shadow of one of these and drawn a line along it, then marked it nine o'clock. He had drawn other lines radiating out from where the two-by-four was sunk in the porch floor and marked these with the different hours of the day.

"Now," he said to Dolly. "Here's you a clock so you'll know what time it is from now on."

But we didn't pay too much attention to Bill's clock. After all, even dinner at nine was six hours after we had eaten breakfast, and we were hungry enough to eat by then. Our next meal came at two, for we ate four a day while we were planting, so two hours one way or the other didn't make much difference.

Dolly did go out every now and then to check Bill's timepiece to see if he had been right. She had to sweep over it every day when she swept the porch but when we moved back to town you could still see some of Bill's marks. When we showed it to some of the blacks, they used to mirate over it and wonder how in the world Bill knew where to draw those lines.

We all slept on the screened porch in the summertime, and Bill decided he would like to too. He bought a Simmons Wheel-a-way and had it brought out, but he never spent the night with us. We used his bed though. Nat, our cook, had a baby too young to leave at home, so Dolly told her to bring Jo Linder along. They put her to bed on Bill's Wheel-a-way.

We had a black blacksmith in town named Gate Boone. He was pretty good with horses, or at least Bill thought he was. Bill took Gate along when he bought the brood mares and the Spanish jack and he moved Gate out to the farm to board with one of our blacks. He wanted Gate there to look after the stock.

The other blacks didn't think much of Gate's know-how about horses, or of Gate, for the matter of that. They used to laugh at him among themselves, though they never let Bill see them do it. Gate had pulled the wool over Bill's eyes, but they didn't want Bill to know they knew it. They figured Bill would find out when the time came, and until then it wasn't any of their business.

I knew Gate had fooled Bill too, but since Bill seemed to think a lot of him it wasn't any of my business either. Bill could have two Gates if he wanted them. We simply let it go at that.

One of the first horses Gate picked for Bill was a mare named Fanny. She was iron gray, gentle, and big with colt. She dropped the foal about a month later, our first colt on Greenfield Farm.

It was born bobtailed and never grew bigger than a Shetland pony. It wasn't worth the space it took up, except as a pet for the children. Roy Butler, a man from town I had taken out there with me when I first moved out, named the colt Jackrabbit, and Jackrabbit she stayed.

Next Bill took Gate with him to a man's place that had been condemned to make way for the Reservoir. He and Bill bought his whole herd of horses. There were ten of them.

They got one good horse in the lot, Shiloh, a saddle mare. We found she was past the age where she could ever have another colt, but I used her for my riding mare. As for the rest, one was the prettiest palomino I ever saw. She had a zigzag white blaze down her face and the devil inside her. She would have what the blacks called "bronco fits." All at once she would begin kicking everything in sight.

No one could handle her. The blacks called her Lightning and that name stuck. I tried to ride her time after time, until one day she threw a fit just as I mounted her and ran sideways into a Coca-Cola truck that had just come out from town. The driver had just stepped out of the cab and she knocked him down and the fellow threatened to sue Bill. We quit fooling with her as a saddle horse after that.

Bub, my oldest boy, used to catch her and ride her bareback till Dolly caught him and made him quit. After the Coca-Cola incident Bill's feeling toward her changed. He told us to take her and work her. He didn't intend to have a horse rule his place.

We took Lightning to the field and hooked her to a plow. We turned her over to James, Nat's husband, who was really good with horses. He got about half an hour's work out of her, then she threw a fit. She refused to move a step and tried to kick herself loose from the plow. We were afraid she'd hurt herself, hamstring herself on the plow point that she had whipping around behind her.

Bill, who was standing there watching, told me to whip her and make her behave before she did damage to herself. I got a willow limb and whipped her across the front legs as she reared up on her hind ones. She tried to paw me. We couldn't do anything with her. The more I whipped, the worse she fought.

Finally Bill said, "That's enough. We won't try to work her any more. She'll lose her colt if she keeps this up and a colt out of her ought to be as strong as leather and twice as tough."

It took all of us to get ropes on her to tie her down so we could get a twister on her nose. Then we led her back to the pasture, where we turned her loose.

Bill had moved Uncle Ned out to the farm from his back yard because he said he wanted to come out there. Uncle Ned was supposed to keep the barn, tend to the feeding and milk the cows, something that would not require too much of him yet make it look like he was working. That didn't suit Uncle Ned. He wanted to take part in everything and boss all of it. He was there with us the day Lightning threw the fit in the field.

"Master," he said. "I used to handle horses for your daddy and I can handle that buckskin. The rest of them just don't know nothing about horses."

"Are you sure you won't get hurt?" Bill asked.

"A horse hurt me, master? I knows all about horses."

Uncle Ned was old. He'd been a slave belonging to my great-grandfather. Dad and Uncle John remembered him from Ripley, when they both used to live over there. When he got along in years and was unable to work steady any more, he came to Oxford looking for them to help him.

Dad looked after him at first and found him what jobs he would take. After Dad died Bill took him over and finally moved him down into his back yard. Then when Uncle Ned wanted to come out to the farm, he moved him out with a black woman named Ella whom he called his companion.

Uncle Ned liked to own his own stuff. He had a cow of his own that he had kept at Bill's, and he brought her along. Then he wanted a pasture of his own, fenced off from ours, so he could have his own cow in his own pasture. Bill drew the line. He told Uncle Ned we were too busy to stop and build him a pasture of his own; he'd just have to keep his cow in the same pasture with ours.

Uncle Ned didn't like that, but he would not dispute "master." However, he didn't bring her to the farm pasture for several days. He kept her tied to a tree behind his cabin. Then her milk started falling off, and he finally began bringing her over, though he took her home every night and milked her there.

Bill had told me to let Uncle Ned do whatever he wanted to around the place. He wanted to work with us so we assigned him a mare and plow and took him to the fields. But whenever he decided it was time to milk his cow he simply told me he was going to the house. Usually I was glad to see him go, he fussed so much about Bill's not letting him have a pasture of his own.

Uncle Ned's setting his own schedule disrupted Dolly's routine too. When he got ready to milk his cow, he milked ours. He brought our milk to the house and whatever time he came, he wanted Dolly to stop whatever she was doing to pour up our milk and wash the buckets so he could take them home with him. He wanted the buckets handy so he wouldn't have to walk to our house next morning but could go straight to the barn with them.

The end came one day when Uncle Ned walked in with the milk about three in the afternoon. Dolly had two of our black women in the kitchen putting up preserves. Uncle Ned wanted her to clear the stove, heat water, and wash the buckets. Dolly poured up the milk, and then threw the buckets at Uncle Ned. She told him to wash them himself.

Some of the blacks were working in sight of the house at that time. They went around behind the barn, and the two women in the kitchen went outside so Dolly wouldn't see them laughing. I took over the milking then. I always did like to fool with cows.

Uncle Ned didn't come around our house for a long time after that. He made trips regular to the commissary for rations, but he never mentioned anything about cows and milking. The next time he did come by home was to say he'd lost his finest rooster. We both had the same kind, New Hampshire Reds. Uncle Ned saw our rooster in the pen and claimed it was his. He said he knew his rooster and that was it.

Dolly sent him away a second time. She didn't throw anything at him this time, but she was right short with him, and he went away mumbling.

So when Bill let Uncle Ned have Lightning, I asked him if he was sure he knew what he was doing. Bill said Uncle Ned knew how to handle horses and it would be all right.

What Uncle Ned really had in mind when he talked Bill into letting him have Lightning was his own fall potato crop. He had already picked a spot to make it, a small clearing in the woods back of his cabin. He got me to haul a plow up there on the tractor and James and Renzi to help him harness Lightning. He left the barn leading Lightning and disappeared into the woods back of where he lived.

About half an hour later, there came Lightning down the road, wild-eyed and whipping that plow behind her like the cracker on a whip. She ran up to the lot gate and came to a stop. We surrounded her and got the plow loose and her inside the lot with the harness off.

I left her with the blacks then and lit out through the woods to see about Uncle Ned. I met him coming down the road over which Lightning had just passed, holding one hand to his hip, limping. He was all over dirt, but he wasn't hurt.

Lightning had thrown one of her fits in Uncle Ned's potato patch, right in the middle of it. With room for her to run in, Uncle Ned had dropped one line and held onto the other, thinking to swing her in a circle and let her run herself out. She wouldn't circle. She dragged Uncle Ned this way and that about the field till she tore his grip loose from the rein. The last he saw of her she was tearing through the woods toward the road, the plow whipping behind her. He hurried after her as fast as he could to see what damage she had done to herself, thinking every minute to find her with her leg broken from the plow.

I told him Lightning was all right. "Thank the Lord for that," he said, then added, "Master ought to have knowed better than to give me that wild mustang to do my plowing with."

When Bill came out the next day, Uncle Ned began limping worse the minute he saw him coming. Bill wanted to know what was wrong and I told him. He jumped all over Uncle Ned about fooling with Lightning in the first place and me for letting him.

"It wasn't any of my doings, Bill," I said.

"You told me to, master," Uncle Ned added.

"I didn't do anything of the kind," Bill said. "It was your own idea."

"But you told me to go ahead."

Bill turned and walked away. He went about twenty feet and stood there a moment, then came back. We all stood waiting.

"The next time you have any plowing to do up to your place, you get one of these blacks to catch up Fanny for you. From now on, you do your plowing with her, hear?"

"Yes, master," Uncle Ned said.

Since Bill thought Gate Boone was so good with horses, he decided to make him his main consultant about all farming. He'd ask Gate where to plant what and when, and Gate would manage to find out where Bill wanted it planted and name that place. Of course, Bill would agree and his opinion of Gate rose. So he decided to leave Gate on the farm full-time as my adviser. He boarded him with James.

Since Bill had told me to consult with Gate, I did. I was a better farmer than Gate, and so was almost anybody else, whether they had ever farmed or not. At least, they had never made a bad crop and Gate had never made anything else, on his sand-hill farm just east of town. Besides, on my own and from what I could learn from our neighbors, I had the prettiest corn crop in our area.

Our blacks said the reason Gate turned into a blacksmith in the first place was he never was able to feed his family on what he could make farming. He'd begun shoeing horses in his barn, then rented a little shed on the side of the road just beyond the turnoff to Yocona. That's where Bill had found him, when he was looking for someone to shoe his horses.

Bill would ride his horse out there and sit and talk to Gate while Gate would spend the whole morning shoeing Bill's horse and agreeing with everything Bill said. That's why Bill decided he knew all about horses, and farming too.

Although I might have been a better farmer than Gate, I wasn't nearly as smart about getting around Bill anyway. I would argue with him sometimes about what we were doing and then Bill would turn to Gate to settle it. Gate always would agree with him.

Gate agreed with me too, for a while, when Bill wasn't there, then one day he didn't. He decided he had Bill in his hand, and it was time for him to sort of take over.

We had finished one field and were moving to the other side of the creek, away from the house, to work out another one. I told the blacks to bring their plows and went ahead to see what needed to be done next. I started across the creek and there came Gate. We walked up to the first field over there and stood at the edge looking it over.

"We'll dirt this one up," he said.

"Let's go see what the others look like," I answered.

"No, sir," he said. "We'll dirt this one."

I turned and looked at Gate.

He stood there looking at me through his eyebrows.

Just above Gate's eyebrows was a wing-shaped scar. It stretched almost from one side of his forehead to the other. It was made when Mac Farmer, who worked for us now, had shot him in the middle of his head with a forty-one caliber derringer. The bullet split and half went one way and half the other, plowing an equal furrow to either side.

I looked at that scar. I had had just about enough of Gate. I started for the house. On the way in I met our other blacks just crossing the creek with their plows, headed for the field where Gate was standing. He was still standing where I had left him, making no attempt to follow me, his head swiveling like a parrot's as his eyes followed me along the path.

One of the blacks, seeing me hurrying toward the house, asked, "What you want us to be doing, Mist' Johnny?"

"Not a damn thing till I get back."

They watched me as I passed, and I heard one of them say, "Gate done done it now."

"Where's my pistol," I shouted to Dolly before I even got to the front steps.

"What do you want with it?"

"I'm going to kill Gate Boone," I said.

Dolly whisked out of sight and I waited on the steps. She took a little longer than I thought necessary, and I was just mounting the steps to go get the gun myself when she came out the door with it.

Nat, James' wife, was cooking for us at the time and as I turned away from the house I saw her ahead of me, running toward the creek crossing. I followed her, walking fast.

When I got over to where I had left Gate he was no longer there. The blacks were plowing in the field, and Nat was standing to one side with her hands folded in her apron like women do, just like men stand around with their hands in their pockets.

"Where's Gate?" I called, when I came up to the edge of the field.

"He gone," one of the blacks answered.

"Where?" I asked.

The black raised his hand and pointed toward the side road that passed our place, leading out to the gravel highway to Oxford.

All the blacks had stopped work.

"He ain't going to be back, Mist' Johnny," Son Martin said.

"What's master going to say?" Uncle Ned asked.

"About what?"

"About you running Gate off with that pistol?"

"How do you know I've got a pistol?" I asked.

I had it in my pocket where he couldn't see it.

"What else you go to the house for? What master going to say?"

"I wish 'master' was here now," I said. "I'd like to shoot him and Gate both. You blacks get back to work."

"Yes, sir," they said and went back to plowing away under the warm sun. Then I heard Mac say, "If he fixing to shoot Gate, they ain't no use in trying it in the head. I done tried that. The bullet won't go in."

The blacks laughed. I had to laugh too. When I did, I was no longer angry.

I looked around a little later and Nat was gone. When I got to the house for dinner, she was in the kitchen singing. Dolly was busy about her household tasks. I put the pistol away. "He wasn't there when I got back."

"I know," Dolly said. "I sent Nat to tell him to get away before you got there."

I said, "Huh!"

I sounded just like Dad used to when he said the same thing to Mother on occasion.

Gate never stayed with us again. He would come out sometimes, but he always stayed close to Bill while they were on the place. When Bill left, Gate left too. Bill never said anything to me about it, one way or the other. But he never did any more conferring with Gate when we talked over crops.

Gate didn't stay with Bill long after that. Son Martin was a better blacksmith than Gate ever was, and from then on he tended to our horses. What doctoring they needed, James did. James and Son both were a lot better with horses than Gate. All Gate was good for was fooling Bill.

Chapter 18

WHEN OUR FIRST FOURTH OF JULY CAME, BILL decided to establish a yearly barbecue on that date. We dug a pit and built a hickory fire in it and stoked it for days to get a good bed of red-hot coals. It must have been three feet deep. Then the day before the Fourth we killed a beef, and the blacks and I constructed a grill over the pit to barbecue the meat on.

Bill was in and out during these preparations, seeing to the quality of the hickory wood we were using and directing the making of the grill. He was having the time of his life getting in everyone's way. Then the morning before the Fourth, he moved in for the duration.

All that day he hung around the pit, mixing the sauce to baste the meat with and telling the blacks when to turn the beef quarters. He poured his sauce over it a ladle at a time. Bill was good at such as that, and the aroma of that steer cooking in his sauce brought some of our nearer guests in a day ahead of time.

We had invited white folks and blacks both, and Uncle Jim Buddy Smith, who lived next to us, came over and so did Uncle Oscar Parham and old Payne Wilson from our own place. They said they could smell that barbecue a mile away.

We had a commissary on the place and what with the arriving guests smelling that cooking meat and drinking a little whiskey from the jugs they brought, we did a land-office business in sardines and crackers and canned salmon. Bill sent the blacks for potatoes and we roasted them in the ashes at the edge of the pit. We had almost as much to eat that day as we did on the Fourth.

Bill sat up all that night, basting his meat and nipping along every now and then with his guests. But next morning, he retired from his cooking stint and turned it over to Uncle Ned.

About eight o'clock we went down to the blacksmith shop with some of our white guests who had arrived early. We sat down around a jug one of them had brought.

There were plenty of boxes and kegs to sit on in the shop. It had a roof on it and was shady. The walls closed it off and it was a good place to sit around a jug. Mr. Lonny Parks was there. It was his jug we were drinking from.

We had got around to talking profundities and Lonny tried to mouth a deep thought. He made an awful mess out of his enunciation and tried again, from the beginning. A second try was no better than the first, and in the middle of the sentence he gave up. He turned to Bill. "I cain't talk good," he said. "I haven't got my teeth in my mouth."

He searched his pockets but his teeth were not there. He had forgotten and left them at home. Bill watched him search for several minutes, then said, "I wouldn't worry if I was you, Mr. Lonny. I've got my mouth full of teeth and I can't talk much better than you can."

He was right too. We had to make him repeat several times before we could tell what he was saying. Bill went home late that evening, and so did our other white guests but most of the blacks stayed on. About dusk more of them started showing up. We had plenty of meat left, still hot over the coals, so I let them have a barbecue all their own that night.

I kept the commissary open, for I had to be there with them anyway. After the beef was finished they began moving up the hill from where the pit was to the front of the commissary. I had a lantern in there. The doors were open, so light spilled a blanket out in front of the steps.

We had soft drinks—Coca-Colas and soda waters—on ice for them, and, full as they were of barbecue meat, they were thirsty. I began opening drinks and passing them out. They would take a bottle and go out on the front steps to drink it, to make room for more in the store. Soon one of them on the front steps brought out a mouth organ and began to play.

The first thing he did after taking the harp from his pocket was to knock it against the heel of his hand to get the crumbs and trash out. Then he slid his lips up and down the keys, sort of warming up. All the blacks stopped what they were doing and listened. He launched into a song they play about a fox hunt. They play the tune and take the part of the dogs too. You can hear them trailing and finally you can hear them tree the fox.

As soon as this first black finished, another one took the organ from his hand and played a train song. You could hear the train starting, running and the whistle blowing. Then a black from across Cypress Creek snatched the harp and played an old blues, "Jack o' Diamonds." The blacks all got stiller than before and one by one they began grinning and patting their feet. Soon they were clapping their hands in time to the tune.

We had a slide that we hooked behind the tractor to pull equipment around the place on. It was of heavy two-by stuff, sturdily built and on runners. In size it was about three-feet wide and maybe four-feet long. It was right there in front of the steps where I had left it after hauling something to the commissary. I had left it there till I would need it again.

The black kept on playing "Jack o' Diamonds," and all at once one of the blacks who had been listening hopped onto the slide and began to dance. Soon he improvised a step and began talking as he danced. He would dance to one end of the slide and then suddenly reach out his hand and shy back quickly. Then he would whirl and dance to the other end of the slide. He'd snort and rear his head back just like a mule when you are trying to put the bridle on him.

That's just what he was, and himself too. He took both parts, trying to put the bridle on the mule and dodging back when the mule threw up its head. The other blacks began laughing and clapping louder than ever, and suddenly another of them jumped up on the stage and pushed the first black off. He took the bridle and caught the mule, all this in dance time to improvised steps, as he needed them. Another black jumped on the slide and led the mule from his stall and took him to the field and hitched him to a plow. Another took his place and began dirting up corn, turning his feet sideways and sweeping them along the edge of the boards. They made a corn crop right there on that slide, three by four feet.

Just then there was a disturbance at the edge of the crowd, and one of our blacks came up to tell me that a white man had come in and was after their women. I went and found him, white trash and half drunk, trying to pull a black woman out of the crowd. I took him to the gate and put him off the place and told him not to come back.

The fun was gone out of the party after that. Soon the blacks began drifting away, by twos and threes. They called quiet good nights and thanked Bill and me for the party and it was over.

It was later on that same summer that I got mad at Bill one day. It was about something he said. I didn't say I was mad but he knew it.

We were out looking at my crops. I was glad to show them. They were the prettiest ones in Beat Two. Some of the old-timers out there told me so. It was while we were looking over the crops that he said something that I got mad about.

"Well, John," he said, "I don't see anything here to complain of."

It was a mighty shy compliment for the work I had put in and the way the crops had turned out. I guess you don't see anything to complain about, I thought. Here you are looking at the best crop in this part of Lafayette County, and don't know what you're looking at.

I turned away and went back to the commissary and sat down on the steps. He stayed down in the fields till I blew the bugle for lunch, then came to the barn where he had parked his car and got in and drove away without coming to the house.

By the next time he came out, we had both forgotten about it. It really didn't amount to a hill of beans anyhow. It was the first crop either one of us had ever made, and Bill knew it was a good one. The neighbors had told him so. I guess he just didn't want me to get big-headed over it. He figured if he praised it, I might get to feeling too good about it and maybe get careless. But I didn't get careless and that fall we harvested a bumper crop and filled our crib.

Along about that time, the price of groceries went up. We had to pay more to the wholesaler, so I marked up the stuff we had in the commissary. Our stock covered everything we needed on the farm—all sorts of staple foods, tobacco, clothes, plow gear. When Bill came out and I told him, he said to mark the prices back down; it was not the blacks' fault that prices went up, and he wasn't going to penalize them for it. So I marked the prices back down.

We had an old log barn in the lot that had rotted on one side, so we decided to tear it down. I will never forget how hard those logs were to pry loose from where they had been keyed to each other. Bill was there while we were dismembering it and he began poking around and found each of the pieces was numbered.

Old man Joe Parks had owned the place years and years ago, so Bill went and asked him about the barn. He found out that the old man had built it, or had hired it done. A group of mid-European woodcutters had come through about the turn of the century, and old man Joe had contracted with them to build the barn.

He had told them the size barn he wanted and they had gone to the bottom and cut the logs there. After a week or so, they began hauling the cut timbers in, each piece numbered as to where it should go, and the barn was erected. A twelve-by-twelve plate was placed around the top before the roof was raised and wooden pins were dropped into holes cut in the corners of the key timbers. Those wooden pins were the only fasteners of any kind in the whole structure. Now, almost fifty years later, as we would pry out one log, the barn would not collapse. It would only sag a little and still stand.

Bill came back and watched us tear that barn down. It took us two days, almost as long, I expect, as it took those men to raise it. That went into some of Bill's later stories, where his characters, skilled almost to the point of artistry, keyed logs into walls that stood for a hundred years.

Bill was running in the money then and bought anything he saw and decided he wanted. Bird season was coming on, and he bought a full outfit of Duxbak hunting clothes. Duxbak is waterproof and that opening day was as hot almost as summer. When Bill came out that morning he even had a sweat shirt on under his coat.

He had told us he would be out that day to hunt, and we were there waiting for him. His new gun had come, and he had it under his arm. It was an Ithaca over-and-under, with his name on a silver plate let into the stock. He had had it specially made for him, to fit his size and weight and arm length. Even the stock at the neck was measured to his grip. The gun had an automatic ejector that would eject either shell fired and leave the other one in the barrel. It cost him somewhere around four hundred and fifty dollars, even in the depression.

Bub has that gun now. He and Bill hunted together a whole lot, and after he died Estelle gave it to him.

After we started hunting that morning, we hadn't gone very far before Bill came out of his Duxbak coat. He handed it to Jimmy. A few minutes later off came the sweat shirt. Chooky tied that around his neck. There wasn't much else he could get rid of, so soon we came back to the house. Our hunt was over for that day.

I had located a few coveys of birds for Bill, but we didn't even get to the first one. There were not many birds on the place then. The farm had been in the hands of the Federal Land Bank for several years, and since it hadn't been posted it had been pretty well shot out. We posted it and managed to save what birds we did have for our own shooting.

Bill laid the law down though. We were to leave so many birds in each covey, to assure a supply for the following years. We remembered and never killed more than a few each hunt, and I made it a point to keep other hunters off the place.

Bill hunted out there often. Once he came out and brought with him a setter given him by Horace Lyttel, gun editor of *Field and Stream*. They had met over at Whit Cook's place near Coontown. Whit had a private hunting preserve over there, and Mr. Lyttel used to fly down from New York for a day or two every now and then. He kept his dogs there and brought only his guns. You could rent horses to hunt on.

Bill used to go there too, and one trip he met Mr. Lyttel, and that was when he gave Bill the dog. He also gave him one of those silver dog whistles that make a note so high you can't hear it, but the dog can.

The day Bill brought that dog and the silver whistle out, I thought it was the prettiest dog I ever saw. Actually it was a show dog and didn't know a damned thing about hunting. It must have been trained on caged birds spaced so many yards apart and thought that was the way to hunt. It would point every hundred yards, whether there was anything there or not. Finally, it went sprinting off toward a nearby ridge and disappeared over the top.

Bill got out his noiseless whistle and began blowing. The dog paid no attention. The longer the dog stayed out there the madder Bill got and the harder he blew. It was the funniest sight I ever saw. Bill blew till he got red in the face, and his hair stood on end. He was blowing so hard he would come up on his tiptoes each blast. And he wasn't making a sound.

Bub and Chooky finally had to run and get into a ditch where he could not see them, and laugh. Later on, Bill laughed about it too, but not then. Although the dog would not come in, it began howling each time Bill puffed through the whistle. He had got it up so keen it hurt the dog's ears. Finally, Bill quit blowing and we went over the ridge, got the dog, and went on home.

Bill started off still mad. Bub and Chooky kept behind him as we walked along, so he couldn't see them. In spite of all they could do, every now and then they would fold over, laughing. Finally we saw Bill's cheeks sort of puff out and quiver, and we knew he was laughing too. We all stopped then, and whooped, and hollered.

After Bill had had the Ithaca for a while, he decided the stock did not fit him, so he got hold of a piece of walnut somewhere and whittled out a new one. He even whittled a cheek piece on it like on a target rifle, the first one I ever saw on a shotgun stock. After using his new stock for a while, he decided he didn't like it, so he put the original one back on.

Bill loved to sit down in front of his fire and imagine hunts he would go on and outfit himself for them. It was a good room to think hunting in, with its big old fireplace and his guns and trophies on the walls about him. He had all sorts of shooting jackets and shooting gloves. Several deer rifles were on the walls, and finally he bought himself a .270 elephant gun.

I think Bill liked to talk hunting almost as much as he liked hunting itself. He'd stop by the places where his hunting cronies worked and talk to them by the hour, usually working himself into a fidget to get back to the woods. But as the years passed, he seldom got around to actually going.

One day soon after his elephant gun came, he talked two or three of us into going out to the river bottom to try it out. This was shortly after the Second World War, and among the ones who went was a returned vet with a service rifle. At that time you could buy one like it for about eighteen dollars from almost any sporting-goods catalogue. Anyhow, as soon as they got to the river, Bill and the boy sat down on the bank and picked out reeds on the far bank to shoot at. Bill shot and missed but the boy hit his.

Bill said, "Let me try that rifle."

The boy answered, "All right."

They swapped rifles and Bill fired at a reed with the old Army rifle and hit it.

"I'll trade you," Bill said.

The boy said, "All right."

And Bill swapped that brand-new elephant gun for that eighteen-dollar Army rifle, merely because he'd cut a reed in two the first time he fired it. They both were satisfied.

I told a friend of mine who had seen the elephant gun and whose mouth had watered over it. "Great God o' mighty. I would have given him a month's salary for it." Then he added, "Ain't that just like Bill?"

After about two years on the farm, Bill's money ran out, and I moved back to town and got a job on the W.P.A. Bill did not seem to have the same interest in the farm after I left it. He did not go out there as often as he had before. He sort of furnished the blacks from in town and let them run it as they pleased. Some of them are still out there.

Uncle Ned moved back to town soon after I did. Bill had someone else in his servant's house by now, so he rented Uncle Ned a cabin in the hollow and continued taking care of him.

The time had come for Bill to make another trip to California and out there he went. He came back with money and put more of it into his farm, but he still did not go out there very often any more. The old tractor wore out and he bought a new one. He had a drain ditch cut across the bottom land to straighten out Puss Cuss Creek and control its overflow. He had a new bridge put across the creek and was in and out during the time they were digging the ditch and building the bridge, but he no longer actually farmed the place. He left that up to the blacks. There were still a few coveys of birds in the hedgerows and fields, and I would see him every now and then in his Jeep with his gun and dogs as he crossed the Square on his way out there for a day's hunt.

Uncle Ned did not stay in Oxford but a year or two after he moved back to town. The urge came over him to go back home to Ripley to spend his remaining years there. Bill took him home and settled him in a house that he made arrangements for and also arranged for his continuing care, even to having someone go in every so often and see about him and mail regular reports to Oxford.

Uncle Ned did not live many more years. He died "at home" and Bill made the trip over there to see to his last rites and had him buried in the same cemetery in which were the Old Colonel and others of our kinfolk.

Chapter 19

THOUGH BILL WASN'T MECHANICALLY INCLINED, he did like to piddle about his yard, and bought all sorts of tools for that purpose. He even got himself a Sears, Roebuck garden tractor to work his garden and mow his yard. When it came he was just like a little boy. He wouldn't let anyone else touch it.

His stepson, Mac Franklin, was there when the tractor came. It was delivered to his back porch, which was open and had a brick floor laid at ground level. Estelle and Bill's yard boy and cook came out to help him uncrate it. He let them assist with that but as soon as they got the crate off he made them all stand back.

There was a book of instructions in the crate and using it as a guide, Bill fitted the pieces together. After he had put gas and oil in it he found a grease chart. No grease gun came with the machine, so he went to town and bought the best one he could find, the kind they use in filling stations. It must have cost him $25 or $30. He filled it with grease and took his chart and greased the tractor. He was now ready to crank it up.

Mac told me about it later. He said the engine fired on the first pull, but Bill had the thing in gear. It was pointed toward the back wall of the house and Mac said he never saw such a fight as Bill put up trying to hold the machine back till he could find the gear and put it in neutral.

The engine on those tractors is four horsepower and that is right powerful for a machine that size. Mac swears Bill and the tractor climbed halfway up the wall, right to the screen door that led into Bill's study, before he got it turned to one side and back down on the porch. Finally, he managed to find the gear lever and pull it into neutral.

Mac said Bill didn't say a word. Just went over his tractor to see that it hadn't been damaged, then drove it out to the garden, hooked on a plow and began plowing.

Bill bought one attachment after another for his new play-thing, till he had about one of everything Sears made that he could hook on to it. Most of the stuff he never used. The mower he bought for it was a sickle bar, like you use to mow a hayfield. That's what he used to mow his lawn.

He always did it himself because he wouldn't let anyone else touch that machine. It mowed his yard about like a hayfield too. He had had a good power lawn mower when he bought the tractor, but he sold it. He said they didn't need two mowers since they didn't have but the one yard to mow.

I remember a party Jill was going to have. I was down at Bill's the day before, sitting in the yard with him, when she came up to where we were sitting. "Pappy," she said. "For God's sake cut the lawn today like you promised. My party is tomorrow. I don't want you running that thing around out here when my guests arrive.

"All right," Bill answered, and got up from his chair to get his mower from its shed.

I went back there with him and helped him crank it, but not before he got out his grease gun and greased it and his wrenches and tightened all the nuts he could find. Bill was a wonder with a saw or chisel, but he didn't know a spark plug from a carburetor. Once satisfied everything was shipshape, he tooled the tractor out of the shed.

I sat on the front porch a while, watching him walk up and down the yard between the plow handles that you used to guide it with. Jill stood beside me till Bill had made several trips up and down the lawn, then, satisfied that he intended to keep his promise, turned and went in the house.

Once, I did manage to talk Bill into lending me the mower to cut my lawn. But he wasn't very happy about it. I kept it longer than he thought I ought, and he came for it. While he was there Phil Mullen, whose family owned our local paper at the time, passed by, and, seeing us together, came in with his camera. He asked if he could take a picture and Bill said yes. He stepped to one side. Phil said, "No, I want one of you and John together."

"Oh, I thought you wanted one of my tractor," Bill answered and came over and stood beside me so Phil could take our picture. It's the only one of us together as adults.

I will have to talk about my writing next, for it was through it that I had my closest contact with Bill through his later years. I believe I knew Bill about as well as any man. You don't love a man for his good qualities. You love him in spite of his bad ones. Bill had his bad ones, but he had about as many good ones as any man I've ever known. I did not get along too well with him through his last years, but I never doubted that I loved him or that he loved me. And I believe he has carried those two facts with him wherever he is now.

I began writing on the farm. It began by my making up stories to tell my youngest son, Chooky. They were later published in a book called *Chooky*.

I was still writing these short stories and having no luck with them, so one day Mother pinned Bill down and made him promise to help me. She called me and told me to take some of them down to Bill, that he was waiting in his yard to look them over.

I picked what I thought were the two best ones and took them down.

Bill was sitting in the yard reading when I came in. I could tell as soon as I saw him that he had got into something he wished he hadn't, and wouldn't have for anyone else but Mother. He told me to leave the stories and then sat there looking straight ahead.

I put the stories on the arm of his chair and got up and left.

I didn't go back until Mother told me to and this time, just as before, Bill was sitting in his chair in the yard. I went over and sat down in a chair beside him.

"The *Saturday Evening Post* will buy these two," Bill said.

I broke in volubly.

"Be quiet now and let me talk," he said. "That's what you came down here for, ain't it?"

I told him yes.

"Then let me talk. I could sign these with you and there would be no doubt about a sale but that wouldn't help you. I would get 90 per cent of the credit and you would have to start all over on your own next time. Send them in. They will take them."

He stopped talking and sat there looking straight ahead again. I knew he was through, and it was time for me to leave. I left.

The *Post* did not take the stories. I went to Bill about it. I never saw him so mad. He was well established by then and believed he was as good a judge as anybody about a story. The *Saturday Evening Post* did not seem to think so, and that's what made him so mad.

I told Mother what had happened, and she went to Bill again and he sent for me.

"A short story either sells or it doesn't," he said. "When you write one, send it in. If they take it, good. If they turn it down, forget about it and write another one. Never rewrite anything. You are wasting your time and talent. Use it on something new."

"No one can help you sell a short story. A novel is another proposition. You write a novel and I will see that you get it published. I can do that."

So I wrote *Men Working* and got fired for it.

The W.P.A. was in full swing, and a nephew by marriage of Mother's, Bob Williams, who had married Sallie Murry, was mayor of Oxford. He was in charge of it. So Mother went to him and he put me on as engineer on the Oxford projects. I had been on the W.P.A. about a year and a half, and when Bill told me to write a novel I wrote one about the W.P.A. When the book came out, they fired me for writing it.

Bill helped me sell that book, but he used the plots of those two short stories of mine he read. It was not stealing, as he claimed to Mother. I knew better and never blamed him for it. His stories were published in *Collier's*, but I doubt if he knew where the idea for them had come from or thought about it one way or another till Mother said something to him about it. That was when he told me any writer will steal from any story.

Of course, Mother got upset about it and called me when she read Bill's stories in the magazine. She had read mine in original manuscript. I always took my stories and showed them to her.

I usually visited Mother every morning for coffee, and we would sit around and talk for a while and then go on to town for my mail. We didn't have free delivery then, and I liked walking. Mother lived between me and town, so I stopped in on the way. Sometimes, Bill would be there, and the three of us would have coffee and talk.

This morning as soon as I came in, she showed me the copy of *Collier's*. And added, "Have you seen this?"

"Yessum," I answered.

"Well, Johncy . . ." she said.

"Look, Mother. Bill didn't steal my story. A writer doesn't know where his stories come from except out of his mind. He may spend forty years picking up a book, piece by piece. Sometimes he doesn't really know he has a book till he picks up the final piece. All he knows is, all at once, he's got a story to tell. He doesn't try to remember where each part came from. The end product is a lot of things he has seen and heard and felt and that have stored themselves away in his mind. All at once a lot of them fit together, and there's his book or story."

Mother had been walking up and down the floor. Now she sat down. "Johncy, Billie told me that a long time ago, except he called it stealing. He said one writer will steal from any other writer."

When Bill used the word "steal," it was a sort of self-flagellation. He was being hard on himself, leaning over backward to do so. It was like him. He was always harder on himself than on someone else. It was his way of demanding more of himself than of another person. There was no excuse in him for his own mistakes.

I finally convinced Mother, but she was not happy about it. She felt her own self, in a way, responsible for what had happened because it was she who had made Bill read my stories.

Later on, Bill told me that that was the reason he refused to read anyone's manuscript. He might remember something he had read and later on fit it into one of his own stories, and the first thing he knew someone would be suing him for plagiarism. He advised me not to also, for the same reason, and I have followed his advice. Besides that, there is no point in one writer reading another's manuscript. He's not going to buy it even if he likes it. A manuscript should be shown to someone who has got the money to pay for it, not another writer.

When I had finished my book, I took it to Bill.

"What's that?" he asked.

"It's that novel you told me if I wrote, you'd help me sell."

"I won't read it."

"O.K., Bill."

"I'll send it to my publisher and tell him I haven't read it," he said.

"Sure, Bill."

I handed him my manuscript and left. I guess maybe Mother had said something to him about those *Collier's* stories in spite of my trying to get her not to.

About a month later, Bill left word with Mother, and she got hold of me. Bill wouldn't use a phone and I won't answer one, so about the only way we could get word to each other was through her or by casual meetings on the Square. We would both be uptown at about the same time and sometimes run into each other. We would usually stop and talk for a while if we did.

When I went down to Bill's after he had left word at Mother's, he was in his study with my manuscript. He handed me a letter his publisher had written him about it. They said my stuff didn't have the fire Bill's had, and they were sending it back. Bill was not pleased because he had told them that if they didn't want it, to send it to his agent in New York. Now he would have to go to the trouble of sending the thing back himself.

He did take the trouble though, and about a month later he had word from the agent that if I would add a little to one place in the book to complete one character, they thought they could place it. Bill told them to return the manuscript to me, and I wrote what they wanted and sent it back.

When they sold it to Harcourt, Brace for a $500 advance, the agent wrote me that it was always best for a publisher to know a writer, especially a new one. My agent thought I ought to come to New York. I went to Bill. I was scared of New York. I still am. Any city scares me. They are too big, and there are too many people in them.

"Do I have to go up there?" I asked.

"If your agent says so, you'd better," Bill said.

"What am I going to use for money to get up there on?"

"Write your agent that if he wants you to come to New York, to send you some money."

I wrote my agent as Bill directed, and he wrote back asking how much.

I went back to Bill. "What will it cost me to go to New York?" Bill thought a while and said, "Tell him to send you $100. No, make it $125."

I wrote for the money and it came right away and I went back to Bill's. "How do you get where you want to go in New York?"

"It's easy," he said. "I'll draw you a map."

We'd been standing out in the back yard. Now we went into his study. He took out a piece of writing paper and a pen and sat at his desk. I stood behind him looking over his shoulder.

Bill made a lot of parallel lines, like the lines on a piece of tablet paper. They went from the top of the sheet clear to the bottom, each line neatly spaced under the other. Then he drew some up and down, like columns in a ledger. Last, he made a slanting line from one corner at the top to the opposite corner at the bottom.

"These cross lines are streets," he said, pointing at them with his pencil. "They run east and west. These up-and-down lines are avenues. They run north and south." He drew an arrow at the top of the page and put an N on it. "This slant line here is Broadway. Take this with you and you won't have any trouble."

He looked at the map a while. "Don't try to stop anybody on the streets and ask how to get somewhere. As slow as you talk and after the time you'll take up saying excuse me and pardon me, they'll be half a block away. And besides that, no one in New York speaks English." He looked at the map a while longer, then he took it and tore it up and dropped it in the wastebasket. "Wherever you want to go, just hail a taxi and tell the driver. He'll take you there."

So that's the way I went to New York the first time.

I thanked Bill for the information and left. Before I went to New York I stopped by Mother's. "What's Bill on his ear about?" I said. "He sold my book for me, and I'm out of his hair now."

Bill had been sort of brusque all through that map business.

"You got a $500 advance on your book," Mother said. "Bill never got but $400 on any of his!"

When I got to New York, I took a taxi as Bill had told me and went around to my agent and from there to Harcourt's. That's where the question of how we spelled our name came up.

Actually there used to be a *u* in it. We came from Tippah County in the northeast corner of the state, and in that county, when my great-grandfather first came there, there was another family of Faulkners. He did not like them.

People, on learning he was from Tippah, would ask him what kin he was to these other Faulkners. He would tell them, none, and he didn't like their even suggesting it. So he dropped the *u* so he could tell them we didn't even spell our names alike.

When Bill started writing, he said everybody thought you spelled Falkner with a *u*, and it was easier for him to change than to try to get everybody else to. So he put the *u* back in.

I had sent my book in under my full name, John W. T. Falkner III. Harcourt asked me if I objected to using the *u*. They said being Bill's brother would not help sell my books, but it might get people to look at them who otherwise wouldn't. They would like to have that advantage in advertising it. *was* Bill's brother, but if they said I was and then my book came out with my name spelled differently, they would think Harcourt might be just trying to put something over on them.

I told them I didn't care what name they used or how they spelled it as long as it helped sell my books. So we put in the *u* dropped the middle initials and the III. And from then on I have been John Faulkner.

I'm sure being Bill's brother did help sell my books, at first, but there was another advantage I got out of the change. I began getting my mail before somebody else read it.

There were three John W. T. Falkners in town at that time (there had been four), and whatever mail came for John W. T. Falkner was put in Uncle John's box. He opened it, along with the rest of his letters, and when I got it it was always marked on the outside "Opened by mistake" and signed "JWTF."

With the *u* in my name they brought my mail to me. I liked it. Now I use the *u* for everything—books, papers, records, legal matters. Bill never used it except in connection with his writings. He was the only living W. C. Falkner, so it didn't make any difference to him. All his papers and legal documents and his telephone were listed as W. C. Falkner.

Since I now had a book to my credit and had had several stories published in *Collier's*, Bill used to talk to me about writing every now and then. It was at one of these times that he told me never to pay any attention to anything a critic wrote. He said most of them were people who tried to write and couldn't, so they were taking a sort of revenge on anyone who could. If they could run down someone's writing that had been published, it would prove they knew more about it than the fellow that wrote it did. If they knew more about writing than a writer, it would prove that their stories had actually been good enough to sell and it was the publishers' fault for turning them down. Bill claimed he never read reviews, and I don't think he did, or letters, for the matter of that.

Bill also told me that a publisher would always send your manuscript back for some more work on it before he finally took it, just to show you he knew more about books than you did. He said the publisher was right too, otherwise he wouldn't have enough money to buy your book.

Another thing Bill told me about writing was that any story must have a conflict in it. You set it up, then solve it. He said the best conflict, the one people like to read about the most, is two men trying to get in bed with the same woman.

It was about this time that Bill made a rule. He said it would be best for us to reach an agreement right then that neither of us would ever have anything to do with the other's work, that we wouldn't even talk about it to anybody else. I told Bill he had been writing longer than I had, and he ought to know more about it than I did. If that was his advice, I'd take it.

We both held to that agreement as long as he lived. I have been offered extra inducements to review his books but I never would. I'm sure he has been offered like propositions and turned them down. All of us have had any number of people try to talk to us about Bill, Mother and I in particular. I kept my agreement in that, and Mother, knowing Bill did not want any of us to talk about him, would not either.

She was inordinately proud of him, as she might well be, but she respected his wishes too. The only times we ever talked about him to others was to foster some of the stories he got up on himself. The three of us foisted many of them off on the public, and I have seen them incorporated in what they call critical analyses. I determined, about ten or twelve years ago, that if I survived Bill I would write a book about him as he really was.

Chapter 20

BILL WAS MORE THAN GENEROUS WITH A GREAT
many of us in his family. He liked being in a position where he
could help us when we needed it. That went for blacks who felt
they had a claim on him because they'd worked for him at one
time or another, and for other reasons too, as well as for his
kinfolk.

There was Mammy Callie and Uncle Ned, for whom he
accepted an inherited responsibility because they had belonged
to us. They had this claim on him the same as we did. Mammy
certainly had been a part of our family. She had given a major
portion of her life to us and all her loyalty. When she had
grown too old to have much left to share, Bill, along with
Mother, accepted her as his charge.

She called on both of them freely for whatever need arose.
Mother did what she could, but her means were limited, so,
whenever necessary, Mammy turned to Bill. Bill footed the bill
for the major share of her upkeep and comfort during her final
years.

Mammy lived down in the Hollow, something like a quarter
of a mile from Mother's. She paid Mother regular visits when
the weather permitted, and if too long an interval passed
between these visits, Mother or Bill would go to her house to see
after her. Bill had arranged for an apartment for her in a double
house. He had also arranged for the woman in the top apartment to pay daily visits to Mammy to see that she was all right.

Once, as she was returning home after a visit to Mother,
she was struck down by a car as she attempted to cross the road
to her apartment. Her neighbors, who witnessed the accident,
got word to Mother right way, and Mother hurried down
there. The neighbors had taken Mammy into her own apart-

ment, and she was lying there on her bed when Mother arrived. She was conscious but feebly irrational from shock.

Mother called an ambulance and went with her to the hospital, holding her old gnarled black hand that clutched at Mother's for support in this strange world into which shock had thrown her.

When the nurses at the hospital attempted to undress her to see to the extent of her injuries, Mammy would have none of them. She would allow only Mother to undress her. When Mother did, she said she had never seen as many petticoats as Mammy wore, or anyone so tiny and helpless when she finally got her undressed. Mother persuaded her then that she must allow the doctors to examine her. It took some doing, but finally Mammy consented on the condition that Mother remain in the room beside her.

Mammy was not actually badly hurt. Her major problem was that she was so old and feeble, which accounted for the extreme state of shock she went into. But even though her injuries were found to be superficial, any injury is serious to someone as old as she was.

As soon as the doctors were through and had got Mammy easy enough for Mother to get away for a moment, she went to the phone and called Bill. He came immediately to see Mammy and provided for her care at the hospital for as long as the doctors felt it was necessary.

Mammy got over this accident and was returned to her own home. Bill went along and made arrangements with the woman in the next apartment for more frequent visits so that a closer check could be kept. He instructed the neighbor to notify him immediately if Mammy needed or wanted anything.

Mammy lived for several years after that. She was up and able to be about after a period of rest, and she renewed her visits to Mother's when she felt she was able to walk the quarter of a mile. She did not come as often as before, but she did come when she could. So Mother began paying Mammy regular visits and so did Bill.

It was after Bill bought the farm and I moved back to Oxford to manage it that Mammy died. Bill was at home at the time. It was between two of his earlier writing stints in Hollywood.

Mammy's death was more from old age than anything else. She died at home, in her own bed, in her sleep. She simply went to sleep and did not wake up. The next morning when the neighbor woman paid her visit, she thought Mammy was still asleep. But it was her final sleep. The neighbor woman notified Mother at once and Mother called Bill.

Bill had Mammy's frail body moved to the funeral home, selected her casket and when she was ready, had her moved to his own house, where she lay on his hearth for a day and a night and a part of the next day, until time for her burial. Bill selected her grave site in the colored portion of our cemetery, and her friends, both white and colored, assembled at Bill's for her funeral. He read the burial service over her himself, and, with his family, followed the hearse to the cemetery to the spot he had chosen for her. After her funeral, he had the monument placed above her which I mentioned earlier.

Bill also cared for Uncle Ned, as I have written earlier, and in much the same way he had Mammy Callie, though he had less reason to.

As to Bill's treatment of his own people, his family, he was best of all to Mother. He gave her whatever she would let him but she was very independent, and her brag was that she supported herself with her painting. She died at eighty-nine.

Bill put money in the bank for her any number of times, but usually she wouldn't touch it. Each January, when he paid his own taxes, he took care of hers too. And every so often he would go by the grocery store where she traded and leave a deposit of one hundred dollars to be applied against her future bills, with instructions to be notified when that ran out so he could deposit some more. He helped others of us on occasion, letting us have money when we needed it.

Bill was especially good to Dean, our brother Dean's child. He held himself responsible for her father's death, since he had arranged for Dean to go to Memphis to learn to fly. And it was in his, Bill's, airplane that Dean was killed.

Bill bought the plane, a Cabin Waco, in 1933. It had to be kept in Memphis, as there was no field at Oxford suitable for its takeoffs and landings. We had a grass strip, but the Waco was too fast, and the area we had was not large enough to take care of it, especially for anyone less than an expert pilot. It was different from the planes Bill had flown, and he never flew it enough to get used to it. Dean did. He became better than good with it, but that was only after handling it for a hundred hours or more. In the beginning, he could not have safely got it in and out of Oxford. While learning, he needed room to compensate for his inexperience, and that's why Bill sent him to Memphis.

Since Bill felt as he did about Dean's death, he extended that sense of responsibility to Dean's child. Dean never saw her. She was born four months after he was killed. Dean's widow married again a few years later and moved with her husband to Little Rock, taking little Dean with them. Bill helped Dean through her public-school years, and when she came to Ole Miss to college, he took over full responsibility for her education. Not only that, he made sure she learned to handle her own finances. Fatherless, she might need to know this later on.

Before she entered the University, he called her down to his house and together they went over her probable expenses. When a yearly amount was arrived at, he gave it to her in a lump sum and left it up to her to spread it out over the school year. And I will say this for Dean, during her four years of college she never ran out of money or had to come back to Bill for more, even in her final year in Europe. After her junior year, she told Bill she had decided she wanted her last year at the University of Geneva, and Bill agreed to this. He gave her their agreed-on sum, and she sailed from New York in June, right after exams were over, and went to a conversation-French school at Aubigny that Ole Miss had set up as a six-week summer-school course. Dean boarded in a French home with another girl, a friend of hers, also from Oxford, where nothing but French was spoken. Soon she was writing Bill in French, and he responded in the same language. They both got a kick out of it. From there she went on to her final year at Geneva and, not too long after her return home, fell in love with Jon Mallard of Jackson.

Bill gave her a wedding like the one he had given Jill. The announcement party was held on his lawn. We each held a glass of champagne while Bill stood on the steps to his side porch with Dean and Jon. Bill said that although his acquaintance with the young man Dean had chosen had been too brief for him to estimate his worth, he had infinite confidence in her good judgment, and he was happy to welcome him into our family. So we raised our glasses and drank a toast to that.

Dean's wedding was in our Episcopal church, as Jill's had been. She walked down the aisle on Bill's arm, and he gave her away. He also left Dean money in his will, a nest egg all her own in case the time ever came when she would need it. I don't think she ever will. We have come to know the man she chose very well and we have found out, as Bill believed, that he had every right to place his confidence in Dean's good judgment.

Bill was as hardheaded as the rest of us and on occasion as stubborn as anyone I ever knew; in fact, as stubborn as a mule. What he said and did, he said and did, and that was it. He never made explanations nor, for the matter of that, would he talk about it later on. Though, at times, his sayings and doings did not suit us, we made no move to oppose him or make him change. Each of us was accorded this same right by the others. I know at times that all of us have done or said things that did not suit the rest of our family.

Bill never tried to influence us any more than we did him, nor did what differences of opinion we had ever lessen the family bond that tied us together. He had his faults as every man does, but his good qualities and his intrinsic worth far overrode them. I know of no man who left more behind him to prove his right to have lived than Bill did.

Another thing, he was as quick-witted as any man I've ever known, with the finest sense of humor. They are good qualities in any man and especially useful in an argument. Bill could turn a point with a laugh or cut you to the quick. I have seen him do both, depending on whom he was talking to at the time. It was a rare occasion when anyone bested him in a battle of words.

The only one I ever knew him to listen to submissively was Mother. He never struck back at her. If he couldn't turn her off with a laugh, he simply stood there and listened. She was even smaller than Bill. He got his small frame from her and other qualities too. That quick, piercing look he could use on occasion came from her.

Either of them could seem to look clear inside you, and give you the feeling they were actually seeing what made you tick. Dad and Mother and Bill, all three, had the same color eyes. They were so dark a brown they appeared black at times. But Dad's didn't seem to penetrate like Mother's and Bill's. Dad's simply glared at you. Their eyes pierced you like a pin.

Bill had many funny turns of conversation. One I remember particulary took place when we were living at the University. We had a tennis court in our yard. One day we were all sitting on the front porch and a squirrel, of which there are many on the campus, climbed one of the posts and became very intent on a section of rope that held the net in place. Dean noticed it. Bill was sitting by Dean on the steps and saw what he was looking at.

"I wonder what that squirrel is doing to that knot," Dean said.

"He's seeing if the knot's tied good and tight before he trusts himself out on the net," Bill answered.

And sure enough, after a little more examination, the squirrel ran out on the net and across it to the other side.

Another of his quick retorts that I remember happened in 1912, right after Lee Russell was elected governor of Mississippi. We were neighbors to the Russells. Mr. Lee was Grandfather's and Uncle John's law partner at the time he won the election and Uncle John was his state campaign manager.

Some other neighbors of ours, the Carter's, lived right across the street from the Russells and didn't like them. Because of our close connection, through Grandfather's and Uncle John's law practice, with Mr. Lee, Miss Minnie Carter, during the campaign took occasion to pick at Bill and Jack and me. There was really no reason for her to do so. We were still under age and could not vote. We were still in high school. It was just that Miss Minnie didn't like the Russells, and every time she saw a Falkner it reminded her of them.

The day after the election, when the returns were all in and it was definitely settled that Mr. Lee had won, Bill and Jack and I were passing the Carter home on the way to school. Miss Minnie was out in the yard working with some flower plants, and as we went by she looked up. When she saw who we were she stood up, with her gardening gloves on and her trowel in her hand. We spoke to her politely.

"Well. I reckon you Falkners are hurrying to get on the band wagon now that Mr. Russell has been elected governor," she said in sort of an acid voice, taking her dislike for the Russells out on us Falkners.

"No, ma'am," Bill answered. "We're jumping down so you folks who didn't vote for him can climb up on quick!"

Changing with the wind or running with the hounds was sort of a trait of Miss Minnie's. She glared at us, and we went along on our way to school. I have known other times when Bill would leave someone without a thing left to say.

We had been friends with the Carters too long not to be back on friendly terms with them soon again. We used to use their front porch for impromptu dances often. It was concrete, smooth enough so that with the application of a little floor wax it made an excellent dance floor. They had a phonograph, and we would bring our girls by, and Katrina Carter would roll the music box out of the hall onto the porch so we could dance.

It was not too long after the election before we were dancing on Miss Minnie's porch again. And she would be there, cordial, hospitable, welcoming us young Falkners to her home and happy that we were using it for our pleasure. Even an election feud didn't have a very lasting effect on our casual social life in Oxford in those days.

Bill was one of the most independent men I have ever known. I never knew him to call on anyone for help for any reason. He stood on his own two feet at all times.

When Bill's first child died, her span on earth had been too brief for her actually to have become anybody. She was named Alabama, after our Aunt Bama. She died at five days old.

Estelle was, of course, still in bed and unable to get out, so Bill attended to her burial himself. He saw no reason for a real funeral since in five short days she had become only a memory. Jack and I, away from home, had never even seen her. So she was placed in her tiny casket, and he carried her to the cemetery on his lap. Alone he placed her in her grave.

Jack and I did not know anything about it till Mother told us on our next trip home. Bill had asked her not to write us, not to disturb us.

Bill's remarks have been quoted time after time, but there are two that remain with me that are as pure Bill as anything in my memory. One, humorous but serious too, was said back in the days of the depression. Bill had watched the W.P.A. bring our independent hill farmers into town and transform them into recipients of public handouts. He didn't like what he saw, what the W.P.A. was doing to them, his people.

He said all their ills might be corrected if they would only stand far enough apart so that they couldn't lean on each other. He wanted them back on their farms, back in their own independence. It was a trait he valued highly in himself and in any man.

The other remark had a wider sweep than just our county. It took in the entire nation. Bill said once that our last frontier was our labor unions. It was not till several years later, in a history class, that I heard my professor make the same remark, and I asked him what he meant.

He said that he was speaking of frontier in terms of the natural resources that man could exploit. Man, in his westward movement across this land, was motivated mainly by a desire to get rich quick, and when virgin country and virgin resources gave out at the Pacific shores, he turned to our one remaining, untapped resource—man himself. He exploited men. He organized his fellow beings into groups and made them pay for joining his organization, then charged them dues each month for the privilege of staying in.

One day, not long after that, I asked Bill if this was what he had meant and he said, "Of course."

Chapter 21

BILL WROTE FOR THE MOVIES, AT INTERVALS, as long as he lived. He brought some funny stories back from his first years out there, and a funny one or two about him came back to us in roundabout ways. To know what makes a man laugh is a good way to know the man.

But none of the funny stories about Bill was the equal of the true one about the time he came home to do his writing. He was under contract then and doing a rewrite on some play. He told his boss he worked best at home and asked permission to go there to finish the job he was working on. The boss thought he meant home in Hollywood. Bill meant home in Oxford. The boss didn't realize he was no longer in California till he tried to phone him a day or so later and had to do it over long distance.

Bill's later writings for the movies were all special jobs and did not require extended stays in California. Most of them were for Howard Hawks, who liked Bill's writings. When he would buy a story he would usually get hold of Bill to make it into a screenplay for him. He would call Bill long distance, and they would make arrangements over the phone.

The deals always called for Bill to come to California after be had finished that particular job and for nothing else. The financial arrangements were different from the weekly or monthly contracts Bill had had before. Mr. Hawks would make a proposition for a flat sum, with a time limit on the finished work. Also there would be a bonus in the contract of so much a day for each day Bill finished under the specified time limit. So far as I know, he never used up his allotted time and always managed to come out with a bonus. And as soon as he had finished out there, he would come home.

Bill was a very compassionate man. He was what is called "an easy mark." With a great deal of money coming in now, he seldom refused to share it with anyone who was really in need. All sorts of hard luck stories were brought to him. He was easy to approach, but not easy to fool if your story wasn't genuine. He got many requests for money through the mail from individuals and all sorts of organizations, but he paid little attention to these. Actually, he probably didn't know about them, for he seldom read any mail that was sent him. After he died, piles of unopened mail were found in his study.

The blacks he helped, the local ones, and our own white people too, were almost without number. Bill knew most of the people here in Lafayette County, or knew of them, and it was a rare thing when he turned one of them down. He made no public display of any of this. Usually, it was only by chance that we learned of it. We would hear it from someone he had helped or from some of their neighbors.

Occasionally, one of us would be present when a request was made. Bill always led his visitor aside where his request could be spoken in privacy. He would listen quietly, and, at the times I have been present, seldom refused to volunteer the money he had been asked for.

Bill had a reputation for unapproachableness. It was a wall he erected to protect himself from any discussion of his writings. He simple refused to talk about them and if you mentioned them to him he shut up like a clam. You could almost see him stopping up his ears. He refused to listen. A criticism of what he had written always hurt him and he devised the only method he could think of to protect himself. That was why he refused to read any reviews of his books, or, in later years, any fan mail sent him.

Only on one occasion do I know of him breaking this rule. A young man from the University, a student working on his master's thesis, came down to Bill's house one day. He told Bill who he was and what he was doing and asked if Bill would talk to him about his writings. Bill told him he would listen.

He did more than that. When he saw that the young man was in earnest, Bill told him what he thought would help his paper. During their talk the young man remarked that he had been unable to get hold of one of Bill's books, the main one he was using for his thesis, except for the twenty-five cent paperback edition. Bill said he reckoned that was about all it was worth.

The young man said, "Don't say that, Mr. Bill. I'm counting on getting my M.A. out of this!"

Bill's feelings for blacks stemmed from his feeling for them as underdogs, exploited because they were unable to do anything about it. Witness his refusal to raise prices at the commissary when the wholesaler raised them on us. The blacks had to have what we had to sell. It was not their fault prices had gone up, So Bill refused to charge them more.

Bill always went for the underdog. That was the reason for his one and only contact with the Communist party. It happened in the 1930's and was purely financial, a donation.

We have a Communist living here in Lafayette County. He is the only one registered in our state. His lonely position enlisted Bill's sympathies, and he gave him fifty dollars. It was not so much a donation to the Communist party. It was simply Bill's tribute to a man standing against the other two million of us. He thought that was worth the fifty.

He never attended one of Mr. Uth's meetings or, for the matter of that, any other political meeting I ever heard of. Even when he drove Uncle John about in his one political campaign, he never listened to him make a talk. He was too busy listening to what the audience might be saying.

This lone Communist of ours was not at all the way we thought a Communist ought to be. We always thought of them with long black beards and funny caps and maybe needing a bath. They carried bombs and were always ready to blow something up. Mr. Uth wasn't like that, and I think his being so different from what we supposed Communists to be fascinated Bill. I think he was as intrigued with our high personal regard for Mr. Uth as he was with Mr. Uth himself.

Actually, Mr. Uth was not only unlike a Communist, he was about like any of the rest of us, except that he was a better house painter than any other house painter in town. He painted some concrete pilasters outside the Bank of Oxford to look exactly like marble, which no other painter could do. He even painted pictures, good ones, and, of all things, they were usually peaceful rural scenes. Some of them even featured soft-eyed cows. Look as hard as we could, Mr. Uth simply did not look or act like a Communist.

Mr. Uth had come to us an immigrant from Norway, speaking broken English, and he still does. He married a cousin of my wife's, and they raised a family of nice obedient children.

They used to live on a farm built by my wife's great-grandfather, a few miles north of town. If he ever created any political uproar in our community, I never heard of it. And if he ever received any contributions besides the fifty dollars Bill gave him, I never heard of that either.

He painted many a house here in Oxford, fancy trim work inside and out. He is the best and charges what he thinks he is worth. Few of us can pay the price he asks for his services.

I know that Bill has been accused of being a Communist, a red, a fellow traveler, a pinko. But Mr. Uth, small in stature and setting himself against two million of us, of all sizes, was Bill's only interest in the Communist party. Actually, his "nonpolitical" contribution was made over thirty years ago.

Oxford seems to exert a lasting influence on people who have happened, for one reason or another, to have lived here for even a short while. Government people, civil service, and military personnel, professors who have taught at Ole Miss for a few years, like the atmosphere of the place and come back here to live when they retire. Our town is full of them. At times our country club seems like an "0" Club during the war.

One such was Colonel Evans. He had been stationed at Ole Miss during World War II as an instructor in one of the programs the government set up at the University. He and Bill had come to know each other then and had become friends. They were both outdoorsmen, loved hunting and walking in the woods and did these things together. Other ties and common interests held them too.

Besides Bill, Colonel Evans had made other friends here and after the war, when he retired, he came back to Oxford to live. The first house he rented was not far from Bill's, and they immediately took up their friendship where they had dropped it.

We have the second largest earth dam in the world, about fifteen miles out of town. It's two miles long and was built to impound the run-off waters from the Tallahatchie River until such time as the Mississippi is low enough for the Tallahatchie to drain safely into it without backing up and flooding our Delta.

In normal times, the backwaters behind the dam are about five miles wide and fifteen long. At flood times the water area is about twice that size. This newborn lake brought something to Oxford we had never known before—water sports and boating.

At about the time the lake opened up, Art Guyton, a neighbor and young friend of Bill's, had built a sailboat. Bill, passing

Art's workshop one day, had noticed Art at work and stopped by to see what he was doing. As he watched the daily progress of the boat he became more and more interested. So when Art launched the boat, Bill went along. After his first sail, he became completely sold on sailing.

Then Colonel Evans moved back here, and Bill took up his friendship with him again. He found out that Colonel Evans also loved boating. It developed that two of their mutual friends, Ross Brown and Dr. Little, shared their enthusiasm. The four of them got together and decided to build themselves a houseboat, big enough to eat and sleep on.

The outcome of that meeting was that Ross and Dr. Little, whose work demanded most of their time, would put up the money, if Bill and Colonel Evans would build it. Bill, who had watched Art build his boat, felt that he was qualified. And Colonel Evans was known as an accomplished do-it-yourself carpenter and cabinetmaker, with a shop full of woodworking tools of all kinds.

Colonel Evans also knew of a supply of mahogany at one of the posts in Central America at which he had served. A friend of his, a classmate at West Point, was commandant down there and Colonel Evans was sure he'd ship the wood to them. It would be ideal for building the boat. He wrote his friend and he and Bill set up shop in the Colonel's side yard.

The mahogany came and he and Bill worked on the boat for months. It was a beautiful thing when it was finished, a mahogany hull fitted out with real brasswork. An electric system was installed, and then an electric stove and a refrigerator. There were bunks for half a dozen people. By the time they were through, they figured the cost in the neighborhood of $20,000.

We had been having a lot of rain. It had been general, all over the country. The Mississippi was lapping against the top of its levee, so the entire runoff from the Tallahatchie had had to be impounded behind the dam. The lake was enormous. From the top of the dam you couldn't see the far end. It simply disappeared into the sky, like trying to look across the Gulf of Mexico.

With the water at this height, it was impossible to launch the boat. We had nothing in Oxford big enough to carry it out to the lake. A company in Memphis had agreed to get the boat to the lake and launch it. They were waiting word when to come. Bill and Colonel Evans began taking daily trips to the reservoir to check the lake level, as they wanted to launch their boat the very first possible minute. But we had had more rain, and the water level was still very high.

Colonel Evans told me about one trip they made out there. He was driving and Bill was sitting on the seat beside him, looking straight ahead through the windshield. They were on the old gravel highway that used to run to Memphis. It skirts the edge of the bottom lands, then turns at a right angle on a levee and crosses the river on Old Iron Bridge.

The upper section of the old bridge could be seen sticking forlornly up out of the muddy flood waters of the river. The road itself simply ran into the reservoir beyond the bridge and disappeared into the yellow flood.

The highway, farther on, was used as a launching site for boats carried out there on trailers. You simply backed your trailer down the road till the conveyance went under and the boat floated. Then you released the boat and pulled your rig back to dry land.

The water was far up over the river's banks. It had spread across the adjacent bottom. The bottom was flat and for every half-foot rise in water level, it spread another hundred yards. Any trailer would have to be backed a mile or two down the twisting, out-of-sight, underwater road in order to get depth enough to float the boat. What Colonel Evans and Bill had hoped to see was the water receding. Instead it seemed to be getting higher and spreading wider.

As they drove along the old highway, Colonel Evans was looking intently across Bill at the high water along the roads. He was exclaiming to Bill at each new high point. Bill was listening to him but looked out ahead at the road, or what normally was road. They went over a small hump, traveling at cruising speed, and Colonel Evans said the next thing he knew he was in a solid sheet of water. He thought for a minute he had run off in the reservoir and had gone clean under. Then the water drained off the windshield, and he could see that they were stalled, about hub-deep but still in the highway.

Colonel Evans said that for a few minutes he just sat there trembling, so scared he couldn't even speak. He turned to Bill and said, "Bill, for God's sake, why didn't you say something? You were sitting there looking down the road. Didn't you see what we were about to run into?"

"Yes," Bill answered.

"What were you thinking when you saw what was about to happen?"

"I was thinking if you didn't stop we were sure God going to run into the water."

The water finally went down to where they could launch the boat. The next day they had a boat-warming. The four owners invited their wives and friends for the occasion.

Most of them had acquired yachting costumes of one sort or another. One of them had completely outfitted himself from the pages of Esquire magazine. Bill had merely asked me for one of my old Navy caps, and I had given it to him.

The guests gathered on the bank and a small ceremony was held, complete with speeches, and then they all marched aboard. One of them, never mind which, though it wasn't Bill, fell off the gangplank and had to be rescued and dried out, but that only added a fillip to the occasion.

So well designed and built was the boat that at first it floated a little light, so concrete had been poured into the hold for ballast. After that it rode the water perfectly and managed well in its few trial runs.

The boat remained on the reservoir for several years and was used frequently. Finally, it broke away from its moorings in a storm and sank. It was never found, though divers were brought down from Memphis and searched the reservoir bottom for an extended distance from where it had last been seen. No trace of it was ever found. Luckily, it was insured.

Then Bill bought a sailboat, which he actually preferred to the power boat he and Colonel Evans had built. Art Guyton had been transferred from the University to the new University Hospital at Jackson, and he sold Bill his boat with the understanding that if Bill ever decided to get rid of it, Art could buy it back. He knew that Bill would, at any time, share it with him as he often had with Bill. Art loved sailing about as much as Bill did.

Bill never did reach the point at which he wished to get rid of it. The boat was in his back yard when he died, where he had hauled it to do some work on it. My oldest son, Bub, has it now, still on its trailer, in a shed at the back of his place.

Pictures were taken of Bill in his sailboat and reproduced on postcards depicting scenes around Oxford. They are in postcard racks in most of our drugstores and bookshops.

Bill used to come by every now and then to take me sailing. I got to liking it too. As usual, when Bill got into something he knew nothing about, he bought books on his new interest. He read up on all its phases-navigation, how to sail, management, and maintenance of his boat. He became better than the average sailing man.

Bill taught me how to sail. I got so I could manage the tiller, gauge by the dimple in the top of the sail whether I was getting the most out of the wind and how to release the sail and glide through a tight spot, crosswind. Sailing, as Bill taught me, was the nearest thing to contact flying I had ever tried. You sail by the seat of your pants almost like you fly that way.

Bill was a careful sailor. Most of the reservoir was plenty deep enough to drown a man, and to us that was deep. Several men have drowned out there, caught in a sudden squall or capsized.

Bill had a marine compass in a neat mahogany box, and he always carried it aboard. Sometimes quick, blinding rains came up, or fog, and unless you had a compass you could get into real trouble. He equipped the boat with life preservers and required everyone to wear one. Both of us were good swimmers, but he insisted on the added precaution. Waves out there get six or more feet in height at times.

Bill also kept an auxiliary motor stowed in the hatch beneath the forward deck. Estelle insisted that he carry it, though I never knew him to use it. He simply bought it to pacify her.

The reason Estelle insisted on the engine had come about because of Bill's stubbornness. One day he had gone out about noon and at midnight that night, he had not returned home. At two o'clock he still hadn't. He finally got in at four.

Estelle had been frantic at first. She'd called around town and asked if anyone knew anything about Bill. They did. He'd sailed his boat out about a mile or so from shore, and the wind had died on him.

Bill sat there in the sun's glare, his boat becalmed and the sails wilted. Several power boats came by and asked if they could give him a tow. Bill said no. He'd come to sail and sail he would. Others passed and offered tows, but the answer was still no. Some of his friends were afraid he might have a sunstroke sitting there in the glare from the water and begged him to come in. He was adamant.

Finally, folks realized they were wasting their breath and let him alone. About midnight a breeze sprang up and Bill sailed in.

By the time he got home just before daylight, Estelle had run the gamut of emotions. From panic, she had gone into a spell of being furious at him. That wore itself out, and when he actually walked in she got tickled. That was so typical of Bill. Bless her heart, as long as Bill lived she never got past the point where she could laugh at some of his quirks and foibles.

My wife says that if she had it to do over again, she'd want no part of a writer. I'm sure Estelle felt the same way about Bill many a time. I guess one reason for this is that most of us spend so much of our time around home. We usually work there. We're always under foot and every wife deserves a husband who spends eight hours away from where she is at least five days a week. No wonder they find us hard to live with.

Along about this time Estelle developed eye trouble. She went to an eye doctor and found she was developing cataracts. There is nothing that can be done about cataracts during this developing stage. They must be allowed to ripen, then they can be removed. This ripening process sometimes takes years.

Estelle did not tell Bill anything about her trouble. There was nothing he could do about it at the time, and she did not wish to worry him. She simply waited out her time and then went to the hospital and had the cataracts removed. With special glasses, now she could see almost as well as she ever could, directly to the front.

It was not long after her operation that I was down at Bill's one day. When I came in he was in his study, just off the hall, looking out the window. His study door was open so I walked in. I spoke to him and took a chair near where he was sitting. He answered without turning his head.

He continued looking out the window. After a while he said, "I've done Estelle an injustice over the last few years. See how clean this place is?"

I looked around. "Yes."

"Estelle cleaned it," he said. "It's the cleanest it's been in I don't know when. Here I had thought she'd got to be a bad housekeeper. Now I find out she's been about half blind."

Chapter 22

MOTHER WAS ALWAYS AN AVID READER. She taught us to read. She showed us that words put together the right way could make a story worth the time it took to read it. She kept us supplied with books matched to our age and comprehension. She was a selective reader too; I never knew her to read a book because "she ought to."

Her reading was all for pleasure, and her literary taste was much like a man's. She was particularly fond of Joseph Conrad, a man's writer, and we came to know him through her: *Lord Jim, Victory* and *The Nigger of the Narcissus*. A collection of Conrad was always on Bill's bookshelf. *The Virginian* was a favorite of hers, and of ours too, as well as George Bernard Shaw and Samuel Butler.

In her later years, she became interested in mystery stories by a few of the topnotchers: Rex Stout in particular, Leslie Ford, Mary Roberts Rinehart and Mignon G. Eberhardt. She would pass her books on to Bill and me.

Bill came by one day when she had just finished reading *The Crimson in the Purple*, by a new writer named Holly Roth. He was looking for more Rex Stout, but Mother did not have a new Stout so she recommended her new discovery. Bill did not know this writer so he was not interested, but for some reason he didn't want to tell Mother this. It was because she was so enthused over it, I suppose.

Anyhow, he thought up a quick excuse that wouldn't hurt her feelings the way a flat turn-down would. He told her he was on his way to town and didn't want to be burdened with it right then. To forestall any future offers of this unknown writer, he told her that besides its being inconvenient right then to take the book, he never read anything any more except Shakespeare and the Bible. And he had just asked her, only a few minutes before, if she had anything new about Nero Wolfe and Archie Goodwin!

It was not long after this that I ran into a friend of mine downtown who told me another one. His name is Jack Odom. He was one of Ole Miss' better linemen.

He was in Gathright-Reed's drugstore one day, at their book counter, looking for something to read.

The Reed in Gathright-Reed is Mack Reed, a close friend of Bill's. It was to Gathright-Reed's that Bill always took his manuscripts to be wrapped for mailing. Mack personally wrapped them for him. Whatever he might be doing when Bill came in with a manuscript, Mack always stopped and wrapped the package for him.

While Jack was there browsing, Bill came in. He, like Jack, was looking for something to read. He came over to the bookrack where Jack was and when Jack looked up and saw Bill, he hastily put down the "whodunit" he had in his hand. He moved down to the classical section and pulled out a book of Greek plays, not wanting Bill to see that he had such low tastes in literature.

With the Greek plays in his hand, he inched back along the aisle and peered over Bill's shoulder to see what his tastes would be. At the moment Bill had in his hand the "whodunit" Jack had just put down! He selected several more from the same section, went over to the cashier's counter and paid for them, then walked out.

Bill had a very real regard for the past, for our taproots were deep-sunk in it. Many of the things people have got away from, because they were old-timey, Bill believed worth the hanging onto. He retained many of the old social customs. On Christmas mornings, for a great number of years, he sent out invitations to his friends and neighbors to come and drink eggnog from a silver bowl in his parlor.

Bill maintained a smokehouse in his back yard and cured his own meat. He raised the meat he cured. No doubt it cost more than if he had got it off a grocery shelf, and it took time to cure. He did most of this himself, but it was the old-timey way and, too, it tasted better when it appeared on his table.

Estelle, believing as Bill did in the old customs, put up canned foods and jellies and preserves from their own garden and orchards. This, against the coming winter, was better than money in the bank.

Bill always kept a log fire in his study when it was cool, and more than once we have gathered there with him on Christmas Eve to drink a toast.

When his grandchildren began coming along, Bill searched Memphis for an old-timey yard swing for them. When he found one, he brought it home himself. It was a latticework affair with standards reaching above it and a trelliswork of braces for children to play on like a jungle gym. There was a foot piece you pushed against to make the facing seats move back and forth, and it was painted red and green. It was all wood; no curved metal and nylon cushions for him.

During Jill's childhood, he provided her a world to grow up in like the one we had known. It was not that he shielded her from today's world. It was simply that he wanted her to know about the good things out of ours, not the least of which was a sense of responsibility toward her home and those who lived in it. It would give her a deeper feeling of belonging to it.

She was taught to tend her own pets, her cats and dogs and the pony Bill got for her. Estelle taught her to keep house and to preserve and can. By her early teens, she was quite an accomplished housekeeper.

Bill had a cart made, taught her to handle it and the pony. She drove it all over town. It was a two-wheeled affair with box seats, facing each other, and she used to take her little friends for rides in it—to town for ice cream and to the swimming pool at the University. The only concession Bill made in the cart was to mount the box on an old automobile axle with pneumatic tires, on account of the noise metal rims would have made on our paved streets.

As Jill grew older, he promised her a saddle horse of her own, for she was outgrowing the pony. On one of his trips to California, he found one that he thought would do. It was registered, of course-what our Blacks call a paper horse.

Bill had flown to California and now that he had the horse, he had no way to get it home. He didn't want to ship the horse the long trip home by rail, for fear some harm might be done it. He wanted to be with it each day, to tend it and be sure its traveling conditions were all right.

Bill was about to buy a car and trailer when he found that a friend of his out there was coming east in his Cadillac. The friend offered to tow a horse trailer if Bill could rent one. Bill accepted his offer.

They made the trip with no trouble and pulled into Bill's driveway just after midnight one night. Bill backed the horse out of the trailer and left his friend holding it by the halter while he went to get Jill. He had to wake her, of course, for she had long since gone to bed.

When he waked her he didn't tell her what for. She was too sleepy to have heard what he was saying anyhow. He led her downstairs and out into the yard and there was her horse. "Look, Missy," Bill said.

Jill had been rubbing her eyes, rubbing the sleep from them. Now she came awake. "My horse," she said, and burst into tears.

When Bill received word he had won the Nobel Prize, I fully believe he was about written out. He had said years ago that if that happened, he'd turn to writing mystery stories. One thing about them, he said, was that once you found a formula that worked, you could keep on using it over and over, by simply changing names and places.

That's what he was fooling around with, I think, in *Intruder in the Dust*, in which an innocent man is saved from a mob and the guilty party caught by comparing the fatal bullet with the weapons belonging to two other suspects. He wrote several other mystery stories, though not of book length. The *Post* published them.

Intruder in the Dust was made into a movie and filmed here in Oxford. Bill didn't have anything to do with the actual filming. He said that was none of his concern; it was up to the company making the movie.

The picture company already knew about Bill and his reputation for wanting to be left alone. They were very nice to him about that. A few of them paid him courtesy calls, but they did not intrude. Whenever he visited the site where they were shooting, they brought him a chair in which he could sit and watch.

He took Mother by a time or two when she wanted to go. He was pleasant about it, to her and to the movie people both. They made on over Mother and she liked that. Bill made it a point to make no suggestions about what was going on, even when they asked him to comment. He simply sat there and watched. When he grew tired, he got up and left.

When the filming was over, a banquet was given for the entire crew in the University cafeteria. That afternoon there was a parade all over town, with the entire personnel in cars or on floats. Many local people were in the show, and the movie technicians made up the floats that were in the procession. The stars and other actors and actresses rode in open-top convertibles.

The parade came along the avenue on which I live, on its way to the University. My wife and I and all our neighbors were out on the sidewalk. When the car with Miss Elizabeth Patterson in it passed, she was waving to people, first on one side of the street and then on the other. She waved toward me and I waved back.

After the banquet that night, there was speechmaking. Each of the stars was asked to step up to the microphone and say a few words.

"I want to tell you something," Miss Patterson said when she was called on. "This afternoon, in the parade, we passed Mr. Faulkner standing on the sidewalk. I waved at him and he waved back."

She thought I was Bill.

It was known some time before the announcement from the Nobel Prize committee that Bill was under consideration. It was even known that he had made the finals. The belief that he would be the winner was so strong among the news services that several of them sent men to Oxford to be on hand if Bill was selected.

The morning the announcement was made, some of them came down to Bill's to ask for some sort of statement. That was the first Bill knew he had won. They found him out in his back lot cutting wood for his fireplace.

In their news flashes about Bill, they called him a fifty-two-year-old farmer. Bill liked that. Although he had never actually farmed, he owned a piece of land and considered himself a man of the soil. There is no doubt of his tremendous love for his native soil and it pleased him to be identified with it.

Bill did know a lot about farming, but it was mostly from the book side. After he bought the farm we had out in Beat Two, he collected literature about farming and really studied it. He talked well about crops, though he had never actually made one.

Bill thanked the reporters for taking the trouble to come out and tell him about the award. That's about all his first statement contained. It was not until the next day that he got around to saying he wouldn't go to Sweden to accept the Prize.

I was down at his house the next morning, and he told me then that there wasn't enough gas left in the tank to go all that distance. I've seen that quoted in other places. The results, I think, are less well known.

When the State Department learned that Bill did not plan to go to Sweden, they were quite concerned. They felt that since the offer of the award came in the name of the Swedish government, if Bill turned it down it might create something of an international incident.

Bill still said no. He said that when he wrote a book and it was placed on the market it belonged to anyone who had money enough to pay the price asked for it; he was still private property and belonged only to himself. He said that if anybody wanted to give a prize to his books, fine, but that nobody had the right to say he had to go abroad to receive it.

The State Department learned of Bill's friendship with Colonel Evans, who was now retired, and got in touch with him. They made him their personal emissary to Bill. Colonel Evans came over, and I don't know how long it took or what was said, but he finally persuaded Bill to go to Sweden, taking Jill with him.

Somewhere along the way, Bill was told he could not go to the banquet in what he was wearing. The affair was very formal and the King would be there; Bill would have to appear in white tie and tails. Bill took that hurdle in stride. He rented a suit of evening clothes. He'd long since outgrown the tails he had in college.

Of course, Mother kept the clippings from the papers. Bill and Jill's stay in Stockholm was well documented, both in print and pictures. They were shown on the snow-covered streets of Stockholm, stopping to smile at the people, and at the edge of a park, Jill feeding the squirrels. There were also many pictures of Bill at the banquet—receiving the Prize, making his acceptance speech.

There is no point in my quoting Bill's acceptance speech. It has been quoted in full many times and was finally published in book form in a special edition. It has been said that his choosing of the word "prevail" to close out his final sentence on man's destiny was worthy of the award, even discounting his other literary achievements.

When they returned to this country, Jill made her first try at writing. She wrote up their trip to Sweden for our local paper, in a series of installments. That was the only published writing she ever did, so far as I know. Her writing was good enough, but I think she was simply not interested enough to keep it up.

That was not what Bill intended her for anyhow. He wanted grandchildren and Jill gave them to him. She finished school, got married and now has three children, all boys. One is named for Bill—William Cuthbert Faulkner Summers. It was the grand-children that drew Bill to Virginia so often that he finally bought a home up there.

After receiving the Nobel Prize, Bill turned out some of his most serious work. It seemed to give him an added incentive. I've never seen anything that could compare to the three essays in *Requiem for a Nun:* "The Courthouse," "The Golden Dome" and "The Jail."

I have read almost everything Bill ever wrote. I liked all of it, some better than others, personal favorites that seemed better written than others. A great many people, I think, try to read too much into Bill's writings. It simply is not there nor was it intended to be. If they would read him for the stories he was telling, they would realize what a good storyteller Bill was.

Some English professors and scholars try to dig through Bill's long unpunctuated sentences a word at a time. They were never intended to be read like that. Read them as you would any other piece of writing, and you will find they are just like thoughts that go through your own mind. They start off with an idea that brings on another idea that brings on another . . . and so on till the sentence is over. Read like that, you will find connections like the links in a chain, that lead from the beginning thought to the closing one, just before the period.

Bill wrote all of his stuff in longhand, if you can call long anything as tiny as the marks he made on paper. Some of them extended the tiniest bit above the others. They were *l*'s and *t*'s and *f*'s and such. Others extended the same minuscule distance below the line. They were *p*'s and *g*'s and *q*'s. All were straight lines, all vertical.

Bill would leave a margin at the edge of the page and write his vertical corrections there. He had to do all his own copying himself because no one else could read what he had written. I don't know how many typewriters Bill wore out. I have written less than half what he wrote and worn out three. But there's one thing I will venture to say: I'll bet Bill used up fewer bottles of ink than he wore out typewriters.

Bill did all his writing on a spindle-legged table Mother gave him. It actually was a writing table, but never intended for the heavy use he gave it. It was of awfully frail construction and belonged in some lady's parlor. He kept it pulled endways up to a window so the light could come in over his left shoulder.

His writing chair Mother had given him too. It was an occasional hall chair, one of the small-seated, tall-backed kind you place against the wall and nobody ever sits in. Bill sawed the back off it and put a cushion on the seat. It was the only writing chair he ever used.

There was part of one book that was not written in that chair or on that table. Bill had a bad back at the time and was unable to sit up. He wanted to finish the manuscript he was typing, so he put the typewriter on the floor beside his bed. He lay across the bed on his stomach, and finished his typing that way.

After Bill won the Nobel Prize, everything he had ever written was reprinted. New editions of all his books began flooding the markets. Publishers began hunting for whatever Bill's regular publisher, Random House, might have over-looked. Bill was back in the public eye again.

A television outfit made a film of his daily life. A crew with cameras and research men was sent into Oxford and Bill was shown walking about the Square, in his home, with his friends. Most of the pictures showed his friends as his old hunting friends, Uncle Ike Roberts, John Cullen, Walter Miller and Big Red. These were the ones most often reproduced in national magazines.

Honors came in a flood too. Medals and citations accompanied them and these he placed in our local museum, along with his Nobel Prize commemorations. The museum has a special show-case to keep them in. It is almost full.

The New York Newspaper Guild's Page One Award was made to him and foreign governments decorated him. He was made a member of France's Legion of Honor and took great pride in the tiny rosette he wore in his lapel. The award was made in New Orleans, and Bill took Mother and Estelle down there. Jack and his French wife came over from Mobile, to be present at the occasion. The award was presented in French and Bill's acceptance speech was made in the same language, which was much appreciated by the officials of the French government who were present.

Shortly after this, a group of Russian writers came to this country under the auspices of our State Department. After their arrival in this country, they were wined and dined by the State Department and the question of their itinerary came up. The choice was left largely up to the Russians.

Almost the first thing the Russians asked for was a visit with Bill. The State Department called Bill and explained. Bill said sure, he'd give them an hour the following Wednesday morning.

The Russians were incensed. They said they expected to visit with him for two or three days. But Bill stuck to his original offer. The Russians did not come.

Chapter 23

THE MOST FERTILE REGION IN MISSISSIPPI IS our Delta. It begins at the bluffs below Memphis and runs to Yazoo City. In width, it is no more than fifty miles at its widest; in length, almost twice that distance.

The Delta has always been cotton country in a state where cotton is king. There has been a government experimental station for years at Stoneville, in the Delta. Each summer, at Stoneville, the Cotton Council puts on a demonstration day.

They have a barbecue and picnic, to demonstrate new trends in the growing and uses of cotton. Notables are invited. These include notables from all branches of the cotton industry, from this country and from abroad. Our governor is usually there and some of our senators and representatives from Washington.

The summer after Bill won the Nobel Prize, he was invited to be one of their speakers. He went and made a talk about farming in Sweden. Bill made a good talk too, having boned up on Sweden's agricultural methods, and held his audience for twenty minutes or more. He received a tremendous round of applause when he finished. And then stuffed himself full of barbecue.

Bill was a big eater and enjoyed his food. His appetite encompassed almost anything but he was especially fond of pork, even in the summertime.

Bill was now in demand as a visiting lecturer at various universities. He went twice to Princeton, for a series of lectures in their school of creative writing, and at the time of his death had for a number of years held a seminar each spring at the University of Virginia.

Jill and her husband lived in Charlottesville, the home of the University. Paul had graduated from that institution and had settled in town as a junior partner in a law firm there. Bill's invitation from the University suited him well, for it gave him every reason to spend a part of each year with his grandchildren. At first, the University furnished housing on the campus for Bill and Estelle, but after a couple of years Bill rented over in town so he could be closer to Jill and Paul and the children.

Bill liked the people in Virginia. He was invited to join one of their hunt clubs and did. He liked his association with the University. Virginia became a second home to him, and he gave a great deal of allegiance to that state.

Finally, he bought a home for himself and Estelle in Charlottesville. He rented out the main part of it to help pay taxes and upkeep but reserved an apartment so that he and Estelle could go up there any time they pleased, whether he was teaching at the University or not.

Estelle lives there now, where she can be near her children and grandchildren, for with Bill gone they are her strongest ties. Their house in Oxford has been turned over to Ole Miss as a combination memorial to Bill and work retreat for senior and graduate students in the School of Journalism. The University believes that working where Bill lived and wrote may be an added incentive to its own aspiring writers. Estelle reserves an apartment there too, so that at any time she wishes she can come home to Oxford.

The State Department availed itself of Bill and his reputation a great many times after he won the Nobel Prize. He made talks in this country and the Department sent him all over the world as a representative of American culture.

One of his talks in this country was before an international gathering of some sort in Denver. That's where he wound up with a continuation of his Nobel Prize acceptance speech about man's destiny, but with a humorous twist. Bill said that if man ever did finally succeed in destroying himself and there were as many as two of him left, they'd be found making a do-it-your-self rocket to leave the world they had ruined. But already they'd be arguing about which direction to take to find some new world to conquer.

Bill went to France for the Department, as well as to Italy, South America, Greece and Japan. He was honored everywhere, especially in Greece, where the government turned the whole country over to him. During this period, he also made two speeches for Jill, at her two graduations—one from high school here in Oxford, the other from Pine Manor College, in New England.

Bill's speech at Jill's high school graduation was of five minutes' duration, the shortest graduation speech on record. When Jill graduated from Pine Manor, where she made the dean's list year after year, Bill went up there and also made the graduation address. I guess it wasn't too much longer.

Jill said a funny and perfectly understandable thing about Bill while she was still at Pine Manor. Of course, being Bill's daughter, she was never allowed to forget that fact. She was not even allowed to be herself. As soon as anyone found she was Bill's daughter, all they wanted to talk about was Bill. Jill finally got fed up with it. She said she had never been as tired of anyone in her life as she was of William Faulkner.

After Bill got back from Stockholm with his Prize money (it was better than thirty-one thousand dollars), he set up a five-hundred-dollar scholarship at the School of Music in the University. Bill kept very little of the money for himself. A great part of it was set up as a fund for the needy of our county. Trustees were appointed to administer this and some of the money is still there, available to those of his people who need it.

Although Bill kept but little of that money for his own use, he began for the first time to realize money's value. Until then he had spent what money he made as soon as he made it, then lived on credit until he made some more. Now, however, he began investing a part of each check.

To add to the money coming in from his reprint editions, he began writing again and in those years turned out some of his major works—*A Fable, The Mansion, The Town* and his last book, finished just before his death, *The Reivers*.

To me they were not as good as some of his earlier novels, but there is no doubt that what they lacked of his earlier fire, they more than made up for in maturity and depth.

Bill's winning of the Prize brought about another change in him. Until then he had been more or less a recluse. Now every paper you picked up had a picture of him and quotes from an interview. He was shown holding classes in Virginia; sitting on a fence with a friend, in hunting togs, talking horses; at the Kentucky Derby feeding a colt, his hand stretched across a fence; in fact, almost anywhere he made an appearance.

When he was here in Oxford, though, he was still the same Bill we had always known, a little queer to some of our people but, without a doubt, a part of our town.

He trained his horses in his front yard, rode frequently on a bridle path that led away from his front gate and on the roads south of town toward Taylor. He also walked a great deal. You could come across him in almost any part of Oxford, on side streets and back streets, walking along with his cane or his folded umbrella. He seemed happier, more content. I think it was because his money worries were over.

The money he was now receiving was many times what it used to be. I remember one day he came by Mother's and was as mad as could be. The movies had just bought an earlier novel of his and he was already in such a high income bracket that the sale of this one story cost him twenty-two thousand dollars in taxes. Bill said his agent should never have sold it. He should have saved it till the next year, when his income might not be so high.

After Bill's funeral, one reporter wrote that seeing me was like looking at Bill's ghost, still walking the streets of Oxford. It was not the only time Bill and I were mistaken for one another.

One time was after I got married. My wife wanted a sewing machine and I bought her one from Mr. Morris, our Singer agent here in town. I bought the machine on the installment plan: five dollars down and five dollars a month.

I had the five dollars to put down and Mr. Morris delivered the machine. The next one or two payments I made, then I missed one.

I did my best to keep out of Mr. Morris' sight, hoping to get the five dollars together before I saw him again. One day I ran into him, unexpectedly, on the Square, and he got after me for promising to make the payment two weeks ago and not keeping my promise. I told him I hadn't made any such promise, I hadn't even seen him. I had made it a point not to. He insisted I had. Fortunately, I had five dollars at the time so I paid up.

What was happening, of course, was that he was dunning Bill, thinking he was me, and Bill, in my name, was promising to make the payment "next week." He thought he was keeping Mr. Morris off my neck for a few more days, to give me more time to get the five dollars up.

Though Bill, in the last years of his life, had the money to buy whatever he wished, his tastes did not run along the usual lines. Most of us who had money bought big cars and traded them in regularly. Bill never cared for cars except as a means of transportation, to get him wherever he wanted to go. He always bought new cars, but when he did get a new one you could be sure the old one was past taking him anywhere.

That new Model A Ford he bought to go to California in 1935 was still his only car ten years later. He ran it till it would run no longer, then phoned the garage and told them to come get it and fix it up so it would run again. The last time he called they told him it was past where it would ever run again, and he would have to get a new one.

The first Christmas I was out on the farm, Bill came out and got us to take us to his home for dinner. He came in that old Model A. It was cold that day. He had the curtains up but the isinglass was out of most of them. We bundled up well, but it was still a chilly ride into town and back.

Bill kept that car till the floor boards rusted out of it. You could look straight down under your feet and see the road whizzing past. Mac, his stepson, said it was a good thing the floor boards were gone; the brakes were shot and the only way to stop the car was to stick your feet down through the floor and drag it to a halt.

It was just after the Second War when the garage told Bill that the Model A was past fixing up. That was when no new cars were available so Bill had to buy the only second-hand car he ever owned. He found a Ford station wagon at the Buick dealer in town and bought it. He kept it only until new cars were on the market again and then traded it in on a gray Plymouth, another station wagon.

Bill wanted no extra gadgets in his cars. The second-hand Ford station wagon had a radio in it, but he made the Buick dealer take it out before he would buy the car.

Bill still had that gray Plymouth when he began going up to Virginia. He might still have had it when he died, I expect, if Mac had not wrecked it in Jackson one night. Bill did not attempt to salvage it. He bought a red Nash wagon, which lasted him the rest of his life. Estelle has it in Virginia with her now.

As soon as Bill got home with his Prize money, the different car dealers in Oxford were sure that the first thing he would do was buy a flashy new car. They began camping on his doorstep, bringing out car after car for him to try out. Some of them became discouraged after a few weeks, but it took the Studebaker man a year to finally give up. He just couldn't believe Bill really meant to keep that gray Plymouth when he had all that money.

One day Bill passed the taxi stand in his old car and one of the taxi drivers said, "If I had all the money he's got I wouldn't let my cook come to work driving a car like that."

"Maybe that's the reason he's got all that money," another driver answered.

Bill's way was well documented after the Nobel Prize came to him. It was lined with cameramen and news reporters, and they took note of everywhere he went and everything he did. Of all the items that came back to us from Virginia, I think the one I liked best came from a student about Bill and his gray Plymouth.

The student was majoring in history and spent a great deal of his time on the battlegrounds around that section of the country, taking notes from the markers there. All the battlefields of Virginia are marked and fitted out with roads so that you can follow the progress of any action that took place within the state.

The student said that frequently when he was out on such trips, he would see Bill in his mud-splashed gray Plymouth following out the progress of some battle, stopping to read the markers, getting out every now and then to more closely examine some particular point of interest. The student said that Bill studied those old fields almost as intently as he did.

Most of Bill's clothes now were for comfort. Though he was no longer the faddist he had been when he was dubbed "The Count," he did have a yen for such as his Virginia hunt club regalia. He also had an RFC jacket that he wore about his house. It was blue, double-breasted with brass buttons and a pocket patch like a club jacket, and it had a red silk lining. Bill derived a great deal of pleasure from it, but I never saw him wear it except at home. When we'd see Bill uptown, he'd be in a heavy suit and flannel shirt, if it was winter. If it was mild he usually wore suntans and an old tweed coat. In summer he always dressed in khakis, a T shirt and sun helmet.

Usually he was smoking a pipe. In extreme cold weather, he might wear a trench coat. I never knew him to own an overcoat. Ever since the First World War, trench coats had been a sort of a trade-mark with him.

Except for khaki pants, Bill did not buy many clothes, but what he did buy was tailored to his own ideas, and expensive. I have seen him out walking on some of our coldest days without even his trench coat on, for the suit he wore was made of overcoat cloth, with a vest. He had a pair of pigskin walking shoes made for him, designed on an Army last and constructed like field boots.

Occasionally Bill would turn up in some, to us, outlandish piece of clothing that had struck his fancy. One day he came to town in semiformal day dress and wearing a derby hat. None of us had seen a derby in forty years. He had seen one in New York and liked it and bought it.

We did not pay too much attention to him. He was Bill and we allowed him what we considered his little eccentricities. He could afford them and anyhow we knew that in a few days he would be back among us in his usual khakis and old tweed coat.

Another day he showed up in town in his Virginia hunting club suit, pink coat and all. He liked himself in it and had come to town to get his picture taken. We watched him walk across the Square and on down to Cofield's photograph studio. A copy of that picture is in Cofield's window now.

In fact Cofield's took a number of pictures of Bill and kept a complete file of them. After Bill's death, they presented them to the University. They hang now in Ole Miss' Mississippi Room, where Bill's sister-in-law, Dorothy Oldham, is curator.

Also in the library's Mississippi Room, there is an almost complete collection of writings by Mississippi authors. That collection bulges the bookshelves. It covers the walls. They say we write more books in Mississippi than we read.

Our scroll of authors is long and many of them distinguished. Bill's writings, of course, are the main attraction.

An oil portrait, finished just before his death, hangs there too. Students must have special passes to use the Mississippi Room for research and the work must be done in the room itself, for no books are allowed to be taken out. Most of the volumes there are first editions. Several years ago some of them turned up missing. That is the reason for the rule now that no volume may be taken from the room.

Bill was no coffee-break man, as are most of the rest of us. Whatever we're doing, along about ten o'clock and three, we usually assemble at whatever coffee counter we patronize, to swap greetings and gossip. I have never seen Bill in one of these groups.

He kept a pot of coffee on his stove at home and drank it through the day. The first thing on visiting him, you were usually offered a cup. When he came to town, it was usually for something he needed; he seldom came just to be coming. He went to the post office for his mail, never having put up a mailbox at home, and then to the store that had what he needed. Sometimes, once there, he would stop at intervals along the sidewalks, usually on the outer edge, and gaze across the Square.

Most of our townsmen let him be. If he saw them and spoke, they returned his greetings. If he did not, they thought merely that he was making up another story and did not want to be disturbed. As to his greatness, they knew that quite a stir was being made over him throughout the world and there must be some reason for it. But to them he was someone they had known all their lives. They remembered him as a boy, had seen him grow up, and though, to them, he was a little strange, he was not enough different to be great. When his name was mentioned, they usually smiled and shook their heads. He was Bill Faulkner, and they let it go at that.

As I think back on Bill, the picture that keeps recurring is the one the student painted—Bill in his mud-splashed gray Plymouth, tracing out the course of battles on those Virginia fields. He was an avid reader of the histories of the War Between the States. He was as well versed in most of them as any professor.

I only wish I could have seen through his eyes what he saw as he followed those Virginia battle markers.

Chapter 24

DAYS WOULD GO BY WHEN BILL WOULD NOT GO to town at all. During these times, his own home interested him more. In fact, his own home and his life there always interested him a great deal more than anything town could offer. And being an outdoor man, except for his writing, most of Bill's activities about his home were concerned with the outside part of it.

A jumping course stretched across his middle front yard and on into his pasture. A white board fence separated the two pieces of ground, and Bill took out a half section of the fence to build a training jump about three feet high. He built a solid ramp up one side and down the other.

A young colt could be led across the ramp at first, to get used to it before Bill attempted to jump him. After a time, Bill would ride him across at a walk, then he would trot him across. Finally a canter and gallop, and the horse was taking the jump in stride.

There were fourteen acres in Bill's original lot. He later increased this to about thirty-five, but the addition was across a lane and mostly woods. In his pasture, across the fence from his front yard, he laid out a complete small riding circle. It was level over there and at one time a part of it had been an outdoor tennis court. In another flat section, over in his front yard, Bill had a croquet layout.

Two of the Linders, Felix and Dewey, our boyhood friends, were doctors now, one an M.D. and the other a retired dentist. They built a house on the old Linder place, not too far down the road from Bill's on the highway to Taylor, one of Bill's favorite riding trails. This was perhaps fortunate, for Bill took some pretty bad falls. They witnessed the worst that happened just about in front of their house.

When Bill first began using the Taylor road for a bridle path, it was dirt most of the way to Taylor. Only a half mile or so from where it curved past the entrance to his driveway was graveled. It went past a few houses, then it was in open country, with fields and woods on either side and only an occasional farmhouse. It was the kind of trail Bill liked. He did not like riding in town.

At the time of his bad fall, the road had been paved for several miles out from town. A factory, the Chambers Gas Range Company, had been set up a mile or so on beyond the Linders', and the road had been paved that far. The rest of it was about as it used to be.

Bill continued to use it even after the first part was paved. He was riding past the Linders' house one morning, and luckily, Felix and Dewey were out in the yard. A piece of paper blew across the road right at the horse's feet. The horse spooked, shied out from under Bill, and he fell flat on his back on the pavement. It was a terrible fall.

Felix got to him at once. Bill was bleeding internally, and Felix said the fall was enough to have killed him. He got Bill home to bed where he had to remain quietly for quite a while until he could heal up inside.

Most of Bill's falls were less severe, and he did have more than a few of them. But they never diminished his love of riding and especially jumping. He said that like sailing, it was almost like flying, and he believed he liked it better.

These lesser falls came mostly when Bill was training his colts. He would be coming at the jumps, and the young horse would balk at the last moment. Bill expected these and was prepared for them. He could break the fall onto the soft turf of his yard with his hands, and they were not serious.

But just before he died, Bill took a bad fall on the bridle path that led through Bailey's Woods. This trail began at his driveway entrance and led through the fences of his two pieces of property into the woods. It went on through to the site of Dad's old ice plant and the swimming hole that Bill wrote about in *Soldier's Pay*. Since the Taylor road had been paved, Bill preferred this woods trail and used it more often than he did the other.

Bill had ridden over to the old ice-plant site that morning. There was nothing much left of it except weed-grown rubble and an occasional piece of machinery rearing up like a rusty tombstone. He had turned back from there and was riding toward home when he was thrown.

The first anyone knew something was wrong was when Estelle happened to look out and saw Bill's horse, saddled and standing at the gate waiting to be let in, its reins dragging. She quickly went out there but could see nothing of Bill. When she called and got no answer, she realized that he must be back along the trail somewhere, perhaps hurt too badly to move. She went over and got Felix Linder then, and together they back-tracked until they found Bill.

He was over half a mile away, hobbling along the path, barely able to walk. The horse had thrown him, he said, and he had been unable to get up at first. After he had fallen on his back, the horse had gone ahead a few steps and then stopped and looked back. When Bill did not get up, it had come back to where he lay and nuzzled him. He had tried to catch the reins but had missed.

The horse had then backed off again and after standing there for a while, had started on down the trail back toward the house. It must have been at the gate for fifteen minutes or more before Estelle noticed it.

They got Bill home and to bed. For some reason, even though this fall had been on the soft bridle path, it seemed to have hurt him more than his spill on the pavement. He was in bed for a good while and suffered a great deal of pain. He had not completely recovered at the time he died.

Mother and Estelle had both, at times, tried to get Bill to stop riding on account of his age, or at least jumping. But he would not stop. He loved riding and intended to keep on doing it, so they finally gave up arguing with him.

One day, a year or so before his death, Bill stopped by Mother's on his way to town. It was summer and she was sitting on the porch. He came up on the veranda and took a chair.

"Billie," Mother said. "I was sitting out here the other evening and someone passed on a beautiful horse. I couldn't tell from here who he was."

"Did he fall off?" Bill asked.

Mother answered, "No."

"It wasn't me then," Bill said, and laughed.

Bill had several falls in Virginia too. These were reported in the papers, so we knew about them. A time or two he got bunged up, but none of them was as serious as the two bad ones he had here.

It was on one of his trips up there that he turned down an invitation to dinner at the White House. The new President had instituted a program of culture. Outstanding poets and writers and musicians and artists were being invited to a series of dinners. Bill, a Nobel Prize winner, was of course included.

When his invitation came, he politely refused it. He said a hundred miles was too far to go for one meal, then left it up to Estelle to write the First Lady.

Bill did a lot of work about his place when he was home. He was forever pottering at something outside. A houseboy was always a part of Bill's menage, a houseboy and a cook. He didn't know how to live without them.

A part of the houseboy's duties, besides shaving Bill, was to follow him about outside with tools in his hands and hand him the proper one when needed. That was about the only contact he had with the tools too. Bill liked to do his own work. After the houseboy handed Bill whatever tool he wanted, he simply stood there and watched. He did mix mortar on occasion, when Bill wanted to lay brick or level up his birdbath. And he shoveled dirt when Bill wanted a hole dug or ground moved from one place to another.

Actually Bill did more than just potter about his place. Besides a brick wall he built as a wing out from his porch, he planned to hire a man or two to help him and build a barn. He already had one, but he decided he wanted another. The first served as quarters for his cows as well as his horses. Now he decided he wanted a barn for his horses alone.

This was five or six years ago and since World War II, skilled labor is almost impossible to come by. All the carpenters are tied up with housing contractors who never seem to be able to catch up with the demand for new homes. They work regularly and have no spare time for projects such as Bill's.

When Bill found he would be unable to hire carpenters to build his new barn, he decided to do it himself. It was a good substantial barn he'd planned and he built it well. And when he had finished the barn itself and stood back to admire it, he decided to add a belfry and a cupola on top. And he did too.

I had been down at Bill's when he was planning his new barn. He took me out and showed me the site he had selected.

I was also aware that he had failed to find any carpenters and had decided to build it himself.

It's not far from my place to Bill's. He lives on one ridge and I live on the one just north of it. There is a valley between, over which sounds carry easily. The sound of his building came easily to my open window and many a day as I worked I could hear the sound of his hammering and sawing as his barn neared completion. I knew when he had finished by the cessation of sounds across the valley, so I went down to see his new structure.

He showed it to me with a great deal of satisfaction, for it stood, to him, as another evidence of his independence. If he couldn't get someone else to do what he wanted, then he could and would do it himself. He pointed out the cupola he had added as an afterthought. He was so pleased with it that he said he thought he'd add a weathervane on top and a barn clock in the front. I don't know whether he ever got around to it or not. I don't remember noticing.

Bill's house is an old one, one of the oldest in Oxford. It was built before the Civil War. Of the colonial architecture, it is two stories high and L-shaped. The front, when he bought it, was columned but was only as wide as the central hall just behind it. A small balcony was overhead, in front of the upstairs hall doors.

On one side, where his study was, the house was only one room deep. Behind it, with a door opening out onto it, was a bricked open porch to ground level. That's where he had cranked up the tractor and it almost got away from him. At first a planked floor had been there, at house level, but Bill had had the floor lowered after he had the place for several years. There was a balcony over this porch with access from the upstairs rooms letting out onto it.

The L part of Bill's house went back three rooms. All the upstairs rooms were bedrooms. With Cho-Cho and Mac there, these bedrooms were all needed. They had a room apiece, Jill had one, of course, and Bill and Estelle had adjoining rooms. Downstairs in that same wing was the parlor, the dining room, the butler's pantry and the kitchen.

Only Bill's study was in the room across the hall. Most of his work was done there. It was not until later on that he raised the back-porch floor, enclosed it and made himself a new study.

He also partitioned off a section for a small withdrawing room just off the dining room and just behind the rear entrance to the downstairs hall.

It was in the new study that Bill wrote his last books but on the same table and sitting in the same chair that he had used for the others. Like in his front study, he pulled the table end-ways to the window, so the light came over his left shoulder.

Bill changed his house several times, by trial and error, until he finally got what he wanted. At first he did the work himself, hiring helpers as he found a need for them, but in later years he hired all the work done. The front porch was extended clear across the width of the house but the addition was not roofed over. Dirt was hauled in to raise the level and when it was well tamped, Bill paved it with brick. It was banistered across the outside and steps led down from each end to the yard.

Bill had just finished his last remodeling when he was invited to New Orleans to receive the Legion of Honor medal. While he was down there, Estelle shopped in antique shops for the furniture she wanted for their new withdrawing room. They came back with the back of Bill's gray Plymouth stuffed full of frail French chairs and love seats.

Though Bill always kept open fires, he installed a central heating system to make the house more comfortable. A basement had to be dug and a huge oil-fed boiler put in. Most of us with big old houses economize on heat. We shut off parts of them in cold weather and heat only the parts we live in. That was not for Bill. He kept the whole house warm any kind of weather and lived all over it. The Lord only knows what his heat bill must have run. But Bill never grumbled.

Bill always claimed the English language didn't have enough words in it. I guess, so far as he was concerned, he was right about that. He certainly used just about every one there was and sometimes some most of us didn't even know we had. Every now and then I would think Bill had made up one, but I'd look in the dictionary and there it would be. That's one thing Bill did for all of us. He made us become familiar with our dictionaries.

Sometimes it seemed like Bill used up all the words he knew in one sentence. It was said that he didn't use enough periods. One day Bill said that the next book he published was going to have a full page of periods inserted in the back with a note that if anyone felt Bill had used too few periods they were free to take as many as they wished from the extra page and put in their own.

Bill was the most meticulous about his pronunciation of anybody I've ever known. He was one of the two people of my acquaintance who pronounced "hiccoughs" the way it should be, with the last syllable like what you do when you have a bad cold. Most of us say "hiccups." Bill never did.

Bill was a pipe smoker all his life and finally got to blending his own pipe mixture. He smoked cigarettes and cigars on occasion, but mainly he stuck to his pipes. He bought good pipes, like Dunhills, which were his favorite, and Ben Wades, Sasienis and the like. He was never a collector.

At first he used to send his pipes off regularly to a "pipe hospital" to have them cleaned and freshened and polished. That's the first I ever heard of a pipe hospital. I was down there one day when a package of his pipes came back. They looked like they were brand new. Later, though, he stopped doing that. He'd buy six or eight new pipes, smoke them until they no longer tasted good to him and then give them away and buy six or eight more. He gave me several after he was through with them and I have them in my collection. I still smoke them.

Bill liked variety in his pipe tobacco. He would blend it differently at times to get a new taste, and every time he would go into a pipe shop he'd buy several selections of ready-mixed tobacco. He would smoke from one can and then another, like a man trying different foods at each meal.

Bill smoked a heavy mixture usually, but in summer he'd cut it with Virginia bright to lighten it. One trick he taught me was that if a mixture seems to go stale it can be brought back by crumbling up a light-strength cigar in it.

Bill's pipes were all for smoking. Most of them were briers, for hard service, the kind of pipe a man smokes outdoors. I never knew him to have but one meerschaum and that was long ago when we lived on the campus. Mac, I think, now has most of the pipes Bill owned. Estelle gave them to him. Mac is a pipe smoker too. Bill taught him, so it was a fitting place for his pipes to go.

Chapter 25

DURING MOTHER'S LAST FEW YEARS (SHE DIED about two years before Bill did) she became subject to those ailments brought on by age that require hospitalization from time to time. Always after these visits she'd have to go through a convalescent period at home in her own bed. We always got nurses for her during these periods, but she never let them stay long in her house. She wanted it to herself. It simply did not suit her to have anyone else in there with her. Argue as we would, she just wouldn't let the nurse stay. At such times, it fell to us to take time about looking after her.

However lacking might be our attentions, the fact that we were making them was pleasing to her and probably was better for her convalescence than the constant irritation of a nurse's presence.

One morning when I dropped by (it was Bill's time to cook her breakfast), she was propped up in bed waiting for him to bring her tray. He brought her bacon and eggs and toast and coffee and she ate it all, a thing she'd refused to do for any nurse. In fact, a nurse could hardly get her to eat a bite.

Soon after breakfast, Bill left and I stayed till dinner, when he came back with a tray prepared by Estelle. That night it was my time and I took her a supper tray Dolly had prepared. But even though she was pleased over this attention from her own family, it never lasted long. Before she should have been, we'd find her up and dressed and going about her daily life as usual.

Bill and I decided she even got enough of her own children at times and at such times we let her alone. She said once that she was too old and crotchety to have anyone in the same house with her. She was as hardheaded as Bill and I suppose that's where he got it from.

I remember one time Bill had been up to Memphis to the airport when I was running Mid-South Airways. Estelle was with him and, I think, Jill. They had been to town during the day and had come by about dusk to pick Bill up and take him home. We had closed by that time so I came home with them. Dolly was already at Oxford, visiting her mother. We would drive back to Memphis the next day.

We were not far out of Memphis before Estelle objected to something about Bill's driving. As I remember it, it had something to do with the car lights. One of them was out or they were flickering on and off. Anyhow, Estelle was uneasy and wanted Bill to stop somewhere along the road and have them fixed. Bill wouldn't stop. He wanted to get on home and figured he could have the lights fixed the next day.

Estelle appealed to me to make him stop. I said, "Bill's driving."

Estelle said, "You Faulkner brothers make me so mad sometimes I don't know what to do. Billie's going to kill us all if he doesn't stop and fix these lights. So far as the rest of you are concerned, even if he kills you too, so long as it's one of you doing it, it's all right. If one of you said, 'Let's go to hell,' the rest of you would say, 'Let's go.'"

It was about this time that Bill started writing and talking integration. It did not set well with the rest of us, but we felt toward him as he had toward Mother about her convalescence. We always felt that way toward each other when one of us did something contrary. If that's what he wants, let him alone. That's what Bill had said about Mother.

Of course, as soon as Bill started talking integration he became subject to anonymous phone calls at odd hours. Mysterious voices cursed him, and his mail was filled with abusive anonymous letters. Since none of us agreed with Bill's views we said, "It serves him right. He ought to have known this would happen."

It didn't serve him right though. It didn't serve him one way or the other. Bill wouldn't talk over the phone and he never opened his mail anyway, unless he thought it might have a check in it, and then he'd only slit the end of the envelope and shake it to see if a check would fall out.

After he died I was back in his study. He had a special rack there full of unopened letters and packaged manuscripts that had been sent him to read, and he'd simply set aside.

Estelle was the one who caught the brunt of it over Bill's integration doings. The straw that broke her back, though, was a record someone sent about the "Murder of Emmett Till." After that I think she quit opening his mail and answering the phone.

This phase of Bill's lasted a few years, and then he had little more to say about it. He had said what he had to say and he was through. During his last two or three years I do not personally know of a single pro-integration article he ever wrote or a speech he made on that subject. We were all relieved, glad that that was over.

One of the English professors out at Ole Miss wrote quite a dissertation on the name "Snopes" that Bill used for one family group whose members turn up time after time in his writings. He had never heard of the word as a family name. He seemed quite fascinated with it, with the sound of it.

His thesis had to do with its phonetic values. He went through the dictionaries comparing it to other words of a similar sound, then compared the meanings of those words with the characteristics with which Bill had endowed the Snopes.

In his research, the professor held mostly to words beginning with the *sn* sound and to short words. He came up with "snarl," "snitch," "snivel," "snipe," but in the main he predicated Bill's selection on "snarl" and "sneak." He said the plural *s* had to be added to the name because Bill himself had described them as a "swarm of locusts."

A great many other scholars have been intrigued with Bill's use of the name. All Bill ever said about it was that it was the luckiest thing that ever happened in his writing.

Although the "Snopeses" began moving in on all sides of Oxford about the time we were growing up here, we knew only those who settled on our side of town. They were share-cropper people who had a little more "git up and git" about them than their neighbors. They were not content to live out their lives as their forefathers had done, scrabbling out less than a living from some washed-out hill farm. They came to town for a better living for themselves and better education for their children, and by their initiative they secured both.

As Bill described them, they moved first into the edge of town, into jerry-built frame houses that rented for only a few dollars a month. Such shacks had, at the most, but one or two bedrooms and into these they crowded whole families and brought in their kinfolk, one at a time, until they spilled over into town. First they took menial jobs, then got into businesses of their own, like cafes and small grocery stores. At last they moved onto our Square and became merchants and town clerks and aldermen.

One of them actually became superintendent of our power plant and in six months' time, had it in such bad shape it would no longer furnish us current. We were without lights a whole summer while new dynamos were being installed. They even got control of our banks and when we needed to borrow money we had to ask them for it. We didn't believe it could happen, but it did.

As boys, we became aware of them at first as their children appeared in our school. They studied harder than we did and most of them made better grades. Even the children seemed to have the same driving urge their parents had. They took advantage of every opportunity. They were persistent and insistent, in an unobtrusive sort of way, like they were part of the landscape. Then they reared up a mountain. Before you actually knew they were coming, to your surprise they were already there.

Some of them moved into Memphis, where their children and grandchildren now hold top jobs in banks and real estate companies and department stores. Others are lawyers and doctors, with impressive clientele and reputations. They live in Morning-side Park and other exclusive residential areas.

Bill never wrote of them as having reached any goal except the original one they set for themselves in Oxford. He saw them only as "locusts that swarmed in and took over our town" or as "termites that undermined an older social order."

There is no doubt that the Snopeses did change Oxford. After we suddenly found them in charge of our banks and biggest stores and town government, we became aware for the first time of the value of human endeavor.

Until then our lives had been pretty well cut and dried. We were entrusted with our city government term after term and it coasted along in the same old rut that we considered good enough for us all. Our banks were in the hands of what we called our upper class, our more substantial citizens, and our department stores were handed down from father to son.

When this new blood was infused into our daily circumscriptions, we didn't like it. It was probably good for us, for it made us hump along more lively than we had before in order to keep ahead or even to hold onto what we had. We still didn't like what we saw happening, really, but we didn't know what to do about it then, and we still don't.

One thing that the Snopes children did, to me was one of our town tragedies. I know it affected Bill deeply, so deeply that it may have been the reason for his choosing the name he did for them. It may explain why he never presented them in any stage other than their most objectionable one.

One of our oldest families had a son, older than we were, who was afflicted with epilepsy. So violently was he afflicted at times that a constant surveillance had to be maintained over him by his family. He could not be sent to school but was allowed the freedom of his own yard, where his people could keep an eye on him.

It was a big old place where they lived, with an enormous front yard enclosed by an iron picket fence. All our homes had fences about them in those days, but not many of us could afford iron.

It so happened that this house was right on the route our first Snopeses had to pass on their journeyings to and from school or town. We, Bill and Jack and I, passed their yard frequently too on our way to school and to the woods where we often played. Always, if the boy was out in his front yard, we stopped and played a while with him, as did all the children in our gang.

We had known him all our lives and saw nothing different about him, except that he was bigger than we were. When we would leave, after having been in to visit with him, he would follow us along the fence on the inside until he came to its far limits. He would wave us good-bye till next time and we would wave back and promise to see him again soon. Then he would return to that part of his yard nearer the house, where he was supposed to stay.

The gates were never locked, for he never made any attempt to leave his enclosure, until after the Snopeses came to town. At first they had noticed that he was different but had paid him no attention other than to move in passing to the outside of the walk or even out into the street.

As they grew more used to his presence in the yard, they began holding to the sidewalk, even to the inside of it, the side nearer the fence. They began picking on him and soon they found they could violently upset him. It was a childish thing on their part but, as childish things so often are, extremely cruel.

It happened several times, and then one day they aggravated him so much that he ran at them. The incident happened just at the yard gate and the boy pushed through the gate which opened at his rush, and chased his tormentors down the street. It scared them badly. They had not known he could get out of the yard. They thought the gate was always kept locked.

They went to their parents and told them what had happened and their parents went to the police. The police had no recourse. They went to the boy's people and made them restrict him to his back yard.

We were all concerned when we no longer saw him in his front yard. We could no longer visit him and have the run of the wide expanse enclosed by the iron fence. Of us all, I think, Bill was the most upset. And I believe that had something to do with his choice of that name and why he never portrayed them beyond the primitive stage. To him, they never got beyond that. They were always the ones who had done that cruel thing to that boy.

A great deal has been said about Bill writing about the kinds of people he did, always portraying their seamier side and their most outlandish doings. They say he presented the worst side of the South, when he could have presented its best. He himself said it better than I can, in *Intruder in the Dust*. In one passage he says that people will believe anything about the South if it is only bizarre enough. He wrote what people will believe, for that's what they will pay to read, and even a writer has to make money.

In *Pylon*, for example, he wrote about two men sharing, time and time about, the same woman. People will pay to read about such things.

Bill always set his stories against the background he knew best. An old admonition to any writer is to write about your own back yard and Bill knew about as much about what he was writing about as any man. He was a writer's writer and a finer accolade can be accorded no man.

Although Bill never did any research for any of his stories, he did do a lot of looking and listening. Most of this was not intentional so far as any story he was working on at the time was concerned. The story would come long after. He was simply storing his mind with what, someday, he might need or use in some story.

Pylon is a good example of this. Bill had his own airplane, and he and Vernon Omlie had flown to New Orleans for the opening of Shushan Airport, dredged up out of a swamp and named for one of New Orleans' commissioners. Vemon had gone back to Memphis but Bill stayed on down there with Roark and Mary Bradford, who lived in New Orleans at the time. Bill was an old friend of theirs, and they put him up after Vernon left.

Mary Rose said that for the final days of the flying meet they did not see Bill at all. One night, after midnight, she heard him calling from the front room of their apartment and she went and let him in. They did not even know he was still in New Orleans.

One day in Washington, years later, she told me about it. *Pylon* had come out long since and she had just read it. She said to me, "Of course I didn't know at the time, but when I finished *Pylon* I did. Bill had this book when he came in and called us that night."

Apart of what Bill writes about in *Pylon* actually took place at that meet. I knew about it before *Pylon* came out or I even knew Bill had been down there. He writes about a French stunt pilot who crashes and burns, and one of the characters, a scarecrow reporter, says, "They ain't human like us . . . crash one and it ain't even blood when you haul him out: it's cylinder oil and the same as in the crankcase."

I already knew about that crash, from the man who taught me to fly. He had gone to New Orleans for the opening of the new airport and it was in his plane, a Taperwing stunt Waco, that the "Frenchman" had crashed. He had rented Doc's plane for a hundred dollars and had crashed in the middle of the field and burned.

Most writers get beat out of some of their royalties when they first start writing, before experience teaches them who in the writing trade they can depend on. Bill was no exception and neither was Brad. Brad's first agent took him for six thousand dollars. He hied himself off to England and, his first Christmas there, sent Brad a leather travel kit. Brad always referred to that as his six-thousand-dollar kit.

One of Bill's early publishers took him. I don't know how much of his money they made away with. Bill wouldn't say, but he did tell me they beat him out of several royalty checks. He told me about it when he arranged for his agent to handle my work. He said he had learned by bitter experience whom he could trust, and he would vouch for the agent. And I found him so. Thanks to Bill, I have never lost anything on any of my books or stories.

There is one somebody who goes into every piece of writing and that somebody is the man who writes it. I have never known anyone who identified himself with his writings more than Bill did. He seemed to be as much a part of the story he was telling as were the characters in it. To see him was to recreate all the stories he had ever told.

Sometimes it was hard to tell which was which, which one Bill was, himself or the one in the story. And yet you knew somehow that the two of them were the same, they were one and inseparable. When we would see Bill we would see him surrounded by his stories. And still he was the Bill Faulkner we knew, the someone who appeared among us on the Square in his khakis and old tweed coat, in T shirt and sun helmet, or even in one of the outlandish costumes we saw him in on occasion.

Little wonder it was as I sat on the steps of the funeral home that early morning, waiting for them to bring Bill there, that I saw his people on the Square just as surely as I saw him and Jack and me. Will Geer, the sheriff in *Intruder in the Dust*, was there. It was at about this same early-morning hour that he, with galluses drooping, was cooking breakfast for his visitors in the jail and, as he cracked eggs into the skillet, saying to them, "If anyone wants more than two eggs, say so."

From where I sat, I could see the section of the Square across which Joe Christmas was led from the jail to the courthouse and where, manacled, he had broken away from his guard and run, chased by Percy Grimm on his commandeered bicycle. And on below the sheriff's house, facing the very road that ran under my feet, was the small frame building where Preacher Hightower lived and from the front window of which he watched at dusk each evening as the ghost cavalry swept past to the sound of falling trumpets.

Everywhere I looked there was Bill and his stories: Oxford, Jefferson, and Lafayette County, Yoknapatawpha.

Bill is dead now. He has stepped into an eternal tomorrow that has left him forever in Yoknapatawpha County; here forever. He can never leave us again.

"Your" Epitaph
(paraphrased by your brother)
If there be grief, it is but the rain,
And this but silver grief, for grieving's sake,
Your green woods will be dreaming here to wake
Within your heart, if you should rouse again.
But you but sleep, for where is any death
While in your blue hills slumbrous overhead
You're rooted like a tree? Though you be dead
The soil that holds you fast will find you breath.